Practicing Sainthood

PRACTICING SAINTHOOD

WALKING THE PATH OF YOUR ASCENSION

Rev. Sidney W. Bennett

Made in Charleston, SC
www.PalmettoPublishingGroup.com

Practicing Sainthood
Walking the Path of Your Ascension
© 2020 by Sidney W. Bennett

All rights reserved. This book or any portion thereof may not be reproduced or used in any manner whatsoever without the express written permission of the publisher except for the use of brief quotations in a book review.

Some materials used by kind permission of The Summit Lighthouse, www.SummitLighthouse.org

ISBN-13: 9781641112772
ISBN-10: 1641112778

Preface

For me, as for so many others, the search began before I even knew what I was searching for. It started as a vague uneasiness and a desire to understand my life at a deeper level. As a young teen I was trying to make sense of why things were the way they were. Why was I born into my family? Why in America and not India or somewhere else? Why did I sometimes feel lonely and out of place, even when I was surrounded by family and friends? Was there a bigger purpose to my life?

My father, who was a doctor, was a lifelong spiritual seeker, and I remember him reading one book after another in his quest for the truth. As I grew older I often talked with him about my questions. One day he shared with me that he believed in reincarnation because it seemed so logical. I was intrigued with the possibility that I had lived before—something I had never heard about in church.

The next day, instead of feeling sleepy in my 10th-grade study hall after lunch, I was wide awake and absorbed in a book he had suggested on karma and reincarnation. It was exciting to have discovered a teaching that answered so many of my questions! Though I loved aspects of the Christian church my family attended each week, I often left services feeling unsatisfied or confused, believing that there was much more to learn. Suddenly I saw my life from a different perspective because the teachings on reincarnation and karma helped explain so much more than the orthodox Christian view. Many of my questions remained unanswered, but I knew I was on to something and I determined to continue searching.

That was only the beginning. I eagerly continued my spiritual quest throughout high school, ever seeking a deeper wisdom and understanding. As I was nearing graduation from high school in southern California, my plan was to attend college in Oregon. At the urging of a friend, I changed my mind at the last minute and decided to attend the University of Colorado in Boulder.

College was a challenging time, as I tried to integrate my spiritual interests with a social and academic environment that often pulled me in other directions. I was always looking for people to talk with about the spiritual path but very few seemed interested.

One Saturday afternoon while I was browsing in the religious section of the university library, a book caught my eye and seemed to "jump off" the shelf at me. It was the *I AM Discourses* by Godfre Ray King. Something about the book clicked with me, so I checked it out and started reading. I vividly remember sitting on the grass several days later, staring at the book and pondering what I was supposed to do with it and the teachings it contained. I finally decided to go back to the library and check out the first two books in the series, *Unveiled Mysteries* and *The Magic Presence*. These three books introduced me to my divine identity and the world of the ascended masters—the saints and sages of East and West who had won their eternal victory. I was never the same again.

I read and re-read those books and told everyone who would listen about Saint Germain and the other masters. At that time I was working in a dormitory snack bar, and one quiet Sunday morning I told a co-worker about the books and the masters. She said, "Wait a minute! I just read something in the classified ads about a store in Denver that carries books about the ascended masters." I eagerly went to the store the following week and found out about an upcoming conference in Colorado Springs.

I wasn't sure what to expect upon arriving at the headquarters of The Summit Lighthouse that Saturday in April 1971. After paying the $5 student rate for the conference, I soon found myself seated in what was originally the mansion's living room that was now being used as a chapel. I was handed a small binder with a few pages of decrees. Since I had no idea what they were, while others said them I just looked around and wondered what in the world I was doing there! Even so, something felt very right to me.

At the conclusion of the decrees, Mark and Elizabeth Prophet entered the room. Mark had a powerful presence and I listened intently as he talked about his life as Longfellow and read one of Longfellow's poems. Then Elizabeth shared a beautiful teaching and meditation on the song "God, God, God!" that affected me profoundly and has stayed with me to this day.

Very shortly it was announced that Elizabeth would be delivering a dictation from Mother Mary. I wasn't raised Catholic and I had never thought much about Mary except at Christmastime. After a musical meditation, I began to hear Mary's words telling us about our path home to God:

> *All of heaven stands waiting and watching... to assist you. But none will ever do it for you, beloved ones; for the joy is so great to do this oneself that no angel or Cosmic Being would be so selfish as to deprive you of that opportunity and that joy. Therefore in rejoicing we cheer you on as though in a grandstand, a cosmic amphitheater. And so it is your time; it is your place.*[1]

I pondered what she said and felt excited without fully comprehending what had happened. But I have never forgotten her teaching that it was *my* time and *my* place.

As I left that day, Mark and Elizabeth were at the door saying good-bye to everyone. At the time I didn't think much about shaking Mark Prophet's hand, but I do believe it created a heart tie that has been a great mercy and help to me these many years since.

Driving home to Boulder that night, I felt more than a little overwhelmed. Nonetheless, something resonated within me, and I was sure of one thing—these teachings were true! An inner soul memory stirred within me, deeply comforting, but just out of reach of my conscious mind. In any case, I *knew* my search was over and my path home to God lay before me. I was filled with profound gratitude and anticipation.

As I learned more about the masters' teachings and applied them, I marveled at their very practical spirituality. I discovered the journey home to God is a path of striving and testing, not to perfect the human, but to become our Higher Self. I began to appreciate that the master-disciple relationship (in the East, the guru-chela relationship) is one of deepest love. The path the masters teach is the greatest adventure of all; it is, indeed, "the sacred adventure," as the Ascended Master El Morya has called it.

In the almost fifty years since that day in Colorado Springs, my outer life has unfolded in many ways much like others'. After graduating from college, I traveled the world, worked in Africa and began a lifelong career in banking and finance. In other ways, my life has largely been a reflection of my spiritual journey. I met my wife as our independent search for God brought us together unexpectedly and almost miraculously. Since our marriage, we have continued to study and apply the masters' teachings and have served in many capacities within our international spiritual community.

Over all these years my love for the masters and their teachings has only increased. They explain the equation of life on planet Earth. They teach us who we are and—surprisingly important—who we are not! They help us understand that the ascension is the goal of life and that our destiny is to walk in the footsteps of Jesus and the saints of East and West. The teachings are filled with the profound mysteries of God, yet are simple enough for a child to understand. My greatest joy is talking about them, sharing and reflecting on their meaning, and helping to make them an integral part of our daily lives until ultimately we *become* them.

In 1987 I became a minister in the church arm of The Summit Lighthouse—Church Universal and Triumphant. The sermons in this book are selected from Sunday services I delivered over a seven-year period. In reviewing them, I discovered many of the same themes are shared in different ways, focusing on key teachings the masters have emphasized on the path to our ascension. And although the sermons have been edited to make them more readable, please keep in mind that they were delivered before a live congregation and therefore have a more personal and informal style.

I enjoy doing sermons because it is often like solving a puzzle. What teaching will God inspire me to explore and share with others? Sometimes the subject comes out of my reading or from a comment I heard; other times it is in response to a difficult initiation that someone shared with me in counseling or that took place in my personal life. Such things make me want to understand what the masters have taught about these tests and the ways that we can master them. I've endeavored to make the teachings understandable, relevant and workable no matter where one is on the path.

The order of the sermons is not chronological. As a result, *Practicing Sainthood* does not read like a "how-to" book with each chapter building on the previous one. It may be helpful to read the sermons as if you had heard them in a weekly service, giving yourself time to pray, reflect and consider the most important keys for your life before reading another one.

I am reminded that in the East a chela or student of a master may only receive one new teaching to guide them through an entire lifetime. Many of the direct quotes from dictations or from the messengers included in this book could fulfill that premise. If you desire to delve more deeply into their meaning, page 348 has a list of the dictations that were played after the sermons.

Our journey home to God begins with searching and finding the truth, and then the work begins in earnest! Gautama Buddha admonished us to "Practice sainthood daily."[2] This path of practicing sainthood—of striving, being tested and giving loving service—is our joyous sacred labor as we work to outpicture our individual God-identity. That's what becoming a saint is really about—putting on our Christhood and becoming the fullness of our true identity while we yet walk the earth. This doesn't happen all at once! But as we apply the masters' precious teachings day by day, our Christhood will increase incrementally until, through many trials and testings and with great love and God's help, we *become* the truth of Being.

It has been a blessing to prepare these talks, and my prayer is that the masters' teachings in this book will help you pass every test on your journey home to God. As our dear master El Morya has said, "The trek upward is worth the inconvenience!"

Rev. Sidney W. Bennett
April, 2020

Note to the Reader

While the sermons in *Practicing Sainthood* are geared toward those who have been practicing the Teachings of the Ascended Masters for some time and are familiar with the terms and concepts they contain, the book can be helpful for anyone seeking a deep spiritual path. Here are a few brief explanations for those new to these teachings.

The ascended masters are our elder brothers and sisters on the spiritual path. They are our teachers, mentors, examples and friends. Having balanced their karma and fulfilled their unique mission, they have graduated from earth's schoolroom and returned to the heart of God in the ritual known as **the ascension**. Through this ritual, the soul reunites with the Spirit of the living God, also known as the **I AM Presence**. This reunion with God in the ascension signifies the end of the rounds of karma and rebirth and is the goal of life for all sons and daughters of God. Prior to the ascension, we are called to follow in the footsteps of Jesus and other saints in the alchemical marriage of our souls to our **Christ Self**.

The ascended masters have emerged from all races and nationalities, all walks of life and all religions. Collectively they are called **the Great White Brotherhood** (white refers not to race, but to the white light that is seen in the aura of the saints). Many of these masters are familiar to us, having walked among us throughout the ages. These include **Jesus Christ, Gautama Buddha, Lord Maitreya, Moses, Mother Mary, Kuan Yin, Zarathustra, El Morya, Saint Francis, and Saint Germain.** (El Morya is quoted extensively in the sermons. He was embodied as Abraham, one of the three wise men, Thomas Beckett, Thomas More and many others.) *Practicing Sainthood* includes teachings from many ascended masters whose names may be unfamiliar, but who are close to us and desire to help us toward our ascension.

God has always sent **messengers** as way showers. **Mark and Elizabeth Prophet** (Prophet was Mark's family name) were two such messengers and their mission was to bring forth the masters' teachings and revelations for the Aquarian age. Mark founded **The Summit Lighthouse** in 1958 and Elizabeth served with him from 1961 to 1973. They married, had four children, wrote many books, and lectured worldwide.

Mark passed on and ascended in 1973 and is now known as the Ascended Master **Lanello**. Elizabeth continued teaching, writing and ministering for decades. She was affectionately called "**Mother**" by students worldwide because of her devotion to the flame of God as Mother. Elizabeth passed on and ascended in 2009. Both are now working from spiritual realms to assist mankind.

Mark and Elizabeth Prophet were trained over many lifetimes to be messengers of the ascended masters. Through the power of the Holy Spirit in the manner of the apostles and ancient prophets, they received thousands of **dictations**—messages from the ascended masters for the upliftment of mankind in this age. Each dictation is a gift of the Holy Spirit and is not something the Prophets made happen themselves. Dictations contain the light and energy of the masters released from the highest spiritual levels as opposed to channelings from lower, psychic realms.

Each of us is created in the image and likeness of God. This **Divine Self** includes the I AM Presence and Holy Christ Self—the Higher Self or Real Self of every man, woman and child. The Holy Christ Self is each one's personal teacher, guardian, friend and the voice of conscience. Your Christ Self is also the mediator between God manifest in your Mighty I AM Presence and your soul evolving in time and space.

The ascended masters teach the **Science of the Spoken Word**, a step-up of all prayer forms East and West. It combines prayer, meditation and visualization with what are called dynamic **decrees**, placing special emphasis on affirmations using the name of God—**I AM THAT I AM**. The masters teach that this form of devotion is the most effective method known today for spiritual resolution, the balancing of karma and soul advancement.

The violet flame is the energy of freedom, mercy, justice, ritual and alchemy. It transmutes negative energy and restores it to positive energy, and is a missing key to vitality, health and inner wholeness on our spiritual path. You can access the transmutative power of the violet flame through the Science of the Spoken Word in mantras, decrees and songs.

Our spiritual work includes overcoming the not-self or synthetic self, also called the **dweller-on-the-threshold**. The dweller is the antithesis of the Real Self, including the negative energies a soul has created through misuses of free will.

It stands in the way of the soul bonding to her Christ Self and it must be overcome for the soul to have her victory.

For more information on the path of personal Christhood, decrees, the violet flame and many other teachings by the ascended masters and the messengers to assist your spiritual journey, see www.SummitLighthouse.org.

Table of Contents

Preface v

Note to the Reader.. xiii

1. Practicing Sainthood..1

2. Love As a Choice 21

3. Pleasing God 43

4. Next Year in Jerusalem..65

5. Nine Mindsets for Your Soul's Victory, Part I............93

6. Nine Mindsets for Your Soul's Victory, Part 2......... 115

7. The Poison of Pride 139

8. A Buddha's Christmas Vow 163

9. Who Am I in God? 181

10. The 49 Percent Challenge 203

11. Seven Ways to Bring Light to the Dark Night.........229

12. Sweet Surrender 263

13. A Walk with the Buddha..................................... 281

14. Claim Your Adeptship!..303

15. Karma, Honor, and Victory 323

PRACTICING SAINTHOOD

Many love Jesus as long as they do not meet with any adversity. Many praise Him and bless Him, as long as they receive consolation from Him. But if Jesus hide himself and abandon them for a little while, they either complain or fall into extreme discouragement.

But they who love Jesus for Jesus' sake, and not for any consolation of their own, bless Him in every tribulation and anguish of heart, as in the greatest consolation.

—THE IMITATION OF CHRIST

ONE

Practicing Sainthood

Chapter 11 in *The Imitation of Christ* entitled "Of the Few Who Love the Cross of Jesus" illumines some deeper points of the path of sainthood for us to ponder:

> *Jesus has now many lovers of His Heavenly Kingdom, but few who bear His Cross. He has many who desire consolation, but few who desire tribulation. He finds many companions at table, but few in abstinence. All desire to rejoice with Him; few are willing to suffer something for Him and with Him. Many follow Jesus to the Breaking of Bread, but few follow Him to the drinking of the Chalice of His Passion. Many venerate his miracles, but few follow Him in the ignominy of the Cross. Many love Jesus as long as they do not meet with any adversity. Many praise Him and bless Him, as long as they receive consolation from Him. But if Jesus hide himself and abandon them for a little while, they either complain or fall into extreme discouragement.*
>
> *But they who love Jesus for Jesus' sake, and not for any consolation of their own, bless Him in every tribulation and*

*anguish of heart, as in the greatest consolation. And even if He should never give them his consolation, they would nevertheless always praise Him and always want to thank Him.*³

It may be easy to read these passages, but the concepts may not be so easy to live by. They might even make us uncomfortable when juxtaposed to our lives. We have rejoiced in the presence of our Lord and been blessed with the light of the dictations and the teachings of the masters for many years. Since the abundance of light we enjoy is almost beyond measure, I wonder if perhaps we expect that God will always be with us and we will always feel this blessing. In fact, we may be surprised when God withdraws his presence or comfort from us for a time. In some ways our surprise is understandable because it's painful not to feel the presence of God—especially when we are used to it, when we know the thrill, the blessing and the glory of the light, and when all things seem possible because of that presence. It's not surprising when that light seems to disappear that we're suddenly very concerned and feel like God has forsaken us. During those times, we need to remember that even in the seeming absence of our Lord he is with us and he is teaching us. He is helping us to understand what it takes to become the Christ, what it takes to put on the mantle of Christhood, to change from mortality to immortality.

In his 1994 Wesak address our beloved Gautama Buddha said,

> *To go from mortality to immortality—can you not imagine the stretch? Can you not imagine what it takes to break the mortal frame with all its limitations, to come out of that prison house of matter and enter in to your*

*immortality, here and now in this body? It takes a great deal. It is possible. And you should know the joy and not deprive yourselves of the joy of having your full God-Reality in all levels of your being.*⁴

Contrary to that, some of us may be thinking, whether consciously or unconsciously, "I'm going to do my decrees, I'm going to do my prayers, I'm going to try and balance my karma. I'm trying to serve while I'm taking care of my family and doing the things I need to do in my life. I'll just trust that at some time in the future I will put on my Christhood."

Many of us may have accepted limitations on uniting with our Christ Self because it's so easy to see our human shortcomings. That's why we need to remember that we are not perfecting the human! Our human consciousness can *never* become the Christ consciousness! So we must beware of falling for the excuses of the human consciousness that postpone our complete surrender to our Christ Self.

In the dictation we're hearing today, Gautama Buddha says, "*What we see... is a certain taking for granted that you will have your victorious ascension in the light if you will give the certain amount of decrees in your lifetime that will be necessary for this to be accomplished.*"⁵ Later in the dictation, he actually says we are somewhat spoiled. We have such an abundance of light. We also have the miracle of the violet flame, which is a grace beyond measure that most of the saints did not have, and Gautama reminds us just how powerful and strong that grace is.

In the midst of all these graces, we need to be careful lest we think—because we have the violet flame, because we have the dictations, because we have the Science of the Spoken Word—we are somehow exempt from the path of our Lord, the stations of the cross, and the walk the saints have taken before us. We are *not* exempt. Nonetheless, it's an easier walk for us because heaven has conspired to give us all these blessings and spiritual tools at this point in time. Some saints who've gone before us did not make their ascension simply because they did not have the violet flame, yet they still had great mastery in other areas.

It is important to study the lives of the saints in order to understand how they thought, what they wanted, and why they embraced pain as part of their path. For the Western mind, it might seem that they had a very different mindset. We're brought up in an action-oriented culture where success is measured by what we do, by what we accomplish in an outer sense—earning money or expressing artistry or whatever it is. These things are not unimportant, but such accomplishments are not the priority of the saints or the would-be saints. Their priority is to love God, to love their fellowman, and to do whatever they need to do to become the Christ, become like Jesus in manifestation.

Learning from the Saints

Many of us yearn for a closer walk with Jesus, but it seems like we can only get so far and no farther. Is it because Jesus doesn't want to come to us, to be one with our hearts as he was with the saints? Of course not. I think it's because something *in us* hasn't reached the point where we can fully receive him, where we can truly surrender our human consciousness and allow him residence, where we give his prayer with a deep desiring of our hearts: "*Jesus, I bid you enter my whole temple now! By my free will, by my God-dominion, I welcome you! And I let go of everything, my Lord.*"[6]

Studying the lives of the saints in preparation for this sermon has truly been a humbling experience for me. We may think we have done a lot and given a lot, and perhaps in comparison to the world we have. However, we must not compare ourselves to the world because we are on a different path. We need to compare ourselves to the saints and the ascended masters. The world may practice the avoidance of pain but we understand its value and the need to embrace it, not because we consider ourselves martyrs, but because the saints have demonstrated that pain is the portal to bliss and true happiness. Pain comes to everyone, but by our devotion and our openness to God the pain he brings to us will be *transformative* because it will free us from our human consciousness and our karma.

Understanding and practicing sainthood is a lifetime vocation. Becoming a saint is a subject Mother taught about over decades, and one that we continue to study. Today I want to look at snapshots of three Catholic saints who all lived in the twentieth century and whose lives are quite an example: Padre Pio, Sister Faustina Kowalska, and Mother Teresa. We will also look at three Christ-like qualities they had in common that I believe are ones we want to emulate as chelas of the ascended masters.

Much of this sermon is taken from three books on these saints that you might want to read for yourself to get a better understanding of their lives. Although there are a number of good books about Padre Pio, an Italian stigmatist who died in 1962, I especially like *Padre Pio: The True Story*. The next book is *Divine Mercy in My Soul*, the diary of Sister Faustina Kowalska, a Polish nun who died in 1938; it is the powerful statement of one who truly had Jesus as the cornerstone of her life and was clearly walking the path of sainthood. And lastly we have the book of beloved Mother Teresa, who was in embodiment up until 1997, titled *Come Be My Light: The Private Writings of the Saint of Calcutta*. I recommend this book not only because it has a profound story to tell, but also because it has much in it that teaches us about our own path and the endurance necessary to finally make it Home. When it was released a few years ago, there was a lot of publicity about the fact that Mother Teresa went through a forty-year spiritual dark night, something we would never guess by observing her joy and how she lived her life.

These saints embodied three God-qualities that are a powerful example for us to follow. Wherever we are on the Path, practicing these qualities will draw us closer to our Christhood. The first is an unconditional love of God and Jesus; for us, by extension, this includes an unconditional love of our I AM Presence, our Holy Christ Self and the ascended masters. The second quality is an unconditional love of others. And the third is an intense love and willing commitment to experiencing the pain that liberates their own souls even as it balances karma and helps others. It doesn't mean that pain wasn't hard for them; it means they saw pain as a way to draw closer to God and serve other souls.

Unconditional Love of God and Jesus

Thinking about unconditional love of God brings up the question, "Why do we love God?" Or perhaps the question should be, "*How* do we love God?" Mother once said there was no reason to be on a spiritual path if we didn't love God. There's really no other reason to be on this journey except to love God and to fulfill his purposes.

The next question that arises is, "How do we love Jesus and our Holy Christ Self?" As the writer of *The Imitation of Christ* suggests, do we love Jesus when he blesses us and fills us with light, but complain when the clouds block out the light of our Christ Self or Jesus leaves us for a while? In short, are we fair-weather friends? This doesn't mean that we can't cry out to God in our loneliness and adversity; Jesus did, and the saints did also. They felt the pain of separation and yet they were willing to keep going because of their unconditional love of God.* Take Mother Teresa, for instance. In 1946 she was on a train to Darjeeling when she felt the call of Jesus (we understand it was actually El Morya). He called her to go minister to the poorest of the poor in Calcutta. She felt a great release of light and love and what she perceived as the presence of her Lord with her. It was the infiring of her mission; it was the charge from God to go forth and do something. She knew it, she felt it, she experienced it; at one level, she was in bliss because of the light and the presence of God. And so she followed the calling, not knowing that the presence of God would seem to be far from her for most of the next forty years.

Amazingly, she went through a *forty-year* dark night of the soul and Spirit. Except for a one-month period about ten years into her mission, she felt devoid of the presence of Jesus in her life. Think about what that must have been like. No one knew this because she did not show it or speak of it. Though her sense of abandonment and exile caused her the greatest pain we can imagine, she persevered with joy and love for decades. Yet to people around her, she seemed the embodiment of Jesus Christ, of the Christian path of love and mercy. The strength of her love for God was so great that even when she felt so bereft

---

* In the audio album *The Living Flame of Love*, Mother teaches the deeper mysteries of the path of reunion with God.

she was able to carry the spirit of God throughout all those years.

The following is an excerpt from a confession that she wrote to one of her spiritual directors:

> *Jesus hear my prayer – if this pleases You – if my pain and suffering – my darkness and separation gives You a drop of consolation – my own Jesus, do with me as You wish – [for] as long as you wish, without a single glance at my feelings and pain. I am Your own. – Imprint on my soul the life and sufferings of Your Heart. [...] If my separation from You – brings others to You and in their love and company You find joy and pleasure – why Jesus, I am willing with all my heart to suffer ... not only now – but for all eternity – if this was possible. Your happiness is all that I want. – For the rest please do not take the trouble – even if You see me faint with pain, – All this is my will – I want to satiate Your Thirst with every single drop of blood that You can find in me. – Don't allow me to do you wrong in any way – take from me the power of hurting You. [...] I beg of You only one thing – please do not take the trouble to return soon. – I am ready to wait for You for all eternity. – [signed] Your little one*[7]

These are the heartfelt words of a soul who loves Jesus so much that she is willing to bear the pain of separation from him. She took a vow early on in her Christian life: "*I want to love Him as He has not been loved before.*"[8] That's an incredibly bold statement that shows how much she loved him. You wonder if those forty years of spiritual dryness were in some ways the answer to that prayer, because she had to love him without experiencing his presence. She saw the work grow and expand

and she saw many people blessed, so she knew Jesus was there. But she still felt emptiness and loss. What a test of love! Can we not also endure the seeming separation for a season without feeling the closeness of our Lord? Is it not right for him to test us so that we understand the love it takes to make it on the Path?

Only the certainty that she was loved unconditionally could have given Mother Teresa enough confidence to abandon herself to God so completely and without reserve. She gave herself totally. Another important thing to note is that the gravity of her vow and commitment did not make her gloomy or despondent. On the contrary, she was full of fun and enjoyed everything that went on. Her joy was not just a matter of temperament; it was rather the fruit of the blessedness of submission. "*When I see someone sad,*" she would say, "*I always think, she is refusing something to Jesus.*"[9]

Mother Teresa received the Nobel Peace Prize, and the head of the United Nations called her the most powerful woman in the world, while she referred to herself as "the little me" or "the little bride of Christ." So we see the joy of God and the pain of seeming separation from God simultaneously in the same person. This was the path of sainthood she walked.

Here is a saying from Mother Teresa that we could almost make our motto if we're brave enough to do so: "*I am ready to accept whatever He gives and to give whatever He takes with a big smile.*"[10] What an affirmation! Accepting whatever he gives and whatever he takes with a big smile—that is embodying the joy flame. Why embody it? Because we love God, we love Jesus, we love the ascended masters, we love our Holy Christ Self. We trust in them. And as we give ourselves to them we have the return current, whether we always feel it or not. That is unconditional love.

We develop unconditional love over time as we ascend the spiritual path. In writing to a soul, Padre Pio gave a teaching on the dark night or purgation of the Spirit and why we need it to take our love of God to a higher level. He said, *"The trial will certainly be a very severe one, but do not be frightened... This new purification will consist entirely in detaching you from what is called accidental spiritual devotion and love of God."* The author of the book adds, *"—in other words from a love of God that is based on his gifts rather than on him, for his own sake."*[11] Do you notice the subtle difference?

We need to be delivered from the consciousness of loving God only for his gifts because that attitude will prevent us from experiencing the fullness of God's love. Without the fire of devotion, when his gifts are withdrawn for a season (as happens to us all), some may leave the Path, blaming God and not realizing they have actually withheld their love from him. We want to have an unconditional love of God no matter what comes our way.

Unconditional Love of Others

We can also develop unconditional love of others. The great philosopher Linus from the *Peanuts* cartoon said, *"I love mankind, it's people I can't stand!"*[12] I think we sometimes feel that way: God bless the world and all the wonderful people in it; but then we have interactions with individuals that lead to frustrations or disappointments or whatever, and we no longer feel universal love. Such interactions help us recognize whether we love others unconditionally or only love those who love us or treat us well.

As part of their love of others, many of the saints, including Padre Pio, Mother Teresa and Sister Faustina, considered themselves to be "victim souls"—those who took upon themselves the sins (or as we would say, the karma) of others so that they might be saved. Jesus told Sister Faustina, "*You are not living for yourself, but for souls, and other souls will profit from your sufferings. Your prolonged suffering will give them the light and strength to accept My will.*"[13] These saints didn't have the violet flame decrees, so when they took the burdens of others upon themselves, it frequently impacted them physically, such as problems with their health that they did willingly bear.

Isn't it interesting that by taking on others' karma, the saints gave those souls extended opportunity, and opportunity is exactly what we have received, is it not? The balance has been held for us for thousands of years by Jesus, by the ascended masters, by the messengers. The saints held the balance for others too. Why did they do it? Because they had an unconditional love for God's people.

I have never heard the ascended masters ask us to be "victim souls." They have given us the Science of the Spoken Word and especially the violet flame to do much, if not all, of the same work the saints did to help others. This has nothing to do with taking on the karma of the fallen ones. This is about taking on a portion of the karma of the lightbearers so that they may be strengthened and resurrected, which is exactly what Jesus did for us the past two thousand years.

Why do we spend hours and hours decreeing? It is to help God's precious lightbearers on this planet. It is our way of being "victim souls," to transmute other people's karma (according to God's will) so that they might have opportunity to move forward on their spiritual path. Great souls who are beset by their own karma or attacks from the fallen ones or even world karma need the light of our decrees in order to be strengthened and saved.

Padre Pio used to go into ecstasies that were sometimes recorded by the monks who were around him. Often these were a dialogue he had with Jesus or his guardian angel, and those present only heard his side of the exchange. Very often he would be pleading with Jesus to take upon himself the sins of this or that individual so that that person might be saved. The other monks could often guess how Jesus responded by what Padre Pio said. He wouldn't give up; we don't know what Jesus told him about particular souls, but Pio would go on and on and on, often praying that the sins of this person would be on him. That is true love.

We can pray for souls through our decrees, always praying according to God's will. We are not on the path of martyrdom but we *are* on the path of service, and by following the teaching of the ascended masters, our service can bring great blessings to souls of light. So if we ask ourselves if we have the unconditional love for people that the saints had, I believe many of us could say we do, as demonstrated by the decrees that we give week after week, month after month, year after year, for the liberation of souls and this planet.

Concerning loving others, Mother Teresa wrote, *"If we really love souls we must be ready to take their place, to take their sins upon us..."*[14] We can do this by being a living sacrifice, invoking light and holding that light in our auras. We know that Mother and Mark bore a great weight of world karma. They are ascended now, and we are called upon to bear some of that karma. Mercifully, we only need to bear a portion of it since it is shared by others walking the path beside us, and we also have the violet flame to make things easier. Even so, this journey takes love, as great a love as Mother Teresa demonstrated for God and his people.

In John 21:15–16, Jesus asked Peter twice, "*Lovest thou me?*" In verse 17 Jesus "*saith unto him the third time, Simon, son of Jonas, lovest thou me? Peter was grieved because he said unto him the third time, Lovest thou me? And he said unto him, Lord, thou knowest all things; thou knowest that I love thee. Jesus saith unto him, Feed my sheep.*"

It seems that Jesus was trying to get Peter's attention because perhaps he didn't understand what it takes to truly love—to "feed my sheep" by loving people with the same love Jesus had for them. Peter needed to go to a depth of love that was not superficial or intellectual. That is the same depth of heartfelt love that we all need to strive for, the same unconditional love that the saints had for God's people.

Jesus' words to Peter make us consider how much we love, how deep our love is, and how much we are willing to do in the name of love. When we hear of hundreds or thousands killed in a war or an accident or a natural disaster, it's hard to comprehend the loss, whereas when we hear the story of one soul or one family's tragedy it is sometimes easier to feel the pain and send them love. Let us strive to hold that same love for the many. It takes great love to bear great pain, which brings us to the third quality the saints exemplified for us to follow—willingness to bear pain.

Willingness to Experience Pain

When we were brought up, most of us weren't taught to experience pain as a blessing on the spiritual path; we were taught to seek the love and care of Jesus and of God. It never occurred to me in my younger years that pain was part of the path Home. Yet the saints counted pain and suffering as their greatest joys. Why did they embrace pain and suffering?

Because they discovered something the world doesn't know—pain is the portal to bliss, to the all-consuming love of God.

Mother Teresa said, "*...I would not wish at any price to give up my sufferings.... I have found real happiness in suffering...*"[15] Padre Pio said, "*I suffer only when I don't suffer.*"[16] Padre Pio also wrote, "*... my good Jesus is very much with me! Oh, what precious moments I have with Him! It is a joy which I can liken to nothing else. It is a happiness that the Lord gives me to enjoy almost only in suffering.*"[17] Sister Faustina wrote in her diary, "*Suffering is a great grace, through suffering the soul becomes like the Savior; in suffering love becomes crystallized; the greater the suffering, the purer the love.*"[18]

With the words "through suffering the soul becomes like the Savior," Sister Faustina gave us the key to understanding the inestimable value of suffering and pain: Pain is a means to an end; pain is necessary to free us from our human self, our carnal mind. It teaches humility, balances karma and brings us to the place of total surrender—the place where we can let go of the human and embrace the Christ.

Remember that the saints had both pain and joy present within themselves at the same time. In the midst of their pain and suffering, the saints had a desire to serve Jesus by carrying some of the pain of the world. They also had an understanding that their suffering gave souls opportunity and could help save many. Likewise, when we are sick or in pain, we can offer that suffering to Jesus, to God, to help other souls. And knowing we are helping others makes the suffering easier to bear. As a corollary to offering up their suffering for others, experiencing pain allowed the saints to feel that they were doing something for God and Jesus. It was a way of expressing their unconditional love for them, and it gave them great joy!

Following their example will assist us in moving beyond asking, "God, what can you do for me?" to the unselfish attitude the saints had of loving and serving God and his people. While it's obviously not wrong to ask for God's help, it's also good to have a deeper understanding that the challenges and sufferings we face are often according to God's purposes. The saints had an absolute trust in God's will, even without the outer understanding of the law of karma that we have.

The following is an excerpt from the same Wesak dictation by Gautama Buddha I referred to earlier. He teaches us how pain relates to our path and our soul testings.

> *I ask that you seriously consider that what will save this earth is your determination to strive for and achieve adeptship. I advise you, the chelas of the ascended masters, to develop a willingness to go through the pain of making yourselves whole through your own Holy Christ Self—who, of course, is always one with the Lord Jesus.*
>
> *Pain, beloved, is not something to be avoided but to be welcomed. Pain, sorrow, the sense of one's own impurity that precedes the sense of one's purity, the dark night of the soul and the dark night of the Spirit—these are the elements of life that let you know that your feet are planted firmly on the path of the adepts and the ascended masters who sponsor you.*[19]

Transcending the Pain Station

We can't measure our success as a chela by all the good things that are happening in our lives, but rather by the type of initiations given to us by God. What we might perceive as calamity may be the reward for our diligence on the Path—the initiations of the fourteen stations of the cross or the like, following in the footsteps of our Lord. Gautama Buddha cautions:

Avoidance of all of these soul testings will surely show you that you are floating on the surface, that you are not in the very depths of the sea or in the very core of the earth itself, where you discover the core of your own psyche and the collective unconscious of earth's evolutions.

Pain is a necessity. Pain is something you experience and call pain, but ultimate pain bears the fruit of ultimate bliss.

Do not practice avoidance, beloved ones. Occupy your total mind. There are those who occupy one-eighth of the mind who may be highly intelligent and highly effective, yet they do not dig deeper because when they dig they arrive at the station of pain.

Yes, the pain station—it is a place in consciousness. Some call it the pain threshold. You must be willing to have pain, beloved, for sooner or later that pain will come upon you out of season, untimely, only to dash your hopes, your health, your highest goals.

It is always well to greet one's karma before it arrives at one's doorstep, is it not? Run down the highway and greet it! Put it into the sacred fire so that it does not even come nigh your abode....

Blessed hearts, those who choose to remain on a plateau will be left behind. We do not remain on any plateau. We keep climbing, beloved. And when we have all reached the top of Everest, we keep on climbing. We do not stay in one place, for we are transformed daily. Therefore seek that transformation, set your sights on victory, keep yourselves steady and do not descend below your Christ consciousness.[20]

How many people move away from the Path when they arrive at the station of pain, looking for something that satisfies their human consciousness instead of delving into resolving their psyche? Perhaps we'll save ourselves some anguish if we realize that moving through our karma and the pain it brings is part of moving forward spiritually. We don't want to walk around with our heads hanging down, saying "Poor me, I'm in the dark night of the soul and Spirit." Although we will experience the pain of being purged, we will also have the joy of knowing we are being transformed, and that joy will increase as we surrender more and give more. I remind myself that the pain of the passage to our Christhood and adeptship is temporal, but the joy is eternal. Countless others have passed these tests, and with God's help, we can too.

So what does it take to be purged, healed and become spiritually whole? For most of us it takes the chastening fire. For some this fire came directly from the messenger. For many now it will come through our returning karma and spiritual tests or initiations.

Padre Pio said, *"To be healed they must submit themselves to suffering, namely, to bloodletting, to the lance, to the razor, to the probe, to the scalpel, to the fire, and to all the bitterness of medicine. In order to be spiritually cured, we have to submit to all the tortures of the Divine Physician."*[21] Powerful images, aren't they? However, that which brings us closer to God is not really torture—it's grace and it's mercy!

This is our path and we are prepared to walk it victoriously according to God's timetable. Let us not get into the mindset that we need to wait for our ascension to put on our Christhood. We need to recognize and accept the possibility and the reality of becoming the Christ *now*. It takes courage to walk this path, but the prize is the greatest of all—our soul's eternal victory. It takes love and it is hard at times, but the saints proved that even the hardest tests can be passed. Others have done it without the violet flame. What wonders can God accomplish in us *with* the violet flame?

This is not only our path; it is who we are. We can ask ourselves, "If not now, when?" It takes courage to ask God to lead us through the path of suffering that the saints walked, but it is the shortest way Home. And I believe it is actually less painful than the fear of pain, which has stopped many souls from finishing. Do we want to come back lifetime after lifetime and walk the via dolorosa? Been there, done that. Let's get through this, surrender our human substance into the flame and walk the earth as Christed ones. The masters have told us we can do it. And it will be the resurrection of the community, the church, and this planet.

Let us all embrace our destiny. Let us walk and practice the path of sainthood daily. God will meet us no matter where we are as we start up the next step on the Path. Let us not fear; let us not lose our joy. For pain as the portal to bliss is a mystery no more.

LOVE AS A CHOICE

Let your love be a demonstration of your Christhood.

—PAUL THE VENETIAN

TWO

Love As a Choice

It was the evening of February 2, 1943, and the U.S.A.T. [army transport ship] *Dorchester* was crowded to capacity, carrying 902 servicemen, merchant seamen and civilian workers.

Once a luxury coastal liner, the 5,600-ton vessel had been converted into an Army transport ship. The *Dorchester*, one of three ships in the SG-19 convoy, was moving steadily across the icy waters from Newfoundland toward an American base in Greenland....

The *Dorchester* was now only 150 miles from its destination, but the captain ordered the men to sleep in their clothing and keep life jackets on. Many soldiers sleeping deep in the ship's hold disregarded the order because of the engine's heat. Others ignored it because the life jackets were uncomfortable.

On February 3, at 12:55 a.m., a periscope broke the chilly Atlantic waters. Through the cross hairs, an officer aboard the German submarine U-223 spotted the *Dorchester*... and after identifying and targeting the ship, he gave orders to fire the torpedoes... The one that hit was decisive—and deadly—striking the starboard side, amid ship, far below the water line.

Captain Danielsen...gave the order to abandon ship. In less than twenty minutes, the Dorchester would slip beneath the Atlantic's icy waters....

Aboard the Dorchester, panic and chaos had set in. The blast had killed scores of men, and many more were seriously wounded. Others, stunned by the explosion were groping in the darkness. Those sleeping without clothing rushed topside where they were confronted first by a blast of icy Arctic air and then by the knowledge that death awaited.

Men jumped from the ship into lifeboats, over-crowding them to the point of capsizing, according to eyewitnesses. Other rafts, tossed into the Atlantic, drifted away before soldiers could get in them.

Through the pandemonium...four Army chaplains brought hope in despair and light in darkness. Those chaplains were Lt. George L. Fox, Methodist; Lt. Alexander D. Goode, Jewish; Lt. John P. Washington, Roman Catholic; and Lt. Clark V. Poling, Dutch Reformed.

Quickly and quietly, the four chaplains spread out among the soldiers. There they tried to calm the frightened, tend the wounded and guide the disoriented toward safety.

"Witnesses of that terrible night remember hearing the four men offer prayers for the dying and encouragement for those who would live," says Wyatt R. Fox, son of Reverend Fox.

One witness, Private William B. Bednar, found himself floating in oil-smeared water surrounded by dead bodies and debris. "I could hear men crying, pleading, praying," Bednar recalled. "I could also hear the chaplains preaching courage. Their voices were the only thing that kept me going."

Another sailor, Petty Officer John J. Mahoney, tried to reenter his cabin but Rabbi Goode stopped him. Mahoney, concerned about the cold Arctic air, explained he had forgotten his gloves.

"Never mind," Goode responded. "I have two pairs." The rabbi then gave the petty officer his own gloves. In retrospect, Mahoney realized that Rabbi Goode was not conveniently carrying two pairs of gloves, and that the rabbi had decided not to leave the Dorchester.

By this time, most of the men were topside, and the chaplains opened a storage locker and began distributing life jackets. It was then that Engineer Grady Clark witnessed an astonishing sight.

When there were no more lifejackets in the storage room, the chaplains removed theirs and gave them to four frightened young men.

"It was the finest thing I have ever seen or hope to see this side of heaven," said John Ladd, another survivor who saw the chaplains' selfless act....

As the ship went down, survivors in nearby rafts could see the four chaplains—arms linked and braced against the slanting deck. Their voices could also be heard offering prayers.

Of the 902 men aboard the U.S.A.T. Dorchester, 672 died, leaving 230 survivors. When the news reached American shores, the nation was stunned by the magnitude of the tragedy and heroic conduct of the four chaplains....

That night Reverend Fox, Rabbi Goode, Reverend Poling and Father Washington passed life's ultimate test.

> *In doing so, they became an enduring example of extraordinary faith, courage and selflessness.*[22]

Isn't that quite a moving story of love—supreme love? For we know, "*Greater love hath no man than this, that a man lay down his life for his friends.*"[23] These four chaplains passed one of love's greatest tests and became an inspiration to the nation.

We might wonder at what point they made the choice to give up their lives for others. When did they make the choice to love? Was it conscious? Was it preceded by many choices to love? Was it simply the manifestation of who they already were, so that it was the natural thing for them to do? Whatever the case, they made that ultimate choice to love.

Love is indeed a choice. Though that may seem an obvious observation, it is important to remind ourselves that each day we make many choices and decisions about how we react to circumstances and people that come our way. It's not a foregone conclusion that we will always choose love. For instance, in the dictation we are hearing today, Paul the Venetian says that when we are angry we "*...have made both a conscious decision to be angry and a conscious decision to forsake love.*"[24] So we can choose love or we can choose to forsake love. It's a choice, a decision.

The Love of the Saints

The subject of love is so fundamental and yet so expansive that it can seem overwhelming to ponder. Let us simply say that love is the foundation of our spiritual path, and we continually receive tests of love whether or not we recognize them as such. Big or small, the tests of love are sometimes the most difficult to pass. We may not be standing on a sinking ship, required to make a life or death decision like the four chaplains. But in the end, the cumulative daily choices we make to love or not to love will have just as strong an effect on our souls, on our spiritual path, and on others, as choosing life or death.

I think at some level we all aspire to the sacrificial love of the saints, which is so inspirational and powerful. Paul the Venetian says, *"There are levels of all-transcending, self-transcendent love, love that is sacrificial—love that is so all-consuming that in its presence one desires to surrender and to surrender again to the arms of Love...."*[25]

What does such love look like in real life? We find one example in a letter written by the Catholic saint Padre Pio in 1914 in response to a woman who had written to him. It reveals that his love for souls was so great that he was willing to pay the ultimate price for their salvation. He wrote:

> *I have very much [taken] to heart all those needs which you have explained to me. May our most sweet Jesus bring peace to all those afflicted hearts. I tell you sincerely, without fear of lying, beloved daughter of Jesus, that my soul can say with the apostle St. Paul: I could wish that I myself were accursed and cut off from Christ for the sake of my Brethren. Yes, (let) our sweet Lord excommunicate me, separate me from him, abandon me and allow me to suffer the shame and sufferings earned by my brethren [their karma]; let him even cancel my name from the Book of Life as long as he saves my brothers and companions in exile....*[26]

Wow! You know he was sincere. He didn't think to himself, "Hmm, do I really want to make this prayer? I'm not sure what will come to me." No! He was totally abandoned to love; nothing else meant anything to him. He couldn't do anything else but offer his life for others because that was the power of his all-consuming love.

We cannot help but wonder how Padre Pio came to the point where his love for others was so great that he was willing to pay any price for their salvation. I can't imagine that depth of love arose spontaneously from nothing. It had to have been built upon the many, many choices he had made to love in that and previous embodiments. He wasn't afraid to love. He wasn't afraid to give his all, because not only had he experienced love, he had *become* it.

Now what about us? What choices can we make for love this very day, this very week that will change the lives of others and ultimately change ours as well? It's likely to be little choices such as subtle vibrations in tone of voice, pausing to notice things, kind actions, compassion for each other, a listening ear. It is choosing to be aware that each day is not just the fulfillment of a routine of what you have to do: "Today I have to finish such and such, take the car to the repair shop, then go to the grocery store, the bank, pick up the kids after soccer practice..." and so on. Although the activities of each day may keep us busy, unless we endow them with love, we're just existing. We're not acting in the way that God has taught us.

Loving Your Soul

Paul the Venetian also tells us,

> *Love Thyself. Love thy Soul. Do not allow schisms within! Go deep in the unconscious and saturate, saturate, saturate again and again and again with Love's fire along with the violet fire of Freedom's love. If you do not love yourself because you have been condemned by parents*

or others, then, beloved, that condemnation will become self-condemnation and it will follow you and follow you like a plague.[27]

Loving ourselves does not mean excusing ourselves or not taking responsibility for our mistakes and karma. However, God does not condemn us, and we should never, ever condemn our own soul or the souls of others. This is such a key point. How can we love other souls if we don't love our own soul? That's where love begins. Jesus put it quite plainly, *"Thou shalt love thy neighbour as thyself."*[28] Love begins with us.

I recently ran into a member of our community. After we had exchanged pleasantries, I innocently remarked to him that my wife and I had been talking about him recently. As soon as I said that, I could see a burden of condemnation come upon him, as though he expected to hear some criticism. When I told him we had been commenting about the example he sets for the entire community by his continual service and willingness to go the extra mile, I could see an instant change in his demeanor and a smile come to his face. I thought to myself, "Here's a soul who gives his all. He's continually serving; he's very unselfish; and yet he's walking around carrying a weight of condemnation."

This man is not unique. Every soul of light on this planet is under the unseen weight of condemnation from the fallen angels. It's an energy we wake up to every day. It's like a constant background noise that goes unnoticed but can wear you down. It can affect our consciousness in subtle and not-so-subtle ways from self-condemnation and depression to criticism of others and serious karma-making actions. It can keep us from becoming the fullness of who we are, which is just what the fallen ones want. It takes will and effort to challenge that condemnation and throw off the weight that is upon us. So be aware and do not allow self-condemnation to penetrate your being.

Begin with love. Love your soul; love your inner child. When Mother Teresa was asked how to bring about world peace, she suggested to start by loving your family. I think we could amend that to say, "Start by loving your own soul." While some people indulge themselves and their human creation, I find that most people tend to be pretty hard on themselves. It's okay to go after those parts of ourselves that we know are unreal, but we should never, ever condemn our soul or the God within us. Our soul is precious; it is innocent. It is the creation of God and the part of us that will become eternal. Our soul has pain and needs help, so we need to comfort our soul even as we comfort our inner child.

Kindness

Love begins with being kind to our souls and to the God within. When we've done that, we're ready to freely extend that love to others. Mother told a story about flying over a California city in an airplane and sending love from her heart to the people below, and they sent back a wave of negative energy. They did not want the love she was extending. So we may offer love, and if people don't want it we send it anyway, just for the sake of loving. And some, if not many, will want it and accept it.

Another question is: How do we love others, not as a "people pleaser" but as someone who loves the God within them? And more importantly, what does that love look like? Paul the Venetian tells us, "*Take measured cups of love, yes, measured cups of love, and give them to those who can assimilate your love as an elixir. Understand this, beloved. All great teachers of wisdom have taught that one must not cast one's pearls before the swinish elements of the human consciousness."*[29] In other words, we need attunement and the discernment of the Holy Spirit as to exactly what we give to others. We need to be aware of what manifestation of love each soul needs at a particular moment, whether physical assistance, encouragement, sometimes even rebuke, or one of the myriad other possibilities.

When we are interacting with anyone, it is generally good to remember the words of Isaiah, "*Comfort ye, comfort ye my people, saith your God.*"[30] A word of comfort, a word of kindness may be all a soul needs to deal with the burdens and trials of the day. Morya teaches that kind words heal. Simple, but so profound. And Mother teaches that true love is a listening heart.

In his dictation "The Vessel of Kindness," Kuthumi says,

> *May you know the one great quality that is sought after that comes from the auric rings of Maitreya and his true bodhisattvas. It is the quality of kindness, almost overlooked in this hurried world, almost thought of as unnecessary. Yet what do you remember most about anyone? A kindness, a gesture, a sincere concern, a practical helpfulness, a perception of your need before you yourself know it.*[31]

In fact, I remember several acts of kindness that were done to me decades ago. I never forgot them because they were the right thing at the right time when I needed it the most. To help us extend love, as we get up in the morning we could say a prayer to be a vessel of kindness, "Dear Father in heaven, position me where I can be the instrument of kindness to a soul that may be in need."

Have you ever considered whether people are glad to see you come and sorry to see you go? Or if they feel loved and worthwhile in your presence? Along those lines, Mother wrote on behalf of El Morya, "*Giving people their dignity is kindness—being so magnanimous and outgoing and supportive of them that they sense in your presence that they have dignity.*"[32] And Mother Teresa said, "*Let no one ever come to you without leaving better and happier. Be the living expression of God's kindness: kindness in your face, kindness in your eyes, kindness in your smile.*"[33]

Have you ever noticed that some people really do have kind eyes? Without thinking about it, when you see eyes like that, you realize that person is kind. You can see the flame of kindness reflected in their face. And how souls yearn for that! It's the yearning for the Divine Mother and her comfort.

This earth is a rough place to live—as though I were telling you something you don't already know! The energies we deal with on a daily basis are pretty intense, and many souls carry a much heavier burden than we know. For example, the book *Unbroken* is based on the story of a man and his experience in World War II. He endured things we can hardly imagine, but he survived. When he was young, his brother had said to him, "If you can take it, you can make it." That became the byline by which he survived the incredible difficulties he faced.

Such stories make us think about the millions who lost their lives in wars or about the various burdens that souls are carrying from just their current lifetime—much less their many previous embodiments. They are probably not even aware of old burdens: the trauma, the losses, the griefs that we can hardly imagine today in modern America with all our comforts and conveniences. We do not know what people carry hidden within their consciousness. Though they may have a tough exterior, they may be carrying incredible pain, so we need to have compassion for them.

Love Heals Inner Pain

In his dictation "The Covenant of Compassion," Lanello reminds us of the sensitive nature of lightbearers, even though they seem to have tough skin. He teaches us to look upon people differently, not as their outer accoutrements or shortcomings or graying hair or anything human, but as their precious souls.

> *Therefore in the bonds of love and service and for the exercise of your own heart, it is well to deal with each one as a tender flower. And remember that those who appear on the surface as having the toughest skin may often have the most sensitive hearts.*
>
> *Thus, into this community of love and understanding shall many be drawn who truly do need understanding. There are many who are sick who need healing, but I have not sent them; for I desire a professional stance from the career son and daughter of God—a point not only of non-condemnation, but the point of positive warmth and giving and welcome.*
>
> *I would like to dedicate this year of my victory to my own Guru, El Morya, who heads the Order of the Good Samaritans. I would like you to think of Camelot and the Inner Retreat as a hospice—a place where the weary traveler may come and find a welcome and food and warmth and shelter, where the needs of the man, and the human, might be seen as paramount, as all know how the human*

problem can weigh so heavy that it must find surcease before the spiritual teaching can begin. But it already has begun the moment you extend love, for this is the essence of your heart and your path.

You will always find that the ascending ones nearer and nearer the goal seem to enter into a life of doing for others often little things seemingly insignificant. And even the recipients of such gifts and graces sometimes wonder, but in each such gesture there is a transmission of love. This increases the capacity of the heart of the giver but also brings great solace and comfort to those who receive, even though they may not perceive it.

For I tell you, beloved hearts, in many the hungers, the pain and the crying is so great that the hurt of all of this is sealed away in some dark corner of the subconscious. And the individual who is striving and determined puts all that aside and goes forth to battle, seeking what he, too, may give to life.

Thus, when the healer comes with the great comfort flame and with love as a mother's heart, when these individuals who have set aside their self-concerns and burdens begin to feel that comfort and they begin to feel the ability to rest and be at ease, for a time perhaps the entire record of the hurt may surface. And then it is that the healing love is most efficacious in transmutation.

In the presence of love, those most self-sufficient may let go and release the burdens, not fearing the opinions of their peers, not fearing to be judged or to be thought any less than the model role that they are pursuing and determining to externalize merely because they, too, may have had some difficulty, some problem, some experience that seems to be less than what the model chela or disciple would have.

> *Therefore, as the strength of each individual is pursued and builded upon, and as that one becomes strong in service, there are cycles also when all that is beneath will pass through the violet flame because of the presence of the Comforter in any one of you and in all of you.*
>
> *Once you are determined to be [to fulfill the office of] that loving Comforter to each and every one, you will begin to be amazed as to how much you can help, how many problems you can heal, how much of a past record can go into the flame—a knot of some past lifetime, a situation that has created almost scar tissue. Your presence, your voice, your comfort, your love, your companionship can dissolve it in a moment. And you will watch how that one will take flight and soar, barely realizing that such a record has been taken and perhaps not even knowing just how much the ruby-ray love of your heart has been a part of the alchemy of release.*[34]

In another part of this dictation, Lanello says there are some records, buried deep in the subconscious, that are not allowed to surface more than once in a century because they are so intense and hard for the soul to bear. Then he tells us that such self-limiting points are best melted by love. Love melts away people's defenses and gives them a surcease from the inner pain they may be feeling.

We can extend that love. This isn't about giving advice or fixing people's problems. Rather, simply being in the presence of love allows souls to work on their own issues, challenges and karma. Being in the presence of love can give them the courage to face and tackle those things that are so very difficult. We all know from our own experience that each of us has these difficult things in our lives, perhaps a deep record, a repetitious record, something that can remain hidden or unresolved until God says, "Now is the time. You have the violet flame, you have community, you can move through this and make it in this life." Such records have to come up, and we have to be ready to be the presence of love and comfort so that the soul (including our own) may go forward in courage knowing they are not alone.

A soul may have tremendous attainment on many rays, but there might be one ray or one chakra that comes up short; therefore they embody for the sole purpose of working on that ray or chakra. So it's not their mastery that shines forth, it's their shortcomings. We may encounter a soul that has certain difficulties in mastering things in day-to-day life. Yet we don't know what their causal body is like, we don't know their levels of great attainment, we don't know perhaps the humility they have chosen to embody in taking these shortcomings upon themselves in order to gain mastery. We have to be careful not to position ourselves or others in an imagined hierarchy of souls: "So and so just doesn't quite have the ability to do what needs to be done to be successful," or the flip side, "Well, that person knows so much about the teachings, they must have a lot of attainment." We may even make such judgments unconsciously.

Mother once commented about a soul in the community. She didn't say who it was, but she said this person came under a lot of criticism from other students. While I don't remember the exact details, the picture that emerged was of someone who wasn't following directions, was always making mistakes, wasn't completing the assignment, maybe wasn't there on time—a person with many frustrating behavioral issues. Mother said that all those things were true about this soul, but she said there was something else true about him—Gautama Buddha was in his heart. I never forgot that. A soul that was not perfect in many outer ways, and yet Gautama Buddha was residing in his heart.

As Paul the Venetian says, we don't give everything to everybody; we definitely need discernment regarding what we give to people. But is there a person in this room who does not like to receive kindness and comfort? Let's see a show of hands. That's a joke, isn't it? We *all* want to feel these things. We all want the presence of the Divine Mother. We may kind of steel ourselves, thinking we're chelas or students of the ascended masters and we've got our karma to balance and we've got a world to save and we've got to be really strong. Well, we do need to be strong, and we need to have enough fire and determination to hold sufficient light to dispel the darkness. But at the same time we also need the presence and the comfort of the Divine Mother.

Yes, we need Kali to fiercely slay the demons and the darkness that assails us, but we also need Mother Mary and the vision of the babe in her arms being comforted by the Divine Mother. We can be that comfort to each other and to all souls, even by just being there for someone in pain. That in itself communicates deep love and can be the encouragement that gives someone the will and the strength to go on. This is one of the blessings of community—being such a force of love that simply being in our aura is transformational.

It's good to remember that it's not so much what you say or what you do, though those are important; it's the presence of love within you that makes all the difference.

Love in Action

How do you get that presence of love? Paul the Venetian says, "*Let your love be a demonstration of your Christhood.*"[35]

When you become the Christ, or you're working diligently toward it and you become a being of love for periods of time, everything else disappears. That is how Padre Pio could sincerely say such things as "cancel my name from the Book of Life"—by feeling the presence of love so intensely that he was willing to lay down his life to save a soul. That is one demonstration of what can happen when love is fully present in a person, and I wonder if some of us are more than a little afraid of that love: "Will that mean I have to let down my defenses and people will see me differently than the way I think they should see me?" Yes, it probably does. Maybe that's the meaning behind the phrase "being a fool for Christ." We need to tear down the walls we have built around ourselves and allow who we truly are to emerge. By grace, that will be our Christ Self, extending the immense love held in the heart of that Christ.

It's not our intellectual attainment or our ability to spout the teachings and the intricacies of the Law that's going to make a difference. We would only be as *"sounding brass, or a tinkling cymbal."*[36] It is the presence of love that will make the difference. To get that presence we must give love—give love to God in praising him and acknowledging his supremacy, give love to our own soul, and give love to others as well.

We shouldn't expect to get applause. In fact, many people who are willing to be love and extend love are criticized. All the saints went through this. Sometimes even their own bands rejected them. For example, Saint Francis thought he was a failure at the end of his embodiment because his own brothers had turned against him and what he was teaching and demonstrating. However, he was the example of Christ's love so no matter what others did, it could not detract from it or lessen it. Padre Pio and other saints wanted to be "victim souls," offering to take the pain of others' sins and karma upon themselves because they had so much love that they couldn't bear for others to experience that pain alone. That's probably not an appealing prospect to most of us, and one might wonder why they would do that. The reason they did it was that the amazing amount of love they had in their heart and being was overflowing. It was the love of a Christ who would lay down his life for his friends.

We can follow the teachings of the ascended masters. We can give the violet flame, which is a tremendous act of love on behalf of others. Yet until we more fully become an instrument of love, we cannot truly become the Christ. In one sense, it's difficult to get a handle on what it means to "have more love" or "be more love." Again, what does that love look like? Well, it begins increment by increment with the smallest acts.

We can determine to have more love and be more love in our interactions with others this very day and week. The bottom line is that although those are powerful concepts, if we are not *changed* by them, they are of no import or meaning to us. I don't think we should announce this week that we're going to be a greater instrument of love. We just have to *be* it. It can manifest in little things. It can be ever so subtle or as simple as listening, as having a concern for the burdens on someone's heart. When someone feels genuine concern, the floodgates often open and we want to be ready to receive what comes.

Try sincerely asking, "How are you doing?" and then be fully present to listen. That's being an instrument of love. It's the opposite of greeting someone with words like "How are you today?" while the vibration says, "Don't really tell me because I'm busy."

Paul the Venetian says, "*Show the Christhood you are becoming. Show it by love.*"[37] And Mother Teresa had a wonderful idea on how to start showing love: "*It is easy to love the people far away. It is not always easy to love those close to us. It is easier to give a cup of rice to relieve hunger than to relieve the loneliness and pain of someone unloved in their own home. Bring love into your home for this is where our love for each other must start."*[38] After we love ourselves and our family, we can expand our home to include not only our family, but also our community. We obviously have karma not only with each other in our families, but also with those in our community, our cities, and our nations. Love will heal that. Love will bring forgiveness, which is the completion of healing that brings wholeness.

We may not feel the immediacy of a ship sinking beneath us, but it is still a good metaphor for us to consider because there are souls in real danger of being lost and what we do each day *will* make a difference for them, will buy time and space for their salvation. It may be in a direct encounter we have with them. They may be inspired by taking a soul reading of us on inner levels and seeing how much love we hold in our being. Saints and avatars have paid the price for us; we are here because of their sacrifice and sponsorship. Perhaps now God is asking us to bear a burden for others that they might also have opportunity.

As love and true compassion grow in our hearts, they will become a collective magnet, a beacon that will draw other souls to these teachings and this path of love. People want knowledge and understanding of the teachings, but the soul's core desire is to give love and to be loved. Everyone wants to be loved.

Each of us here does have love and we do give love. We are motivated by love every time we make the decision to go to a service, to give our decrees for the saving of souls and the planet. Yet we also know that whatever love we already have now must increase, for our own soul's victory, the victory of all lightbearers, and the victory of this planet in a golden age.

There is a time to study and show yourself approved to God, and there is a time to impart knowledge. There is a time to impart love, and there is a time to simply *be that love*. Where do we start? We start today, this week, this month, and this year by making the choice—the choice to love.

PLEASING GOD

See, then, and understand that pleasing God does not require gymnastics of the mind or ultimate feats of this and that but simply the gentle heart. Oh, the gentle heart, the heart of kindness, the heart of Maitreya, the heart of the Bodhisattva!

—**LANELLO**

THREE

Pleasing God

A Christian minister told the story of what happened when he asked those attending a Sunday service how many of them really wanted to please God more than anything else. Every hand went up. Then he asked them, *"How many of you think God is really pleased with you?"* Out of at least four hundred people, one eleven-year-old boy and one ten-year-old girl raised their hands. That was all.

He commented, *"Very few believers actually believe that they are pleasing God. Most feel some degree of forgiveness and maybe acceptance, but to think that the Lord is actually pleased with us is another matter. A person can choose to love you because of his or her goodness, but to be pleased with you, they actually have to like your performance. Right?"*[39]

Now, don't worry, I'm not going to ask you to raise your hands, but you can ponder what your answer about pleasing God might be. I think for most of us it could be, "I please God some of the time, but not all."

I remember being surprised when I heard a master say in a dictation that the Darjeeling Council often talks about us with "fondness." I had always assumed that for the most part they were pulling out their etheric hair (if that were possible) over us or some of our antics.

There's a razor's edge here: we can't rest and be comfortable in the bosom of Abraham thinking all is well, nor can we simply think all is not well. El Morya tells us that he overlooks the little things many times but not always. So we may be at peace with who we are, as long as we are striving to do our best each day and to please God.

Do we have doubts about whether we are really pleasing God? If we do, then we need to figure out what actually does please him. The fundamental question we need to ask ourselves is, "Am I more concerned about what others think of me, or what God thinks of me?" The way of the world and the way people have learned to get ahead often rests on superficial considerations: "What's my teacher going to think of me today?" "What's that girl over there going to think of me?" "What's my boss going to think of me?" Having such human concerns is rather natural until we understand who we truly are. How many of us make our daily decisions based on what God would think? When we think more of others' opinions than God's, we are defending our egos.

The title of Saint Germain's dictation we're hearing today is "Pleasing Your Mighty I AM Presence Is the Greatest Honor You Can Ever Achieve." That pretty much says it all. Why should we spend so much time and energy in the never-ending effort to defend our human identity and please others? Doing that can consume all our being—and to what end? Now, of course, we should still try to please others by doing our best, whether our teachers, our employers, our families. Yet, if we give God the credit for our good works, we please God by not compromising our true identity and our path.

So how do we know what pleases God? After all, God is God, and who are we to fathom what pleases him. Hmm...that statement sounds rather like a way to escape responsibility, doesn't it? Well, the point is we *do* know what pleases God.

One source I found listed sixty-eight scriptures in the Bible that refer to pleasing God, and of course, this doesn't count what we've been taught by the masters. Here are a few noteworthy Bible verses.

Baruch 4:4 in the Catholic Bible says, *"Israel, we are blessed because we know what is pleasing to God."*

We are *blessed* because we know. Because we know what to do, and thereby receive the blessings of service to him.

Hebrews 11:6 is familiar: *"But without faith it is impossible to please him: for he that cometh to God must believe that he is, and that he is a rewarder of them that diligently seek him."*

Isn't that what we've based our life on—that he is a rewarder of those that diligently seek him? I remember one of the masters saying in a dictation that we come into life without a memory of our past lives and what we have to do because we have to *discover* our mission. We have to *discover* where we must go, what we must do. By that striving, we please God.

Colossians 1:10: *"We're praying this so that you can live lives that are worthy of the Lord and pleasing to him in every way: by producing fruit in every good work and growing in the knowledge of God."*[40]

We must produce fruit. God must receive a return for his investment in us. Let us remember Gautama Buddha said not one of us could be on this path without sponsorship. The masters must receive a return for their sponsoring of our lifestreams, and so they expect fruit. Are we growing in the knowledge of God, both in our book learning, so to speak, and in our experience with God?

Hebrews 12:28: "*Therefore, since we are receiving a kingdom that can't be shaken, let's continue to express our gratitude. With this gratitude, let's serve in a way that is pleasing to God with respect and awe.*"[41]

Isn't that a wonderful sentiment—respect and awe? Doesn't that feel a lot like love to you?

Hebrews 11:5: "*By faith Enoch was translated that he should not see death; and was not found, because God had translated him: for before his translation he had this testimony, that he pleased God.*"

Of course, we think of translation as the ascension. God came and took Enoch, and I wonder if he made a physical ascension because he was found no more. And his testimony was that he pleased God. He made his ascension by pleasing God, something that we can consider as well.

And finally, here are the words that each one of us lives and breathes and does all that we do in hope of one day hearing for ourselves:

Luke 3:22: "*And the Holy Ghost descended in a bodily shape like a dove upon him, and a voice came from heaven, which said, Thou art my beloved Son; in thee I am well pleased.*"

What a day of celebration that will be! If we follow the path that Jesus taught, that the ascended masters teach, we are pleasing God. It can be done!

The Ascended Master Lanello, in his birthday address in 1992, made it easy for us to know what pleases God. He said,

> *Yes, beloved, wholeness is the goal. It is achieved through love, yes, and wisdom. But as you have been told, without God's will, without that faith, without that fire of the true-blue chela, you will find it difficult, [yea impossible, as the scriptures say] to please God. And, blessed heart, if you are not able to please God, then you will become among all people the most miserable.*[42]

Ponder that—if you aren't able to please God, you will become among *all* people the most miserable. Lanello continues:

> *See, then, and understand that pleasing God does not require gymnastics of the mind or ultimate feats of this and that but simply the gentle heart. Oh, the gentle heart, the heart of kindness, the heart of Maitreya, the heart of the Bodhisattva!...*
>
> *Let the power of God that you love as God's holy will make you humble—humble before your God and truly humble before the God in each and every one upon earth. Humility is the key, beloved. Be humble and let God raise you up. Always remain humble.*[43]

The Gentle Heart

"The gentle heart"—doesn't that bring a feeling of comfort and peace, of letting down your defenses and just being with that person who manifests that gentle heart? Humility is a recognition that I of myself can do nothing, only God can do things through me. We cannot please God if we think we are the doers. And if we know what pleases God, then logically we know what does not please God but is a burden on him and others, not to mention on our own souls.

One day when I was fairly new on the path, I was caught up in my zeal for Saint Germain, and I remember kneeling at an altar and promising him that I would do all these wonderful things. As I concluded my prayer, something didn't seem quite right, and I wondered why my offering to him didn't feel like it was accepted. I pondered this and in due course it came to me that my prayer that day, at least in part, had a vibration of pride: I am going to do all these great things! What a friend I am to Saint Germain! While my zeal may have been commendable, it was not the humble prayer of one who knows that God is always the doer.

That was an important lesson for me. It was even more important because, left unrecognized and uncorrected, that pride was dangerous to my soul and to others around me. The challenge of such tests is greater when they are subtle, especially if we have a blind spot that we cannot or will not see.

A number of years ago, Mother called me on the phone and said she had a message for me from El Morya. He gave me an incredible teaching on my psychology. The problem was so obvious when I heard it, and yet I had not seen it. It was right there in my psyche, yet I had been totally blind to it. Ever since then I am more prayerful that I not be blind to those things that need changing in my life so that my offering may be acceptable to God.

Discord of any kind (and isn't pride a form of discord?) is not pleasing to God. Furthermore, discord does great harm to us because it results in us becoming disconnected from our Holy Christ Self. You cannot be discordant and be one with your Holy Christ Self. It's as if discord automatically turns off the switch to connecting to your Christ Self.

Mother and the masters have taught that when we are disconnected we revert to our carnal mind and our mental body.

You can do many things with the mental body, and that's what most people operate on in the world. They develop the mental body and become very good at certain things. They can be successful in the world, successful in politics or whatever field they choose. But living in your mental body or for the success of your human self does not please God. It is not the acceptable offering. When we do this, we must immediately recognize our mistake, call upon the law of forgiveness, and do what we need to do to reconnect with our Christ Self.

Jesus gave the antidote to discord in lesson 25 in *Corona Class Lessons:*

> *Let my words to Martha concerning Mary be recalled: "And Mary hath chosen that good part"*[44]*—and let my disciples of today also learn to choose the better part on the stage of life that they might play it well. Dedicate yourself to outpicturing nobler ideals in more Godly characterizations, thus following the path that leads to the Life victorious— your ascension in the Light attained through the overcoming of every discordant manifestation on the Emmaus walk of dedicated discipleship.*[45]

"Dedicated discipleship" is Jesus' clear and strong description of what it takes to pass our tests over every discordant manifestation.

Dedicated Discipleship

We have been taught many ways to overcome discord in our lives. If you haven't ever heard or recently listened to the album *Imperil*, I strongly recommend it. In it Mother gives profound teachings on the poison of irritation. I remember being in the audience when she gave it, and at one point she stopped and said she was getting an overwhelming feeling of a guilty conscience from all of us. We were all squirming in our seats because who has not felt irritation? But no one had ever told us how bad it is! People tend to think, "Oh, it's just part of life. Everybody gets irritated every once in a while, so what's the big deal?" When you're on the path of the ascended masters, when you're on the path of putting on your Christhood, such things *are* a big deal.

It takes dedicated discipleship and daily effort to pass our tests if we're going to put on our Christhood. It's not so much following the letter of the law as it is humbly recognizing and clearing those things in our psyche and being that are blocks to us wearing the mantle of our Holy Christ Self every moment and every day of our lives. We can't perfect the human; it's impossible. But we can work on our discipline and our chelaship in order to prepare the chalice of our being to receive the Christ and the great light of the Christ that the world needs so desperately. And we do not want to lose that precious light through inharmony or discord. What a karma that would be! God wants to protect us from that karma by not giving us more light than we can hold in harmony. So the difference is we are not perfecting the human, but we are learning to manifest the discipline and mastery that are required to hold the light that God would grace us with.

As we pursue our Christhood and become aware of things that do not please God, we need to understand it is for our benefit and be careful not to condemn ourselves. We need to realize these things are not who we are, but rather a habit or momentum to be overcome. On the other hand, you can't just excuse yourself, "Oh, that's not the real me, you know, I'm not going to worry about it." It may not be the real you, but it happens to be in charge of your temple at that particular moment, and that's why you need to be diligent about overcoming it.

In the book *Understanding Yourself,* Kuthumi wrote of those who earnestly want to please God but are caught up in old momentums:

> Men cry out that they wish to please God. They beat their breasts, and they vow with fierce determination that they will never again depart from the law of their being. Yet the record is clear: old and crusty momentums often draw more of their kind into the world of the individual and they pull down the otherwise buoyant craft of self into the rapids of life where experiences blend into a montage of whirling energy, a movement too fast to stabilize.[46]

Interesting choice of words—"old and crusty momentums." Let us not think it is beneficial to be referred to as "crusty." We are sincere; we really are. I don't think God questions our sincerity. We *are* trying. But are we dedicated disciples who work every day to overcome these momentums so that we make progress? Can we please God if we don't work on these patterns?

Mother has explained that for students of the ascended masters, the worst kind of discord is the *subtle* kind—a small irritation or a little bit of self-pity. Most of us—if not all—have blind spots or karmic patterns or mental habits that can be so subtle that, if we do not identify and correct them, they will cause us to do things that can compromise our path, our service, and our desire to please God and the masters.

The forces of darkness are always waiting to play upon these crusty momentums in our psyche. If we're not aware, we can fall into any number of traps—hopefully not every time. We have to be alert and awake! Gautama Buddha said, *"I am awake!*" We want to be able to say, "I am awake to who I am and I am awake to who I am not. I know there are parts of me that are not real, and I must deal with them because they make me vulnerable." Jesus taught us to be ready so that when the devil comes he won't find anything in us. When we have points of vulnerability, the fallen angels and the little demons will play upon them in our psyche to trap us into making karma. These vulnerabilities become more important the further we are on the Path because the tests become increasingly more subtle and the consequences of wrong decisions can be much greater.

Working on Points of Vulnerability

We can each look at the perversions of the twelve lines of the cosmic clock† to help identify points of vulnerability in ourselves that we think are most perilous to our soul's victory. When we identify weaknesses or negative patterns, we need to go to work on clearing them, and we can begin by including them in our daily dweller-on-the-threshold decrees.

Besides putting such negative momentums in your dweller calls, you can ask the angels or your Christ Self to help you recognize when you are engaging in them—to catch yourself in the act, so to speak—lest you lose contact with your Holy Christ Self. It's great to make calls on something, but you have to also be alert to when you're falling into a bad habit. You have to catch yourself so you don't reinforce a momentum.

Take it one step at a time. God has been patient with us for a long time, and he will honor us if we work on even one point of

---

† A spiritual tool given by Mother Mary to chart the cycles of your returning karma and opportunity so that you can meet life's daily challenges and transcend yourself.

vulnerability at a time. He knows that when you gain victory or mastery over one point, it's easier to gain it over others.

Many years ago, I started to make daily calls on self-pity, self-condemnation, self-justification and self-delusion because I could see how they could trap me in patterns that could undo so many of my positive efforts. It's amazing when you see how quickly this happens; a series of thoughts, one leading to another, can easily turn into self-pity or any of the other perversions. If you are sincere in asking for it to be brought to your attention, it will be. A simple call will work: "Beloved Holy Christ Self, when I do these things, please knock me on the head or do whatever is needed to make me aware of it."

The carnal mind is slippery and serpentine in the ways it leads us astray. Then, as I mentioned earlier, we are also subject to projections from the little demons that sit on our shoulders—just like the ones described in *The Screwtape Letters* by C. S. Lewis—and add fuel to the carnal mind and negative momentums. Mark Prophet said that if we could see how little the demons are that whisper in our ears to sway us, we wouldn't be swayed by them anymore.

When the angels or your Christ Self or God bring something to your attention, it is an "Aha!" moment. Besides being surprised, you will be amazed how a series of seemingly innocent thoughts brought you to a point of discord or wrongdoing. You have to laugh at yourself and be grateful that God has helped you see what was happening. It is a great feeling to catch yourself in the act and stop it on the spot!

You weren't aware of what you were doing because it's a pattern, a "crusty momentum" in your psyche that repeats itself until God says, "*Whoa!*" We want to arrive at the place where our Holy Christ Self is so strong that we can't miss the fact that we're misusing energy, that we're doing these things and reinforcing patterns, no matter how subtle they might be.

When you recognize what you're doing, you can stop immediately and make a fiat: "God deliver me from _____ (fill in whatever the momentum is, such as self-pity or self-condemnation or pride) and anything else that is keeping me from holding my harmony!" Doing that makes you feels great! With God's help you've recognized a pattern, you've made a call on it, and you've stopped it in its tracks. The pattern may come up again, but it happens less frequently as you raise your awareness, focus your decrees on it and build a momentum of keeping in contact with your Holy Christ Self.

Mother has taught us to think of a pendulum swinging from side to side, with your Holy Christ Self on one side and your carnal mind, your dweller, your human consciousness on the other side. Sometimes we swing over into our Christ consciousness. We all have a momentum of sometimes being in the Christ. You put the Christ on incrementally, and as you do that you spend more time on the side of your Christ Self. Then something happens and you lose contact and swing back to the human side. Then back to your Christ Self, then, uh-oh, back to your human. You start gaining momentum just like a pendulum does, and ultimately you will swing to your Christ Self and you will not swing back; you will stay there. You will have put on your Christhood.

We work on this daily; we work on it incrementally. This is about gaining mastery. This is about honoring our teachings by living them. This is how we please God. God cannot entrust us with great light if we cannot hold that light in harmony. Good intentions are wonderful, but they of themselves do not demonstrate mastery. And while it is good to try, it is better to succeed. Gaining mastery is a way to please God.

Perhaps every morning we should recite the prayer from today's children's story, "*O my holy Guardian Angel, take good care of me today and do not let me displease the good God. Amen.*"[47] or change it to "Holy Christ Self, take good care of me today and do not let me displease the good God."

Putting God First

But so far I have omitted perhaps the strongest teaching on what God requires for us to please him.

Matthew 22:36–40 says, "*Master, which is the great commandment in the law? Jesus said unto him, Thou shalt love the Lord thy God with all thy heart, and with all thy soul, and with all thy mind. This is the first and great commandment. And the second is like unto it, Thou shalt love thy neighbor as thyself. On these two commandments hang all the law and the prophets.*"

We must put God first in all things, before anything else in our lives. If we can't trust God enough to surrender all unto him, then how can we please him? Do I love my family less because I love God first and most? I think the opposite is true. The more I love God, the more I love my neighbors.

In the same Corona Class lesson cited earlier, Jesus said:

> *My words to Peter, "Simon, son of Jonas, lovest thou me more than these [the net full of great fishes]?" were designed to teach my apostles, and the many other disciples that should follow in their footsteps, that learning to love God first and more than all else is a prerequisite for discipleship.*
>
> *Summarizing early requirements, let me say: Put aside the desires of self-importance and cultivate the thoughtform*

that will allow your own God Presence to exalt you in due time.[48]

Self-importance is what the world teaches, isn't it? It's the attitude, "Let's work to get to the front of the line. Let's work to be number one. Who cares what happens to the others, let them fall to the wayside. I'm the one who's important."

No, God is important. If you love God first and foremost, then even if all things of the world are taken from you, you will not be lost. You will have the anchor of your relationship with God.

Mother gave the example of losing the cup of victory because you don't love God more than you love your victory! Isn't that sobering? You can lose your victory because you love that victory more than you love God. Ponder that; think about what it means: God first, victory second.

What is going to save the world in this hour of great darkness? What is going to save America and all the nations? And what is our part in this? Mother said our part *"is to walk the earth as the embodiment of the I AM Presence, because it's the only thing that will help the world."*[49] Of course, our decrees and prayers are helping but, ultimately, becoming one with our Christ Self and our I AM Presence is what will save the world. We can't wait for God to do something through us. We must put on our Christhood so that it can be the one acting in the world.

If God is the doer, how can we be anything but humble? Jesus embodied true humility, yet he challenged the greatest darkness on this planet. Being humble doesn't mean you are passive. You *are* active, not for your own gain but for the gain of God.

Let us overcome the fear that if we give God the glory for each accomplishment and seek only to walk the earth as the embodiment of our Christ Self and I AM Presence that we will somehow lose our identity, somehow cease to exist in the way we like. Yes, you will change. You will be free of that dweller who is the spoiler in your life—and has been for thousands and perhaps hundreds of thousands of years. You will be free. You will be free!

A man once told me of an experience he had while doing inner child work, and he gave me permission to share it. While working with a very skilled therapist and invoking the masters, this individual actually saw himself as his Holy Christ Self during one of his sessions. Think about that. He saw a vision of himself in his mind's eye, but it was him in the full presence of the Christ. He said his face was full of light and joy. Although the image was clearly him, it was quite different from how he appeared physically on the outer. He said he looked so free, so happy. He was very excited to see what he could become. His story shows that you don't lose anything by putting on your Christhood; you gain everything. And at the same time, you will still be you.

Everyday Mastery

Of course, we want to please God because of who we are. But as Saint Germain suggests in the dictation we're hearing today, we sometimes put limitations on what we believe we have the strength to do. When we remind ourselves that God is the doer, can we not expect more to come from our strivings? If we can't do more physically, then we can do more spiritually by focusing light in our bodies and in our being. That is what Igor did—the humble man who quietly saved millions of lives in the Communist revolution in Russia and who is now an ascended master.[50] As Lanello said in the quote I read earlier, God does not require gymnastics of the mind or ultimate feats of this and that, but a gentle, kind and humble heart. The fruit of these heart qualities can be the mastery we need to hold the light the world so desperately needs, and hold it in harmony.

I recently witnessed what I thought was an extraordinary example of mastery—in a grocery store, of all places. I was traveling and went into a Safeway store to get something to eat. I went to the deli area that offered custom sandwiches as well as Chinese and other cooked food. It was late in the afternoon and people were picking up things for dinner. There was one young woman (in her mid-twenties, I would guess) serving both the sandwich area and the hot foods area, which were separate but not too far apart. There were lines at both places and she was going back and forth between them.

I could see the other line clearly and saw the fatigue on the faces of people who had probably put in a long day's work and wanted to get their food and be on their way. The store needed at least one and probably two more people at that time of day to service the lines, but there was just this one young girl. What I especially noticed was how she kept her harmony, going from one station to the next, always smiling and genuinely interested in helping people. When my turn came, there was no one behind me in line, but there were seven or eight people in the other line. You can imagine what they were feeling, looking over at me, just one person compared to how many were in their line. I could feel the negativity coming toward me.

The girl who was helping me was Asian and her English was somewhat limited, so the order for my sandwich took much longer than it might have otherwise. I had to correct her a couple times as she just wasn't getting it quite right, or perhaps I wasn't communicating clearly. As she was patiently helping me, the people in the other line were getting more and more irritated. While my bread was toasting, she ran over to serve a customer in the other line and was back to me just as the toast came up. Even after I got my food, I lingered and watched her. There was never a look of exasperation or injustice on her face or any indication of being influenced by the obvious irritation and even anger being directed at her.

Have you ever been in a situation like that? You're tired, you're waiting in line and all you want to do is get whatever you came for and go home. It's easy to direct negative energy at the man or woman behind the counter, thinking, "It's all this store's fault; they don't give customers the support they need; they should hire more clerks...." It happens, doesn't it? It's human nature. But this sweet soul was always harmonious, always peaceful, and always greeted the next person with an eager desire to serve. It was very humbling.

I have to confess that this week I had my own grocery store test. You know how it is when you go to the store and all the lines at the checkout are quite busy, and you pick the shortest line, or so you think. Well, I picked the line with only one couple in front of me. Though they had a large grocery basket, it was clearly the shortest line, so I got in line behind them. I was watching this couple, and the lady appeared to be meditating on every article as she took things out of her basket. She'd look at it, she'd study it, then slowly move it over to the checkout counter. I thought to myself, "This is a test."

Don't expect your tests in big, grandiose situations. Expect them in your everyday life. This is how they come. Most of us aren't in the halls of government or places where big deal things go on. We're here in Montana—or wherever we are on the planet—with a day-to-day life. And that is where God will test you. Be alert to that. Don't expect the sounding of trumpets every time you're going to get one of these subtle tests.

Just work to gain mastery, and be able to laugh at yourself when you recognize a test you need to pass.

Wherever you live or work or go to school, rest assured that Maitreya will bring you those situations where you will be called upon to demonstrate your mastery. As I said, it could be the grocery store, the bank, the dinner table, or anywhere you are.

Why do we strive for mastery? Because we love God and we want to please him. Because we love God's people and we want to do everything we can to help them. We also know that in our current state, we aren't doing as much as possible to help them. We have to do more.

Do you ever feel that if you could only take the next step, get over the next hill, you could do more for God and more for the planet? I feel that way. Yes, all our calls, decrees and vigils do make a difference. But the time has come to let go of this human consciousness and move on. To help with this we can say a simple prayer such as: "God, deliver me from these human reactions that I might be free of these patterns in my psyche, these old crusty momentums that do not serve you and do not serve my soul. I am tired of them. I want to be free of them. I want to walk forward in the light."

A prayer like that will open the door because it means "I want nothing else besides you, God, and I want to be of greater service to you. I want to put on my Christ Self and be more of you and less of me, so that I can do the things that not only please you but also help those in pain, those who are suffering on this planet, those who are without hope—the Christians in North Korea, the women and children who are abused so unmercifully, the holy innocents who are aborted."

If we put on our Christhood, put on that light and hold it in harmony, if we follow in the footsteps of Jesus and our messengers, we *are* going to be different and this planet *is* going to be different! We don't have to wait until we ascend to put on our Christhood. We can do it here and now. The goal of the masters is to have us walking the earth as Christed ones. We don't expect the laurels of the world nor will we get them. But we *will* get the joy that comes from serving God.

There is a freedom in being who God wants us to be; there is a joy, a lightness, a peace that passeth all understanding, even though the world be in turmoil around us. True freedom is not having to defend our egos but learning to embrace God. We have spent enough time in this world of maya as a human. It is time to fulfill our divine destiny. It is time to put on our Christhood, step by step, initiation by initiation, surrender by surrender.

Won't that please God?

NEXT YEAR IN JERUSALEM

And there does come a time in your life, beloved, when nothing else will satisfy your hours, your moments or your days but communion with the Lord. These are the moments before your entering in, when the happiest occasion, even celebrated with lightbearers, will have something missing for you because you are about to experience the marriage of the Lamb, the true marriage, beloved, whereby you are bonded to my Heart.

—JESUS

FOUR

Next Year in Jerusalem

"Next Year in Jerusalem" is a centuries-old prayer with a history behind it. After the destruction of the Jewish temple in AD 70, the Israelites were scattered from their homeland in the great diaspora that lasted for almost two thousand years. Over time it became a Jewish custom, at the end of Passover and Yom Kippur each year, to recite the prayer "Next Year in Jerusalem" to celebrate their eventual return to their homeland.

With the re-establishment of the Jewish state in Palestine in 1948, many considered their exile to be over. They thought their goal had been realized, especially after the Six-Day War in 1967 when Jews were at last able to pray at the Wailing Wall that was part of the Jewish Temple built by Herod. An Australian Jewish Rabbi, Aron Moss, was asked what a modern-day Jew living in Jerusalem was supposed to pray since "next year" was now. I loved his answer, which I'd like to share in part with you today. He said:

You can be miles away from Jerusalem even while living there. And you can be on the other side of the world but only a step away. Because Jerusalem is much more than a city. It's an ideal that we are struggling to reach.

The Jewish story can be summed up as a long journey from Egypt to Jerusalem. Beyond being just geographical locations, they symbolize two opposite spiritual states. The journey from Egypt to Jerusalem is a spiritual odyssey. Both as a nation and as individuals, we have always been leaving the slavery of Egypt and heading towards the freedom of the Promised Land. By analyzing the psychological Egypt and the inner Jerusalem, we will see how this is a road that we are still traveling.

The Hebrew name for Egypt is Mitzrayim, which means limitations, restrictions, obstacles. It represents a state in which our souls are trapped in our bodies, enslaved to material desires and tied down to physical limitations. It is a world in which righteousness, justice and holiness are held captive to corruption, selfishness and egotism.

Jerusalem means "the city of peace"—a place of peace between body and soul, heaven and earth, the ideal and reality. When our body becomes not a prison for the soul but rather a vehicle for the soul's expression; when we live our lives according to our ideals rather than our cravings; when the world values goodness and generosity over selfish gain—then we are in Jerusalem, we are at peace with ourselves and the world....

The Jewish people were born in Egypt, in slavery. But they were told that on the other side of a vast desert lies their destiny, their Promised Land. As our forefathers walked out of Egypt—3,323 years and some-odd weeks ago—they were taking the first steps of a long journey to Jerusalem.

> Every generation since has pushed further forward along the road to Jerusalem. The journey continues with us. But we haven't got there yet. Even if you are living in the city called Jerusalem, as long as there remains suffering, injustice and unholiness in the world, we haven't reached the Promised Land. As long as we remain slaves to our own negative instincts and selfish desires, we are still struggling to truly leave Egypt.
>
> As we sit at the Seder, we note that another year has gone by, and we have yet to complete the journey. But we are getting there. We are that much closer to the Promised Land than we were last year. We have advanced a few more steps in a march to freedom that has spanned generations.
>
> Perhaps this year, our efforts to better ourselves and our world will bring the fulfillment of the words of the Haggadah‡: "This year we are here, next year we will be in the Land of Israel. This year we are slaves, next year we will be free."⁵¹

Rabbi Moss's description of the spiritual odyssey from Egypt to Jerusalem could be equated to our own spiritual journey from unreality to Reality. Perhaps we also believe, "This year we are here, next year we will be in the land of all that 'is real'!" This year we are slaves, next year we will be free." But will we? It's interesting to note that even with the return of the Jewish state to Jerusalem many Jews did not physically return. They liked it where they were. It always feels much safer when our goal is in the future and we don't have to decide if we are going to make the effort to fulfill it today.

While it's easy to raise our cup and say "Next year in Jerusalem," are we at last ready for that day to come in our

---
‡ the text repeated on the first two nights of the Jewish Passover.

spiritual journey? Perhaps, as with the Jews' long-awaited return to Jerusalem, we have always kept our final victory in the future. And perhaps this has been necessary in some ways because, after all, Rome wasn't built in a day, and it takes many days or years or lifetimes to put on our Christhood. There is admittedly a certain comfortability with a goal always being in the future. But in today's vernacular, *the future is now*. As Rabbi Moss pointed out, even though the Jews have returned to Jerusalem there is still work to be done. And I think we would be the first to admit there is still work for us to do.

Journey to the Promised Land

When we find these teachings, when we find this path, when we find out that we can make our ascension in this life, we're obviously very excited and overjoyed. In our exuberance, few of us are thinking about the initiations that will be coming our way down the road. So when those initiations come, do we lose that enthusiasm? Is it tempered? Do we go back to our familiar way of life and say, "Next year in Jerusalem"?

The danger comes when we equate *learning* the teachings with *becoming* the teachings—the big difference between the truth being sweet in the mouth and bitter in the belly.[52] The journey to the Promised Land of our Christhood and ascension is not an easy one. If it were easy, many more people would have ascended. When Moses led the Israelites out of Egypt to the Promised Land after God freed them, they found the going a bit rough, to say the least. In Exodus 16:3 they lament, "*...Would to God we had died by the hand of the* LORD *in the land of Egypt, when we sat by the flesh pots, and when we did eat bread to the full; for ye have brought us forth into this wilderness, to kill this whole assembly with hunger.*" You can almost hear their grumbling:

"Egypt wasn't so bad, was it? Even though we were slaves, we had full stomachs, a home to go to at night and a place to rest. But now we're wandering around hungry in the middle of the desert, and if I have to look at manna one more time, I don't know what I'm going to do!"

The Israelites learned the hard way that they could not take the flesh pots of Egypt with them if they wanted to make it to the Promised Land. They spent forty years in the desert partly because they did not pass the initiation of leaving Egypt behind them. That generation did not get to the Promised Land because they weren't ready to let go, to surrender to Moses as their guru, and to trust in their God. Even though God had freed them, they kept themselves in bondage by their unwillingness to let go of things they held dear.

Although it's easy for us to wax philosophical about their plight in Sinai, I think we can understand that it was hard for them—they were hungry and uncomfortable and tired, and day after day all they saw was the desert sun and sand and manna. It was definitely a test and an initiation for them.

It may be easy to just sit here thinking, "Wouldn't it have been better for them to let go, to surrender and trust in God so that a journey that should have taken days would not take forty years?" Perhaps some of us were among them, and that forty years is a drop in the bucket compared to the lifetimes some have been pining after the old ways. Of course there were problems with the old ways, but they were comfortable compared to facing the challenges of the Path.

Now our test is to let go of our attachment to the old ways and old things and the unreality of our lives. God is very patient and loving and he has allowed us time and space to hold on to portions of ourselves until we're ready to let go of them, but even God runs out of patience at some point. It's time for us to decide: Are we going with the masters to the Promised Land or are we staying as slaves in our human Egypt? We can't have it both ways.

Part of the title of Jesus' Easter 1992 dictation is "Do Not Postpone the Day of Your Initiation." In this dictation Jesus says,

> *For there are those who when seeing the abyss of their own human creation and the abyss of planet earth and beholding Death and Hell itself will step back and say, "I will not take the initiation of the dark night of the soul this day or this week or this month or this year, but I will tarry in my level of comfortability and insulate myself from these true initiations of the saints."*[53]

There have always been some who have been willing to take the true initiations of the saints, while we have stood by and watched. I remember a dictation by the Goddess of Purity describing how we were together in the temple on Lemuria some 250,000 years ago, and there came a certain point in our initiations when we had to decide whether to stay in the temple and complete them or go out into the world. The master said we chose to go out into the world, and we are still here, while she's been an ascended master for a very long time.[54]

Those who choose comfortability and insulation over the initiations of the saints continue to follow the path of *next* year in Jerusalem by excusing themselves, "Oh, yes, I'm really going to focus on my path, but right now I've got some issues in my life that I have to work on." Of course we all have issues, yet we cannot let opportunity slip through our hands again because we're "busy." We've fallen for that trick over and over; maybe we even *want* to be tricked so that we don't have to stand and face these initiations. Sometimes our anxiety and fear of an initiation is far worse than the initiation itself. Morya has even talked about us "charging" through the initiations of the dark night of the soul and the dark night of the Spirit when we are prepared.[55] So they don't have to be a specter that keeps us from moving forward. As chelas of El Morya, let us take him at his word and charge through our tests!

Assessing Our Goals

At the same time, it's natural for us to wonder where we stand on the Path. Gautama Buddha reminds us, *"There comes a time in the life of every man (and every woman) when he must assess his goals, when he must assess, 'What will be the fruit of my effort at the conclusion of this incarnation?'"*[56] Older people who are getting closer to the time when the Lord will call them Home do this in hindsight. They ask themselves, "What did I do? What did I accomplish?" Think how much better it is to consider this when you're young, when you have your life in front of you and you are setting your goals.

The masters have given us the goal of balancing our karma and making our ascension, and for many of us that is our main goal. But what else do we want to accomplish? What record do we want to leave in the ethers of planet earth as someone who took a stand and was willing to go through the initiations and the trial by fire[57] in order to win their victory? That record—whether it is known on the outer or only on the inner—will be our message to every soul, and it will encourage other people of God to also move forward.

Though we may all have the goal of making our ascension at the end of this life, are we clear about what it will take for us to get there? It is one thing to acknowledge the initiations of the Path at an intellectual level, but another thing to prepare for and pass those tests in our life. It's easy to watch other people's initiations when we can sit back and say, "Look what the master is doing. Now all so-and-so needs to do is this, this and this, and they'll be victorious!" But we all know that life is not a spectator sport and passing tests is not quite that simple.

Have some of us shied away from the goal of walking the earth in the fullness of our Christ Self? Are we ready to make the final trek to the Promised Land? Can we kneel before the altar of God and say, "Enough! Enough! I am done with this human nonsense—my human creation, my indulgences, my delays, my embracing the world of maya and duality in hopes of postponing the day of reckoning with my God."

We may be so comfortable with certain aspects of not only our human consciousness but also the human consciousness of others—silently agreeing in sympathy, "I'll indulge your sin if you indulge mine"—that it takes a lot of fire and determination to say, "It's enough! I am *done* with this!" We know that at a certain point in his final lifetime Godfre did just that, basically saying, "I'm *done* with this dweller-on-the-threshold! I am *done* with it!" Does that mean that Godfre never made another mistake? I doubt that, but the sacred fire descended to affirm his fiat and call. It will affirm it for us too when we say, "I am ready, Lord. I am ready to take my stand. Give me the strength, wisdom and understanding I need to pass my tests."

Today many of us are finally willing to go through these tests or we wouldn't be here, we wouldn't be on this path. Jesus knows what will happen when we reach the place where the fire and determination and yearning after God becomes so great that we won't settle for anything else. He says:

> *And there does come a time in your life, beloved, when nothing else will satisfy your hours, your moments or your*

days but communion with the Lord. These are the moments before your entering in, when the happiest occasion, even celebrated with lightbearers, will have something missing for you because you are about to experience the marriage of the Lamb, the true marriage, beloved, whereby you are bonded to my Heart.[58]

Our souls are destined to be the bride of Christ. We feel it and we know it. Perhaps we're closer to it than we have been for many thousands of years, because (as the saying goes) we can almost taste it. We can almost taste the victory, it's so close; yet it's not a victory in the sense that we haven't fully achieved it. Nevertheless, we can feel the stirrings in our being, "This time I'm really ready to go for it!"

Many of us are at that point, and there is no doubt it represents our soul's progress on the spiritual path. But when we reach that point, do we expect that the remaining steps and tests of the Path will only be filled with light and love and the joy of the Lord, with the angels strewing rose petals in front of us? We know that isn't the way, don't we? In his dictation, Jesus clearly tells us it isn't: *"You will knock, beloved, and the door will not be opened. And you will knock again and again and again and the door will not be opened. And you may be burdened by the weight of oppression and the depression of the world itself."*[59]

We wonder, "How can this be? It seems to contradict the biblical teachings of our Lord, *'I am the door: by me if any man enter in, he shall be saved, and shall go in and out, and find pasture.'"*[60] I understand I'm in the midst of the dark night, but what does this sense of darkness mean?" Well, it can signify that we are drawing so close to God and his Presence that our *"remaining darkness and the ugliness of the human creation"*[61] reveals the contrast between God's perfection and what remains within us.

In other words, we are down to the dregs of our negative substance and they are not pleasant, but we have to face them. We cannot use these dregs as an excuse for failure nor can we pretend that they are not there. As we consider reality and unreality in our life, we know we have a certain amount of misqualified energy that could be hundreds of thousands of years old that has not been transmuted. When it comes up, we can't just say, "God, take me as I am, let's deal with that later." We have to deal with it now!

Man, Know Thyself as God

On one hand, we are waiting to greet our Lord, to walk with him in the alchemical marriage and the bonding of our soul to our Christ Self forever. On the other hand, we still have karma and substance that we have to transmute; we can't give it more power than it has nor can we ignore it. Perhaps this is why the saints went through some of the most intense things in their lives just before that bonding.

How do we stand in that same hour of intense initiation the saints faced, when we feel overcome by discouragement and disillusionment and think that God has abandoned us? *We stand knowing who we are and who we are not!* That is the key to our victory.

Think about the words "maya" and "duality." Maya conveys the Hindu understanding that the world we live in is an illusion, that ultimately it is not real. Although it may not be real in the ultimate sense, that doesn't mean the pain of this world does not impact our souls, our path, and other people. That's the nature of duality—two seemingly opposite things existing at the same time. It's easy to say that we live in a world of illusion when our stomachs are full, but not so easy when they are empty. Yes, the world may be maya, but we know it has the *appearance* of reality to us and others. It sure feels like we're living in reality, doesn't it? And if no one had taught us that this wasn't real, it might be harder for us to comprehend that.

So here is the Zen koan of this: All this is unreal in the ultimate sense, but it is very real in the sense that we have to demonstrate the unreality of it by putting on our Reality. We're here because we have unfinished business, and it's not just the unfinished business of our karma. It's the unfinished business of the ascended masters and our God, because many (if not most) people on this planet remain caught up in unreality.

Remember the fiat we give: *"Evil is not real and its appearance has no power!"* In other words, ultimately, evil cannot survive in God's universe; but right now there is a manifestation of it that is outwardly expressing itself, and the pain is real, even though it is temporal. The tragedy, the grief, all seem real to our souls. We have to move through and beyond them to be healed and transformed. We cannot escape the world by becoming metaphysical and simply saying, "Don't worry about that, it's not real anyway." That kind of attitude will get us many more embodiments in this unreality. We have to understand that even though it's unreal we still have to master it. "Well," you might say, "if we still have to deal with it, why are we concerned that it's not real?" The answer is: Because we *believe* it's real. And as long as we believe it's real, then we cannot know who we really are, and what the reality of our souls and our lives is.

Are we God or are we man? Let's be honest with ourselves and answer these questions: Do we see ourselves and God as separate beings? Do we see ourselves as being in a certain place and God in another, perhaps in the Great Central Sun? Well yes, God is in the Great Central Sun, but God is also in you and in me. As long as we see ourselves as *separate* from God, we *are* separate from God. That does not mean we make one affirmation and suddenly we're one with God. It means we know in our hearts that we are truly one, and once we get through this unreality—this maya that has surrounded our lives—the oneness will be all too apparent. But if we *don't* work to get through the unreality, if we say, "Well, since I am really one with God, there's no rush," then we're back where we started and probably worse off than before.

We need to think differently. Proverbs 23:7 says, *"For as he thinketh in his heart, so is he."* Do we truly know who we are and who we are *not* in the depths of our heart, at the core of all that motivates us and is reflected in how we live on a day-to-day basis? I recently read a teaching that said, "God is not far away; he is within you." That's a basic concept of the ascended masters' teachings, right? But for some reason it dawned on me anew, "Oh, God is in me, right within my heart! It's a reality, now what am I going to do about it? Am I going to wait until next year or am I really going to focus my life on knowing God and being an instrument of his will?" So, yes, God is in the Great Central Sun, but yes, he's also in our hearts.

Do we see ourselves as a hybrid, half-man and half-God? Or do we believe the words inscribed on the ancient temple, "Man, Know Thyself," which Mother taught means "Man, Know Thyself as God!" If we know ourselves as God, free from maya and duality, then we see clearly and not "through a glass, darkly."[62]

What is Reality?

During a Darshan on the guru-chela relationship in 1997, Mother spent considerable time explaining why the chela needs to be chastened by the guru. She said:

> It's because I know something that you don't know. And he [El Morya] wants me to tell you this: I know that everything that is negative in this world is unreal. And I have such a conviction in this truth and such an awareness of nonreality that that nonreality is what I go after every time I wrestle with you.
>
> You don't know that what is around you is unreal, is not real. And as long as you think that the burdens, the life, the karma, everything about you is real when it's not real—only you in God is real—then I will continue to be intense about going after you. We are in a plane of unreality and we have to know that so that we don't lean on the notion of our own unreality.
>
> So, as I was processing everything that we have said tonight, I realized that the one thing I haven't put inside of you is the knowledge that you are real and everything else that's around you, that puts you down, that torments you, that drives you is not real. It is unreal. And it's as if I want to come to you and shake you and say to you, "It's not real. This thing you think is real is an illusion!" And when you know that, you will walk out of this maya universe into your kingdom with God.[63]

It's not real—it's an illusion! Yet we can't pretend that we don't have to deal with the manifestations of energy around us. So for now we have to straddle the contradiction: Knowing what's unreal but also knowing we still have to master it.

In the early 1970s, The Summit Lighthouse distributed a small record (remember record players?) with a recording by Mark Prophet that started out with the question "*What is reality?*" Right after college (and after I had met Mark and Mother), I had that question posed to me in an interesting way when

I was traveling around Europe with my former college roommate. We met an American couple on the train one day and they asked us what we were doing. As we were sharing our story, the guy looked over at me and said, "When are you going to wake up to reality?" Though he was saying it in a different context, I can imagine El Morya speaking through him, "When are you going to wake up to what the reality of this planet really is?"

The things we think are real are an illusion. We can understand that intellectually, but we must *know and internalize it*. That concept is a challenge to grasp even at the intellectual level, let alone at the core of our being. Akshobhya, one of the Five Dhyani Buddhas, describes this challenge as *"the realization of the self in the sea of maya."*[64] Isn't that beautiful? The realization of self, of who we really are while we live in this sea of maya that is our point of initiation on the Path in time and space. How are we going to do it? How are we going to realize who we really are when we're surrounded by this unreality? In the dictation we will be hearing today, Akshobhya promises to teach us the way out of maya and unreality. He is doing this because we *need* it. The understanding of who we are and who we are not is absolutely crucial if we are going to be victorious and ascend.

If we are to be free of the concept of duality, we have to stop thinking of ourselves as separate from God, while still living in the world of cause and effect and our karma. I remember a master saying a family dog often thinks it is human because it lives with humans. The irony is that we can be the same way—because we live with humans, we think we *are* humans!

In addition, confusion is increased by orthodox Christian doctrine that says, "You are a worthless sinner! Fess up to it. The only reason you're going to get to heaven is because Jesus is going to carry you there." But we are *not* worthless sinners! The precious souls who receive that condemnation are *not* worthless sinners. They may have sinned or erred and made karma just like we have, but they are not worthless sinners. How will they make their ascension or how extraordinarily difficult will it be for them if they don't know who they really are? What a *crime* that the teachings of our Lord have been corrupted to that extent.

We have to have more than an intellectual understanding of our true identity. We can acknowledge the truth of it, but until we live that truth will it really change us? I can remember nodding my head when I heard this teaching years ago, thinking, "Oh, yes, I can see that. That's really true, isn't it? Yes, that's really true. I wonder what time lunch is?" Honestly, haven't we all done something similar, even though we're sincere chelas? We really want to know and to do the right thing, but so often we can't quite get there. We can't quite get there because we can't seem to translate the teaching from our intellect to our heart—from outer understanding to inner knowing and being. That's the challenge.

Talk to God

The final leg of this journey to the ascension is a perilous one. Even with all our knowledge, there are snares and pitfalls that can entrap us along the way, including our psychology and the debris in our electronic belt.§ These can sometimes be quite subtle and cause time-consuming detours. We need to

---

§ The momentums of an individual's untransmuted karma orbit around the lower portion of his physical body to form what looks like an electronic belt of misqualified energy. Diagrammed at the point of the solar plexus and extending downward below the feet in a negative spiral, this misqualified energy forms a dense forcefield shaped like a kettledrum. Referred to as the realm of the

implore God and our guru to get us back on the straight and narrow if we are deviating from our homeward path. We don't live in fear of going astray precisely *because* we trust in God and the guru. We trust that by our devotions, by talking to God and *listening* to God, we can be brought into alignment. We no longer have the outer chastening of the Lord through Mother as the embodied guru, but if we're attuned, we can receive an inner chastening that can be just as powerful in stripping us of energies and vibrations that keep us from seeing and doing the right thing.

To avoid mistakes, it's good to be on our knees, saying to the guru or teacher or master that we feel a tie to, "If I'm going the wrong direction, please do something to help get me back on the right track. Please help me align with the will of God." We need to do this because, as Mother has explained, in this world of duality and maya, we *can't* see clearly until we put on the fullness of our Christhood. We *think* we can, but we *can't* because of what is around us. When we're in that state, we're prone to making mistakes—well-intentioned mistakes, but mistakes that can hold us back on our path.

How do you know when you should do something differently? Trust your teacher; trust your guru; trust your God to tell you—and be willing to hear the truth! While the guru may have an inconvenient or difficult truth for us, our soul would want that instead of a convenient lie. We need to be willing to separate reality from unreality and know that when negativity comes up from our electronic belt or karma hits us head-on it affects how we see things.

In another part of that same Darshan I mentioned earlier, Mother says, "*Talk to God, and talk to God, and talk to God.*"[65] She

---

subconscious and the unconscious, the electronic belt contains the records of unredeemed karma from all embodiments.

repeats it three times in a row. I think that was a hint to ask God (or the guru or master that you're closest to), "What am I missing? What do I need to know for my next step?" And then listen!

As we humbly ask for assistance and guidance, God will show us the truth, and then it's up to us to act upon it. Of course, there will be times when we don't necessarily feel God or the guru, as Jesus told us, and in those times we have to rely upon what we know, upon our Holy Christ Self and our ability to draw forth light to help us.

Unfortunately, some people fashion their guru the way they want the guru to be. That's like saying, "Yes, I'll be your chela, but you have to be the guru that I design, not the one you are." So even though such a person may have a picture of his or her guru on the wall, in essence they're making that guru over in their own image and only hearing what they want to hear. All the while they're very sure that what they're doing is right and that the path they've taken is the correct one.

There was a radio program in the 1930s and '40s called *The Shadow*. The introduction to the show has become part of the American idiom: "Who knows what evil lurks in the hearts of men? The Shadow knows!" We might ask, "Who knows what evil lurks in the electronic belts of chelas? The guru knows!"

Ah, the guru! There is no greater love than the love between the guru and chela. Every one of us has been sponsored on our spiritual journey or we wouldn't be here. We can't make it without that sponsorship. Mark Prophet said he could not have made his ascension without the help of Mother Mary. Mother Mary did not do it for him, but she was there. We're in the same situation of needing the guru to help us make it. Yet, in Western cultures, the concept of a guru has been vilified and muddied for the true people of God because it has been connected with destructive cults. A true guru will never harm you in any way.

A true guru will not win your victory for you, but they will be there to help you. The guru is teacher, disciplinarian, mentor and, yes, friend. The guru does not indulge you, but he will love you. There will be times when you are so filled with the love of the guru you fear that you will not be able to contain such love. However, we must not mistakenly interpret the love of the guru as an indulgence. Although the guru may look beyond certain things we do in our lives and turn his eyes away for a while, there comes a day when God's law requires us to be accountable for our actions.

There will be times when it feels like everything you do is not good enough and that you have been abandoned. But as long as you are honorably striving on the Path, the guru will not forsake you or stop guiding you. So take the hand of the guru because the guru is the best friend you will ever have to help you get Home.

Getting to Know El Morya

You might wonder who your guru is. Mother said, *"El Morya is the first Guru we encounter when we join this organization. Some people think that it's a matter of choice, but it really isn't. This is his organization. It's his ashram, his place, and you can't go anywhere except to the heart of El Morya when you come here."*[66] We also know that other masters assign their chelas to El Morya to help, let's say, smooth out the rough spots a bit. And Jesus said, *"It is an hour when all must count themselves as chelas of El Morya, who does lead you in this way of ultimate overcoming. Do not lose the way, beloved!"*[67]

To keep from losing the way, hold fast to the hem of Morya's garment. Hold fast to Mother or your chosen guru. Let's do whatever we need to do so we don't lose the way. We're close to our victory, we're very close, and if we keep striving, keep praying, keep opening our heart to God, keep surrendering, keep letting go of the human consciousness, then—with God's help—we can make it!

I have been studying this beloved book, *Morya I*, almost daily for the past year or so. It is a compilation of the first thirty-four dictations given by El Morya after he founded The Summit Lighthouse in 1958. While I gained many things by reading this book, two in particular stand out to me that I would like to share.

The first is that I feel that I know Morya much better than I did before. The tenderness of his love for us, his hope and sacrifice for us, have become powerful motivations for me on my path and in my desire to serve him. If we had time, I would read you a number of excerpts that are so sweet and caring that you could hardly hear them without a tear. His love for each one of us is so pure that he will not indulge our unreality no matter how much we cling to it. That is one of the main reasons I trust him.

Ralph Waldo Emerson penned the words "Hitch your wagon to a star," and I can think of no star in heaven that we need more today than El Morya. If you want an example of the profound love between a chela and a guru, read Mother's introduction to *Morya I*. In it she advises us, *"If you are smart, my friend, you will seek and find him. And when you do, you will implore his intercession in your life. For as chohan of the first ray he holds the key to the will of God in your life."*[68]

If you ever have any second thoughts about giving up your human life for the life of being an ascended master, read this book. During the winter months, Morya warms himself and his chelas at a cozy fire in his study. He rides his stallion in the hills surrounding Darjeeling. He meets in conference with the Brothers of the Diamond Heart and the Darjeeling Council and probably many other cosmic councils. While we can identify with such activities, we can't truly know the freedom and joy he has as an ascended being. He is safe from the wiles of the fallen ones, while we are not as yet. He has immortal life, while we are still striving to attain it.

Procrastination is a common pitfall among chelas and is part of the problem. We say, "Oh, God, I'm going to do this, I'm going to do that, I'm going to fix that, I'm going to correct this...," but for some reason we don't always follow through. But Morya has done what we are trying to do, and he is willing to help us. *Help us*, but not do it for us. Morya says:

> You see, beloved ones, I have stood before the Karmic Board on numerous occasions on behalf of various students throughout America, and I have pled with the Karmic Board to hold back some specific karmic act that was intended to be leveled upon their heads.
>
> Well, you know, beloved ones, I do not have to do this. I am a God-free being, and it is not necessary in the great cosmic law that I intercede between the cosmic hammer and an individual lifestream. And if necessary, I can stand aside and not deflect the blow. I can let it fall in order that the lesson may become more paramount in your minds, and perhaps the quality of mercy might be better served if I did. We shall see in the future months by the responses to the great light and its expansion as to whether or not this is so.[69]

Morya also says that very often the Karmic Board grants him that dispensation. So, as tough as our lot is or as we sometimes consider it to be, I wonder how much worse it might be, save for the intercession of the gurus.

Dress Yourself in the Will of God

The second thing I took away from this book is a greater understanding of the will of God, its importance to our ascension and Morya's devotion to it. In one of his dictations, Morya speaks of his *"vast momentum"*[70] of devotion to the will of God that has been unwavering for *"aeons and aeons."*[71] If we turn from the will of God, then eventually, whether it be *"ten or ten thousand years,"*[72] we will return to that exact place on the path and be faced with the same choice of embracing God's will or not. We're on a merry-go-round until we determine that this time we're going to stop riding and get off, we're going to embrace the will of God and get on the path to our Christhood.

I love the phrase "embrace the will of God." Morya tells us:

> *Teach this to your children. Teach them there is no profit in sidestepping the will of God, which is the honor of God, which is the protection of God, which is the perfection of God, which is the faith of God, which is the power unlimited of God. To dress yourself in the will of God, to bathe yourself in the will of God, to give the mantras and give them again—"Not my will, not my will, not my will but thine be done!"*[73]

Isn't that wonderful imagery—getting dressed in the will of God? What a concept to impart to a child or an adult! "I'm getting up today and getting dressed and doing everything I need to do before I go out into the world, but I'm not going out before I dress myself in the will of God! I still see through a glass darkly. I need the will of God as my protection, as my power, as the light and Presence of God within me to guide me lest I stumble along my way or lest I stumble and hurt another of God's children."

The will of God is the key to our ascension. Yet some fear it. Akshobhya teaches us that those who *"fear reality embrace unreality."*[74] The antidote for fear is trust. Mother teaches:

> *Lean not unto thine own understanding. As long as we're in duality, our own understanding is always incomplete. So we can't listen to that. We always go back to God. You see, trust always takes us back to God.... So, trust: it all comes down to this. Do you trust the guru? If you don't, you might as well not be here. Trust is not merely a word; it is a way of life.*[75]

What a profound teaching: trust in God and in the guru is *a way of life.*

So, we all know we have to be free of maya and duality in our lives. We need the guru to help us with that because, as Mother explained, as long as we're in duality, our own understanding is incomplete. That's why we ask, "What should I do, God? I need some help." And God answered before we asked—he brought us the guru. The guru comes to us with a price, and that price is letting go of the human consciousness and all that has blocked the flow of God's light and consciousness within us. How can we consider that a price? It's our liberation; it's our freedom!

Ponder Morya's dedication to our souls as revealed in his words:

Blessed and beloved ones, I love each and every one of you. If I seem to chastise you, I do it but for the love of God. I do it but to increase your cosmic capacity for good in the will of God. I do it to stop your blessed feet from stumbling, and I do it in the memory of all those endearing young charms (which you are) which I gaze on so fondly today. I love you. I love you. I love you. I am the chohan of the first ray. I am the will of God ever manifest, ever the strength, ever the courage to be true, to dare to do, to be and to be silent when necessary.

Blessed ones, you stand before a great golden door of opportunity and the glories before your consciousness not only tonight but every day of your life. As you knock upon the gateway of that door, as your hand reaches out to turn the latch and to open it, know that I stand beside you. And I am not alone when you adore the will of God. Beside you is blessed Archangel Michael, beside you is blessed and beloved Jesus—an infinite procession of cosmic masters extending back into the very beginning of time, to the beginning of the chronicles of mankind's existence upon this planet. There is hope for all.[76]

Hope for All

The masters have hope for us! They know our souls and who we truly are in God—which much of the time we don't. They know our divine destiny, and they know the perils involved in getting all the way Home. Can't you imagine them pleading before God for our souls and our victory? They know they can't do it for us and that we have to do it. But they love us so much, I think they would step through the veil to help us if they could. However, we cannot coast on their love. Instead, let it be a goad for us, an incentive that lights a fire within our beings to win this victory with their help!

At long last, after many lifetimes spent wandering in the Sinai of the nonsense of human consciousness and human karma, it is the hour when we are returning to Jerusalem—to the inner Jerusalem, to the Holy City which is our true abode, to the Reality that is right within us. We're close to our victory and the masters are all around us, watching us, standing with us and cheering us on.

It's not enough to go to sleep at night knowing we are loved by God and his holy angels and the ascended masters. It's not enough to be loved. *We also have to love.* When nothing else satisfies us, we have to *become* that love and the Reality of our being.

Yes, the world demands certain things of us and people have certain things they need from us. God's people have needs and we are meant to be God's instruments in fulfilling those needs. We can do that when we become more of who we truly are, when we have finally decided: "Enough! I am moving beyond this human condition!" And as we say the words, know that they will be challenged: "Oh, you think you're done with this? Let's see how much determination you have." We will be tested to be sure we are willing to meet every challenge of the Path, and to trust that God's light and his grace are sufficient. We know what to do, and we *want* to do it, so there doesn't have to be anything on heaven and earth that keeps us from doing it!

Where do we begin this final leg of the journey Home? On our knees, surrendering to God, embracing the will of God, doing the best we can when God doesn't give us the answer to every problem or situation that faces us. God does not tell El Morya how to run the Darjeeling Council; he's got to figure it out for himself. Likewise, we have access to the master, and yet we also know there are times when we must look within our own hearts for the answers.

Jesus said we will knock and sometimes it won't be answered. That's part of the Path and we need to humbly accept the rules God has ordained. There are certain tests we must pass and rules we must follow, so let's follow them. Let's embrace the will of God. Let us understand that that which is around us is unreal, and that God is Reality within us. Let us be God's hands and feet as we go out to give comfort, love and service to those yet caught in unreality.

What an exciting proposition! What tremendous hope! We don't have to wait until we get to heaven to be God in action. Heaven has plenty of ascended masters and we are needed on earth. Some of the masters have even told us heaven can wait for us to balance 100 percent of our karma!

We know there is hope for all. Hope becomes a living reality in each of us when we are free from maya and duality, when we are in the world but truly not of it. Only we can answer the question of *when* that will happen in our lives.

Let us decide, "Enough!" Let us, with God's help, be done with unreality. Let us move forward knowing who we are and who we are not and continually remind ourselves so we *never* forget.

The future is now. Let us not keep God or our souls or other souls of light in need waiting any longer. Let us affirm with the fire of our being, "**This** year in Jerusalem!"

NINE MINDSETS FOR YOUR SOUL'S VICTORY

PART I

There is a moment in our lives when our best is no longer good enough. We get content with our best. We get content that we're on top of things. Everything's under control. Everything's going right and we're in command of our job. We're in command of our soul. And all of a sudden God comes along, pulls the rug out from under us and says, "It's not enough. I have a higher calling."

—MOTHER

FIVE

Nine Mindsets for Your Soul's Victory

Part 1

If you were to ask the average American familiar with our history to name one naval hero from the Revolutionary War, I would wager that most would say John Paul Jones. Many of us know what he said. But do we really know who he was and all that he did?

Let's find out more about him in these excerpts taken from The Naval History and Heritage website.

> *As an officer of the Continental Navy of the American Revolution, John Paul Jones helped establish the traditions of courage and professionalism that the Sailors of the United States Navy today proudly maintain. John Paul was born in a humble gardener's cottage in Kirkbean, Scotland, went to sea as a youth, and was a merchant shipmaster by the age of twenty-one. Having taken up residence in Virginia, he volunteered early in the War of Independence*

> to serve in his adopted country's infant navy and raised with his own hands the Continental flag on board the Navy's first fleet. He took the war to the enemy's homeland with daring raids along the British coast, and of course, his most famous victory over the ship, the HMS Serapis. As John Paul Jones' ship began taking on water and the fires broke out on board, the British commander asked him if he had struck his flag [wanted to surrender].[77]

Imagine: You're on your ship, it's on fire and it's sinking. What do you do? The enemy is urging you, "Be reasonable, John Paul. I think it's time to give up the ship." But he was *unreasonable*. He replied, *"I have not yet begun to fight!"*[78] And amazing as it may seem, it was the British commander who surrendered in the end.

> Jones is remembered for his indomitable will and his unwillingness to consider surrender when the slightest hope of victory still burned. Throughout his naval career Jones promoted professional standards and training. Sailors of the United States Navy can do no better than to emulate the spirit behind John Paul Jones's stirring declaration. He said, "I wish to have no connection with any ship that does not sail fast for I intend to go in harm's way."[79]

How is that for an attitude? He clearly had a mindset for victory! And I think we all agree the ascended masters have a mindset for victory; I don't think they know anything else *but* victory! But what about the rest of us? Do we truly have a mindset for our personal victory and the supportive mindsets that we need to get all the way Home?

In the dictation we're going to be hearing today, the Elohim Hercules¶ tells us that many people reach a certain point on the Path and decide that it is just too demanding or hard to go on, so they leave. That point may be before the Path really begins or even decades after they have been on it.

The sad and tragic truth is that the person often leaves at the exact point where they previously left the Path, not just once, but many times, perhaps even predating Lemuria! Leaving at that same point has become a habit—a dangerous pattern *that has to be broken.*

We may or may not have reached that point in our personal chelaship. But would it not be wise to think about what we can do to prepare for the time when this test will inevitably come, if it hasn't already? When this initiation comes to our doorstep, we want to take our stand and say, "By God's grace, I will pass this test!"

A few months ago, a friend of mine sent me the book *Put Your Mindset to Work*. It made some powerful points that apply not only to the workplace but also to our chelaship. The authors explain mindset this way: *"The much quoted Oxford English Dictionary defines mindset as 'a habitual way of thinking.' That's why we think of mindset as much deeper and more profound than anything just on the surface. For us it is the internal lens through which you see and navigate life. Mindset influences everything you see as well as everything you do."*[80] Webster's dictionary defines mindset as a "mental attitude or inclination and a fixed state of mind."

¶ Hercules is the Elohim of the first ray of power, faith, and God's will. He is one of the seven Elohim that created the physical universe and is millennia older than Greek mythology. The origin of the figures in Greek mythology is a distant soul memory that there were great beings of light who walked and talked with mankind during past golden ages.

But before we go much further, I want to put aside the idea that mindset is just a mental exercise. For the student or chela on the Path, it is a "heartset"; it is a "soulset." It is our being, how we approach life. It's not just a mental-body exercise, though it may involve the mental body.

The authors of this book asked thousands of top employers what they really look for in their employees. Here is what they found: *"Given the choice between someone with the desired mindset who lacks the complete skillset for the job, and given someone with the complete skillset who lacks the desired mindset, a total of 96 percent of those surveyed picked mindset over skillset as the key element in those they seek to retain."*[81]

It's interesting, isn't it? We may come prepared at some levels for this path, but if we don't have the right attitude, it's going to clearly influence how successful we are. Perhaps if we can take an honest look at some of our mindsets (cherished as they might be to us), we can better prepare for the tests that are coming. And if we have the right mindset—a wisdom, an understanding and a heartset—we will have a much better chance of passing them.

As I began to read the book, I started to reflect about the mindsets of a successful chela. I thought, "Are there key mindsets that we can all benefit from that will help us on the Path?" Well, I got more than I bargained for! One day I had a particularly long wait in a doctor's office so I decided to write down some mindsets that I thought might be helpful. By the time the nurse called me in, I had come up with thirty-two of them and I thought, "Oh boy, what do I do now? This is far too many. They've got to be prioritized if they're going to have any value."

I prayed and pondered a lot and narrowed it down to nine mindsets that I felt could be helpful. This is clearly not an exhaustive list. They may or may not be of benefit to you, and you may come up with your own. But hopefully these will bring up something in you, in your way of thinking, in your approach to the Path, that will help you get those mindsets that you need for your victory. Maybe you don't work with all of them at once, but just pick out the ones that you know can really help you.

As I started to write these down, it became abundantly clear that this was not a one sermon exercise, so I have divided it into two sermons. I also want to say that I didn't necessarily put them in any order of importance because they are all important. So here we go.

Mindset Number 1:

I WILL GET UP EVERY TIME I FALL DOWN

The Ascended Master El Morya teaches that you only have to get up one more time than you fall down in order to make your ascension. It sounds simple, doesn't it? But how many people reach a certain point on the Path, the point where they've been many times before in other lifetimes, and they say something to themselves like: "(Sigh!) I have been on this path for so many months, years, decades, whatever, and I have made a big effort, I really have. I've read my *Pearls of Wisdom*, I've done my decrees, and, you know, it's just not working. This is just too hard. Maybe I'm just not cut out for it!"

Pretty easy to rationalize, isn't it? But what if we knew that the initiation or test we are receiving might be the *exact point* where we have failed in many, many lifetimes, and that we have developed a *habit of failure* on this particular point? It may have come in different guises but the initiation is the same. So what do we do?

We can surrender any sense of self-pity or sense of injustice or whatever we have, and affirm in our being, as the Apostle Paul does in Romans 8:28, *"And we know that all things [not some things but all things] work together for good to them that love God, to them who are the called according to his purpose."* Another translation of this verse from an old Catholic Bible puts it this way, *"And we know that to them that love God, all things work together unto good, to such as, according to his purpose, are called to be saints."*[82]

So if we are called to be saints—and we know we are—then we have to trust the good Lord that, as we do our part, the circumstances of our lives and the situations that come to us will be for our good and are necessary for our victory. That's easy to say, especially to someone else who is going through an initiation or major test. But it's not always easy to see things so clearly in our own lives. When we reach a point like this, let's be honest, admit that it's hard, and say something like, "God, this is really hard; it's really painful. I don't really understand why this is happening, but if you brought this to me, it must be for a reason. I will not give up. I will keep on trying because I love you. *I am willing to pay the price for my Christhood."*

That's a question every single one of us must answer: Are we willing to pay the price? And it helps to remember that the price is getting rid of our human consciousness and clearing our karma. Is that too great a price? I think not—it is a bargain!

When tests come to us, we must be careful not to be attached to past failures and use them as an excuse for not keeping on. The teaching we've been given on the "failure syndrome" can really help with this. The failure syndrome is a convenient way to get out of making the effort by telling ourselves, "Well, I've failed at this before; maybe I'll pick it up some other time." We have to challenge that! It also helps to understand that when we have a momentum on failing, it can be amplified by negative and anti-victory projections that try to stop us from passing our tests and to take us from the Path.

Dave Barry, the humorist, tells a story about his screened-in patio and his dog. When the dog wanted to go outside, he would first have to go out of the house and into the patio area and then go through the screen door of the patio into the back yard. Well, by-and-by a bad storm hit the area and destroyed the patio and the screen door—just blew them away—and only left the doorframe where the screen door used to be. So there was nothing to prevent the dog from going directly from the house into the yard. But what did the dog do? He went and stood where the screen door used to be and waited for his master to open it for him![83]

Well, maybe God has cleared a new way for us to go and we just haven't noticed it or made an effort to look for it. Perhaps our victory is closer than we think, and if we fall, we simply have to stand up, dust ourselves off, and try again!

Be willing to do what is necessary for your victory, and that begins with getting up each morning, forgiving yourself and others when mistakes are made, self-correcting and even showing up where you need to be. For example, only seventy or so people attended the quarter of Summit University sponsored by the Great Divine Director. Mother said that the master told her two hundred people were supposed to attend, but when the others saw at inner levels the price they would have to pay, they didn't come.

We have to be willing to pay the price. We have to have the courage to get up again even if we don't feel like it. When everything else in our being says, "No, I've done enough, I can't do any more," we have to summon the will, the fire and the determination that this time it's going to be different. If for nothing else, we can do it out of our love for the honor of God.

Mindset number 1: I will get up every time I fall down.

Mindset Number 2:

I WILL NOT BE AFRAID OF PAIN, EITHER MY OWN OR OTHERS'

Experiencing emotional or physical pain is hard enough, but being afraid of pain can be much worse for, as we know, *"fear hath torment."*[84] We have heard the teaching that pain is the portal to bliss, but are we willing to experience the pain to get to the bliss? Most people in the world want the bliss, but they've settled for a temporal bliss, one that will not last, because they have been unwilling to walk the sacrificial path to receive eternal bliss.

There's no shortcut. We have wonderful tools like the violet flame, but we still need to walk this path. There is no shortcut to our Christhood, to the everlasting bliss of God, and *the journey through pain is one we all have to take.* Yes, it is hard. But we cannot allow the *fear* of that pain to be worse than the pain itself, because if we do that, not only will we not reach our goal, but we won't make as much progress.

I think virtually all of us reach a point on the Path where pain is the *only way* we can learn something, especially if we have failed or avoided the same test many times in the past. Mother cautioned us about people who have walked away from the Path and said, "I'm going to do it another lifetime. I don't think I want to do it now. This isn't really my time." Well, it *is* our time or we wouldn't be exposed to this teaching.

When you are going through a particularly painful period, allow yourself to experience the grief, the sorrow, the hurt, the loss. Process it and let it pass through you; don't let it overcome you. A few ways to help deal with pain are: talking to someone you trust, reading comforting words from the masters or the Bible, working on your psychology, singing and walking and talking with God. You can also ask yourself questions like, "Why am I reacting this way? What makes this so painful for me? What is it that God is trying to teach me?" Allow yourself to dig deeper during these times.

It helps to stay balanced in our lives through good habits and the rituals of prayers and decrees, so that when pain comes our way we will be centered in our heart and have the strength to deal with it. Don't try to blot out pain or run away from it. We have run away from it so many times before; we can't do that anymore. There are worse things than pain, and running away from it is certainly one of them. Be balanced, get exercise, and be willing to surrender whatever God is asking you to let go of. One of the most helpful rituals for doing this was given to us by Mother Mary—*The Fourteenth Rosary* (aka the Surrender Rosary).***

Many years ago I was in a very difficult situation, and even though intellectually I knew what I needed to do, emotionally I wasn't ready to do it. I felt like I was wrestling with the angels. "God, you know, I'm just not going to surrender." I may not have said it that way, but that's the way it manifested, and it took a long time for me to reach the point where I was willing to

---

*** *The Fourteenth Rosary: The Mystery of Surrender* is a devotional ritual released by beloved Mother Mary to help us let go of all struggle, fear, pride, ambition, and any false identity or counterfeit of our Real Self. The Surrender Rosary is a tremendous gift for the devotee who is desirous of submitting to the sacred fire all that impedes their soul's ascent to God.

surrender, to let go and trust God. Only then did things start to work for me.

Be willing to surrender. This is a journey and it may be a long one, but when it's over, it's over! When the toothache is gone, you don't think about it anymore, do you? But if you fear pain, you may think about it continually in this life and beyond. Instead, be courageous like John Paul Jones and say, "I'm going to go in harm's way. I'm going to allow myself to experience pain. I may not seek it out, but if God sends it to me, I will allow it to occur."

Besides our own pain, there is the pain of others. How many times has some tragedy befallen a friend or family member and you deeply felt their pain and loss, but you were uncomfortable approaching them. It's hard to be in the presence of another person's pain, but let us be willing to share that pain, to just be with them and not think we have to fix it. Sometimes we just have to be present.

Mother has taught that sometimes God has allowed pain to come to people for a reason, and we cannot deny them the opportunity to experience it. That doesn't mean we leave people to themselves. Sometimes a note or phone call or just being there with compassion is all we need to do. The tradition of bringing a meal to those who are bereaved sends a powerful message. Doing something simple and loving shows that you care, that you're not afraid of their pain and that you're sensitive to what they're going through.

Mindset number 2: I will not be afraid of pain, either my own or others'.

Mindset Number 3:

I AM THE DEBTOR TO GOD, AND ALL BLESSINGS ARE GRACE

How we view ourselves and our relationship to God is crucial to how we view and react to the tests God sends us or to the karma that descends upon us.

Do we go around with a subtle sense of superiority—so subtle that perhaps we can't even see it? After all, it's easy to think, "Aren't we God's chosen people? Didn't many of us come from Venus with Sanat Kumara? Have we not been faithful chelas, supporting the Brotherhood's messenger and organization? Don't we have knowledge beyond what 99 percent of the world has? And don't the masters and angels love us?"

There's a danger in thinking ourselves special or separate from the Law or above taking the tests of the Path. As we seek humility and shun pride, let us remember that we are unascended beings with unbalanced karma and a record of leaving the Path other times. We have also created a dweller-on-the-threshold that is so powerful that it is a real threat to our soul's victory and the victory of others as well.

Yet many of us act surprised when karma or a major initiation comes upon us, and we ask, "What did I do wrong?" Well, interestingly enough, we might not have done anything wrong. In a lecture Mother gave in 1991 titled "On Healing and the Four Types of Fear," she shared a key perspective on the times when people have an initiation on the Path that they don't understand:

Does anybody here tonight doubt that you have a higher calling in God than the one you are now fulfilling? Not a

> hand should go up, right? So we know that we are balancing our karma. We are bearing our burdens. We're working through things in our psychology.
>
> And we know that there is a moment in our life that will come, it comes to all of us, when the calling that we are fulfilling will not be enough. We say, "What have I done wrong? Why haven't I pleased Morya? I tried my hardest. I did my best. What happened?"[85]

Have you ever been in that place? I think everyone who's been on the Path a long time has been there, probably more than once. Mother continues:

> It's because there is a moment in our lives when our best is no longer good enough. We get content with our best. We get content that we're on top of things. Everything's under control. Everything's going right and we're in command of our job. We're in command of our soul. And all of a sudden God comes along, pulls the rug out from under us and says, "It's not enough. I have a higher calling."[86]

When that happens, it's a difficult experience because it shatters who we thought we were. Everything about ourselves—our attainment in the world, our spiritual progress, our service, everything that made up our identity that we were pleased and happy with—God sees it all and says, "It's not enough. You have a higher calling." And so we must become remade in Christ. God will no longer accept who we were before.

If we think we are God's chosen people and that we have great attainment, then we may be dumbfounded when this initiation comes. "Why is this happening to me?" This confusion can be the exact point where a lot of people leave the Path because they don't know who they are anymore. All that they had thought their own is now gone. It's been stripped from them. Some may go into a fog of self-condemnation and think themselves failures, while others may react in pride with a sense of injustice and anger. I think we've all seen that in people. Even if we receive this initiation with humility, it is a very difficult one because it strips us of who we thought we were and tells us we must come up higher.

How do you keep the right perspective or attitude when this happens? How do you keep the balance of knowing that God in you is perfect, while having to walk this journey through your human substance?

One of the best tools to have by our bedside is *The Imitation of Christ* because reading it helps us keep the right mindset for a student on the Path. Not an attitude of self-condemnation, but acknowledging that we are on a journey and we have tests to pass. We have things hidden in our psyche that we are blind to and God is going to go after those with cosmic surgery. We have to allow him to do it without thinking that we have failed or that God has rejected us. It is helpful to understand that there's a difference between our human creation and our Christ Self, and to humbly acknowledge that God is the doer in all things.

We need to keep things in perspective. And again, we need to be very careful not to indulge in a sense of injustice. As long as we do, we can't progress on the Path. That doesn't mean we don't find these initiations difficult or confusing, but we have to ultimately trust that they are what we need.

Remember the story of Peshu Alga, the first one who fell. He cursed God when his son was taken from him. His anger and sense of injustice was so great that he even subverted

Archangel Lucifer. Did you know that? He caused Lucifer to fall, and we know what happened after that.

While we stand in the dignity of our Christ Self, let us not think we are exempt from the law, either spiritual or physical. Until 100 percent of our karma is balanced, we are debtors. And all that God has given us—these teachings, this path, this opportunity, the violet flame—is grace.

Let us be humble before God and the Path, never forgetting that we need to fulfill the Law, and not only win our victory, but also help to win the victory of the earth. So let us acknowledge that we are debtors to God, that we have the grace of his blessings in our life, and decide that we will keep on and not succumb to the subtle vibration of a sense of injustice.

Mindset number 3: I am the debtor to God, and all blessings are grace.

Mindset Number 4:

EVERY DAY I AM IN THE ULTIMATE BATTLE BETWEEN MY SOUL AND MY DWELLER AND THERE WILL ONLY BE ONE WINNER

While that is not a pretty thought, it is a mindset that cannot be sugar-coated. As the Elohim Hercules tells us in the dictation we're hearing today, we must be alert to what is going on in our worlds and what comes to us. I think it was somewhat of a shock for all of us when we first learned about our dweller-on-the-threshold. We wondered, "Who is this guy? Is it me? Is it someone else? This is confusing!" But as sons and daughters of God, we understand that we have created a human consciousness, a not-self, that is not of God but is comprised of all our mistakes, wrong feelings and wrong thinking. We've given it so much power that it can overtake us. It's the sorcerer's apprentice. It's sobering to think about this and ponder, "*What have I done?*"

What do we do about our dweller? Well, fortunately God has given us the answer. We can overcome it with his help. We can't overcome it on our own; the masters have made that very clear. If we're going to challenge and bind our dweller-on-the-threshold, we must have the help of God, the angels, and use the decrees that we have been given to do that.

In the beginning stages of the Path, parts of our dweller are removed fairly easily. We had some worldly habits that we heard weren't right and some of them weren't so hard to get rid of. However, as we get farther along on the Path, we begin to deal with some very core issues, such as anger, fear, hatred and rebellion, that can even go back to our soul's first fall. Admittedly, tackling those does get harder.

All of us want to put on our Christhood. But perhaps, consciously or unconsciously, we are not totally ready to give up parts of our dweller. With the parts that are overt and obvious, it's easy to say, "Yes, God, you can have those." But it becomes quite subtle when there are parts of the dweller that we are unwilling to give to God because we have become comfortable with them and we kind of like them. They are so much a part of us that it would take great effort to dislodge them.

So we have to affirm that the days of trying to get one foot into heaven and keep one foot on earth are over. It doesn't work. We've been doing this for hundreds of thousands of years, and we're not ascended. Why? Perhaps one of the reasons is we haven't adopted the mindset that our soul is going to be the victorious one, not this dweller-on-the-threshold.

We have to recognize the seriousness of this battle. *It is our own personal Armageddon!* Though it's a battle, we can take comfort in the fact that the masters have told us we can be victorious over our dweller if we make the effort and give our daily calls. We need to take advantage of that.

We need to look at our reactions to people or circumstances. The masters (and psychologists as well) have taught that the things you don't like in others are often reflections of the same things in yourself. So when God brings those things to our attention, let us take the opportunity to really look at them, no matter how hard it is.

The Elohim Hercules warns us to be alert for the dweller in others as well, for it comes in many guises, even in *"sweet souls"*[87] with good intentions. Interesting, isn't it? We might have our guard up for the demon or the devil that may come after us, but what about the subtlety of sweet souls with good intentions that may divert us from our path or from where we need to be.

I had a very close friend many years ago at the Ashram of the World Mother in Los Angeles, and someone not in this community asked him, "How do you know what's wrong in the world if you don't experience it for yourself?" That's not so subtle, really, but unfortunately this individual fell for that. Now he is long gone from the Path and engaged in things that are detrimental to his soul. We have to be discerning—not fearful of everyone who walks through the door, but alert; we have to be alert.

We all have blind spots and don't always notice our dweller outpicturing its darkness. So observe yourself and your reactions, and if you don't like what you see, be willing to go after it. And do you know what happens? After a certain period of time, you start to feel better. You don't even know exactly why, but you feel a new lightness, a new enthusiasm, a new joy in your life because you have been freed from certain human momentums and patterns.

If we understand and acknowledge the freedom that will come from moving through the hard parts, it's a sacrifice *not* to walk this path. Why wouldn't we want to do it? Why wouldn't we endure a little bit of difficulty or pain for the victory that is ready to be plucked, ready to be won? God is ready to receive us if we are willing to keep striving. We all know who the ultimate winner in this battle is going to be. It's going to be our soul bonded to her Holy Christ Self because we are *not* going to allow our dweller to continue to spoil our lives and the lives of others.

Have you thought about what brings you unhappiness? Of course, in some ways it's your negative karma. But what has caused you to make that karma? Well, it's what you have allowed into your consciousness. At one point in his dictation Hercules tells us, *"There is someone else, besides the fallen ones, who is blocking the light of the Cosmic Christ in you. Guess who? It is you yourself, your own worst enemy! And I do not speak of your dweller-on-the threshold. I speak of you—you, you, you, you, you, you, the very you!"*[88]

He says we think it's our dweller, and we visualize our dweller as some beast chained in the corner of our subconscious that periodically leaps out and does something that we get blamed for. He explains that we are so enmeshed with the dweller that it's not as much a separate entity as we like to think it is. It's us, and we have to extricate ourselves from it. God helps us do that, because it is so much a part of who we are that we can't do it on our own. It is really an ongoing cosmic surgery; it doesn't happen all at once. But as we call to God and sincerely ask for help, and we work on those things in our lives that we can see are patterns that are not of the Christ, then portions of the dweller will go and the balance scale of the Real and unreal within us will start to tip.

Many years ago, Mother said some people in the community had gotten to the point where their dwellers had shriveled up to almost nothing. Even if that is true for us, it's not the time to rest on our laurels, but rather it's the time to keep on keeping on. There will be one winner—one victor in this battle of our personal Armageddon—not two. We have to have the fire and determination to keep on because that dweller is not going to go easily; it's not going to go without a fight, and we have to be prepared for that. That battle is part of the Path. It's not going to rule our path or be all we think about day and night, but it's something we're going to be aware of—that the dweller must be displaced; it must go; it must be no more!

Mindset number 4: Every day I am in the ultimate battle between my soul and my dweller, and there will only be one winner.

Today we've covered four of the mindsets for victory, and next time we'll look at others. Until then, think about any of these mindsets that have struck a chord with you and any other mindsets you *want* to embody.

Also think about any other mindsets you already have—good and bad. If you don't know if you have mindsets that you might want to change, think about how you react to things that happen to you. At a soul level, we know where we've come up short, where an attitude we hold hasn't allowed us to go forward.

Let us wake up in the morning and get up (Hercules tells us that's our first decision of the day) and be ready to meet the next test that God will send us, the next challenge of our human consciousness or the next step we must take on the Path.

Just think about it. *At long last*, after what may have been thousands and thousands of years for some of us, we have the knowledge, the tools, and the opportunity to be victorious! Is that not a reason to be joyous? Is that not a reason to keep on keeping on and to encourage each other?

Now is not the time to placate the human consciousness, but rather it is the time to embrace the Christ within each one of us because it *is* possible to succeed! It is possible to finally get past the point where we have previously failed in this or other lifetimes. Whenever we reach the point where circumstances have been very tough to deal with or the rug is pulled out from under us, let us say with John Paul Jones, "By the grace of God, I have not yet begun to fight!"

NINE MINDSETS FOR YOUR SOUL'S VICTORY

PART 2

Forgiveness is the foundation of your healing of the mind and the subconscious. Leap! Run! Seize the violet flame! Call upon the law of forgiveness! Be purged of it! Tell God you forgive every part of the whole universe you have ever wronged or who has ever wronged you. Mean it! Feel it!

—MOTHER

SIX

Nine Mindsets for Your Soul's Victory

Part 2

We'll begin today with a reading from *The Imitation of Christ*, chapter 19, "Of the Practices of a Good Religious."

The life of a good religious man ought to be eminent in all virtues, that he may be such interiorly as he appears to men in his exterior. And with good reason ought he to be much more in his interior than exteriorly appears; because it is God Who beholds us and we should exceedingly stand in awe of Him, wherever we are, and like angels walk pure in His sight.

Every day we ought to renew our resolution and excite ourselves to fervor as if this were the first day of our conversion and say:

Help me, O Lord God, in my good resolution and in Thy holy service, and give me grace now this day to truly begin, for what I have hitherto done is nothing.

> *According to what our resolution is, our progress will be; and he has need of much diligence who would advance much.*
>
> *But we must always resolve on something definite, and in particular against those things which hinder us most.*
>
> *We must examine and order well before our exterior and interior; because both are necessary to our advancement.*
>
> *If you cannot continually recollect yourself, do it sometimes, and at least once a day, that is, in the morning, or evening.*
>
> *In the morning resolve, in the evening examine your performances, how you have behaved this day in word, work, or thought; because in these perhaps, you have offended God and your neighbor.*
>
> *Prepare yourself like a man to resist the wicked suggestions of the devil....*[89]

The language is a little archaic but I think we all get the message: The path of Christhood is a daily path. What we do each day matters. How we respond to situations and circumstances determines whether that day is a victory or a setback, whether we've taken one step forward or one step back. The reason we may not go forward every day is that there are some tests we still need to pass and some lessons we need to learn. But we need to be striving to move forward *every* day because that is how we get Home.

It's easy when we feel the presence of God and the light in church on Sunday to make resolutions and to have that fire and determination, "I'm going to go out"—and as Mighty Victory says in the dictation we're hearing today—"*and literally beat the world into submission.*"[90] Then Monday morning comes, and we don't always feel the same, do we? Yet we need that fiery consciousness to make the effort each day to be where we want to be. Having the right mindset and attitude is critical if we are to be successful in overcoming those things that are blocks to our victory and service.

As I shared in Part 1 of this sermon on "Nine Mindsets for Your Soul's Victory," there are many mindsets or attitudes that are important for winning. Nine is an arbitrary number, but it's a place to start. Each one of these mindsets gives us things to reflect upon. Mother lectured for hours and hours on them, so this is an extremely scant review of them. We already know them at some level, but we sometimes forget about them and fall into the same patterns that we've been in for a long time.

The messengers and masters have given a lot of teaching on momentum. When we think a certain way, we respond a certain way, and we tend to repeat that over and over. The problem with some of these momentums is that they are not just from one lifetime; they are from many, many lifetimes. These patterns are so ingrained in us that we don't even realize we have them. It takes the teacher or the guru to expose the patterns, and it takes work on our part to recognize them and even more work to change them. It's easy not to recognize an ingrained pattern because it's the way we've been doing something for a *long* time. This is the hour we need to change that.

Although I've chosen nine particular mindsets to help us be victorious, if I were to choose them today, I might choose different ones. The value of these mindsets is that they may help us to avoid some common mistakes that hinder progress on the Path. Just because they're common doesn't mean they're not difficult to overcome. In fact, sometimes people leave the path for almost trivial reasons, which somehow seem very important to them. So we examine ourselves daily to determine what we need to do to avoid mistakes and to move that next step toward victory.

In the first part of the sermon, we covered four mindsets, and now we will look at five more.

Mindset Number 5:

I WILL NOT MAKE IDOLS OF MYSELF OR OTHERS

In Exodus 20:3 God gives Moses the Ten Commandments, including *"Thou shalt have no other gods before me."* And Exodus 34:14 states, *"For thou shalt worship no other god: for the* L{\scriptsize ORD}*, whose name is Jealous, is a jealous God."* Did you know God's name was Jealous? But truly, we can put nothing else before God if we're going to become the fullness of who we are.

How often Mother warned us of making an idol of her! She explained what a burden it was when people did that, because at some point people will tear down their idols. Then they often lash out and feel angry or disillusioned.

We might not think of idolatry as being one of our major issues, but it can come in subtle ways. People can even make an idol of a previous embodiment. It's interesting that some people have a fixation on the past lives of themselves or others. There are many reasons God doesn't necessarily show them to us. There can be a tendency for people who know or think they know of a past life that is famous or noteworthy to try and "ride on their own coattails," to rest on their past accomplishments.

In her lecture "9 Cats, 9 Lives," Mother talked about the embodiments of Al Capone. He was a saint in one of his lifetimes, and yet look what happened to him as a Chicago gangster in the 1930s. So let's not idolize ourselves for the good we did in the past or condemn ourselves if we think we were someone who did some terrible things. We all hope that we have past lives that have accomplished great things for the Brotherhood, but God is more interested in who we are now. And we should be too.

We have to be so careful of the subtle seeds of pride creeping into our consciousness, like thinking we are special people because we've had many embodiments with the masters, we have accomplished great things for the Brotherhood, and on and on. Pride can be subtle, it can be very subtle.

In a dictation given on March 27, 1970, Djwal Kul addressed this issue of subtle pride. He said:

> *For when individuals become enamored with their own unique qualities, they are sometimes victims of a subtle pride that seems to set them apart and above their fellowmen. This often occurs upon the spiritual path and has been the cause of the downfall of many avatars almost. And when I say the modifying word "almost," I am referencing souls who have come so far upon the Path that the crown of the avatar was actually held over their head and the hierophants were prepared to lower it when the pride of the individual was read as a part of the life record of that individual embodiment, and then the challenge was issued by the advocates. And the advocates, in issuing their challenge, found that the judges could not help but deny the crown to the individual at the supreme moment of conferment, simply because the individual's pride would not permit the law of God to act and confer it. Thus we understand that pride goeth before a fall and that God resisteth the proud but giveth grace unto the humble.*[91]

Pretty sobering teaching, isn't it? A person can have the attainment of an avatar and yet they cannot receive the crown because of the subtle seeds of pride. It seems like we should be on our knees daily asking God to deliver us from that pride because surely it is a danger to our souls. We don't want to idolatrize who we are or who we think we are, for God is the doer in all things.

Look what traditional Christianity has done to Jesus—they have made him an idol, someone to be worshiped rather than emulated. Well, we also know that we cannot make idols of other people: a husband, a wife, a child, a friend (much less athletes or musicians or Hollywood stars). We can have *no one* before God. Of course we can love other people, have wonderful relationships with them and give of ourselves; but God comes first.

There was a chela in our community many years ago who wanted to get married. His prayer to God was for a wife who loved God more than she loved him. In other words, he didn't want a wife who was idolatrous of him or others. Interesting, isn't it? He had his priorities right.

We also have to be careful not to make idols of our leaders in church or state. They are chelas on the Path just as we are. As Mark Prophet taught, trust no man's human consciousness, but trust only the God within each one.

Some of these tests and mindsets are subtle. We really have to be vigilant to catch ourselves when we start doing things that we don't want to do. For example, James 2:2–4 says,

> *For if there shall come into your assembly a man having a golden ring, in fine apparel, and there shall come in also a poor man in mean attire, And you have respect to him that is clothed with the fine apparel, and shall say to him: Sit*

thou here well; but say to the poor man: Stand thou there, or sit under my footstool: Do you not judge within yourselves, and are become judges of unjust thoughts?[92]

Yet don't we all tend to do that very thing if we are not attentive to our thoughts?

Another type of idolatry that is important to look at is when we make a "god" of someone because we haven't forgiven them. Let me explain. When we don't forgive someone for some terrible or traumatic thing they have done to us, then in essence we're making a god of that person because we are giving them so much power over us. And because we won't forgive and let go of what this individual may have done, it intrudes on our consciousness every day of our lives. Some people become so focused on a person and what this person did to them that it not only prevents them from moving on, but it becomes the most important thing in their lives. When we do this we have exalted the other person to the level of a god. And if we allow them to make us bitter and angry, then we are karmically tied to them; we are not free from them.

I was recently rereading *Messages from Heaven*, which is a wonderful book. In it our brother talked to us from heaven and said, *"It is possible to let one person keep you from your ascension. Ask yourself, is there anyone that I am allowing to keep me from my spiritual progress because I cannot forgive him?"*[93]

Can you imagine losing your ascension because you can't forgive one person? We're on the journey Home and we can't allow any person or thing or circumstance to stand in the way of the victory that is God's will for us. Whether it's idolatry of ourselves or others, whether it's pride or non-forgiveness or something else, we must avoid idolatry in all its forms.

Mindset number 5: I will not make an idol of myself or others.

Mindset Number 6:

I WILL EXPECT TESTS AND INITIATIONS EVERY DAY OF MY LIFE UNTIL MY ASCENSION

Over the years I've observed that one of the biggest problems for chelas comes under the category of mismatched expectations. We all think we have an idea of what the Path is and how it should work.

I remember when I first started applying the teachings, I was working at a bank and we had about fourteen volumes of policy and procedure manuals. Whatever you wanted to know, you looked in the manuals and there was the answer in black and white and you knew what to do. I kind of thought that's the way the Path should be: we should have reference materials, know exactly what's going to come our way and happen, and what to do. Well, I found out it doesn't work that way.

Expect the unexpected! God will give us tests and initiations every day of our lives. It's the only way we're going to prove our mastery and get Home. It's good to remember that the reward for passing initiations and giving service is the opportunity for more initiations so we can progress on the Path. I've learned the hard way that you can't try to outthink the masters or what they will do or the initiations you will get. So expect the unexpected!

No test or initiation can come to us unless God gives it to us or allows it, so we have to be careful not to have a sense of injustice or anger because of our testings. Why do we sometimes act surprised when the big initiations come to us and think, "I don't want to be here, God, I don't like this one bit. Are you sure you still love me?" or "I must be a terrible person. I must have done something really bad in another lifetime if this is coming upon me." So we can get into self-pity and feeling sorry for ourselves. Well, I always take comfort in the fact that Mother and Mark came into embodiment with less than 50 percent of their karma balanced. Look at the attainment they brought with them, yet these two extraordinary souls were below 50 percent, like I suspect most all of us were when we came. Isn't it exciting to think that we can get to where they are? That they came in the sackcloth of their karma just as we have? I never heard Mother or Mark complain about their karma or get into self-pity and say, "Oh, boy, this is just too hard, this is just terrible...." That certainly wasn't their attitude or approach.

Another aspect of soul testing that I have learned the hard way is that an initiation isn't over until Lord Maitreya determines it's over. I know when I've had some big initiations I reached a certain point where I said, "Okay, God, I understand your point here. I know what I had to learn, I've done what I needed to do, and now I'm ready to move on." But Maitreya doesn't see things that way. Even when I have pointed out to God that I'm finished, he's not necessarily ready to let me go. Do you know why? Because the masters take advantage of every opportunity. They go to enormous effort and trouble to arrange these initiations for us—to bring us the right people, the right circumstances or the right consciousness so that we can face a test that perhaps we've failed a hundred or more times before. They carefully arrange all the details so that we have the opportunity to finally pass this test, and they are not going to let us move on until we have gotten the most out of it.

The analogy that comes to my mind is the old-style washing machine with the tub in the bottom and a wringer on the top. The wet clothes are passed back and forth, back and forth through the wringer until the excess water is squeezed out. It seems that's what Maitreya does with us, continuing an initiation, back and forth, back and forth until it's complete. And how many of us have said, "How long, O Lord?" Well, God determines how long. It's certainly a good thing that we don't determine it humanly, because at a soul level we really do want to get the most out of any test or initiation. We really do want to pass our tests, even though they're hard at times.

Be aware of your reactions to tests—they can help inform you as to why you are having them and what you need to learn. Be careful not to project your shortcomings on others who might be serving as a mirror. Be willing to work on your psychology so you can pass the test and move on. Don't be too quick to dismiss the tests that you have. Don't try to deal with them at a surface level that is not getting you to the core of the issue you're dealing with. That's important. Someone recently told me that Mother made the comment that you may pass every requirement for your ascension, but if you haven't resolved key elements of your psychology, you'll be coming back into embodiment. So we shouldn't delude ourselves that we'll be okay simply because we're doing all the right things. If we don't work on our psychology and the negative patterns we have, then we may not win our victory.††

We should expect to be tested and initiated every day until we ascend. It's a sign that God loves us and we're truly on the Path!

---

†† The ascended masters have given us spiritual dispensations and tools to assist us with the healing of our psychology, including the Child's Rosary, the violet flame, and decrees and mantras to heal the inner child. Mother and the masters have also emphasized the study of psychology books and the support of a skilled therapist for help in resolving deep-seated issues.

You know what would be worse than being tested? If God didn't pay any attention to us at all. Wouldn't we be forlorn?

I'm not suggesting that all our tests are easy. We do have major initiations that are very difficult because of where we are on the Path and the patterns we have brought with us from other lifetimes. I'm not dismissing the difficulty and challenge of these. Passing them takes work, it takes perseverance, it takes fire, it takes determination, and most of all it takes love. These initiations can be very painful. But if we are going to be on this path, we need to understand that we are going to be tested in little and great ways. And we can't ignore the little ones; they come to us for a reason. We need to keep that mindset. We don't suddenly get to a certain point and then relax and say, "Now it's time to put my feet up." If you balance all your karma, I can assure you there is plenty of world karma that God can give to you.

We're working on getting to a certain point in balancing our karma, building mastery and putting on our Christhood. The masters continue to grow in attainment even after they're ascended. So we shouldn't limit ourselves, because the more good we do and the more mastery we gain in this embodiment, the more we will have to give to God when we make our ascension.

Some of the masters have shared that they wish they had written something during their lifetime to leave a record and create a tie with aspiring souls so they could help them from the ascended state. That's a reminder that what we will be able to do after our ascension will largely depend on what we do now. When we have that mindset, we're not going to feel sorry for ourselves or look at our neighbor and say, "Wait a minute! I'm on the Path and that guy is not, but he seems to be enjoying himself and look what's happening to me!"

That's right—you *are* on the Path! You've made the choice. And when you make that choice, tests and initiations come with it. But thank God they do come with it because that is what is going to get us where we want to go.

Mindset number 6: I will expect initiations and tests every day of my life until my ascension.

Mindset Number 7:

EVERY DAY I WILL WORK TO SURRENDER MORE THAN I DID BEFORE

Surrendering is a process. Thank God we don't have to surrender everything all at once because, quite frankly, I don't think we could do it. But we want to be surrendering something every day. Many of us have been in the teachings for decades. Remember when you first came into the teachings and you had to give something up? It may have been who knows what—a behavior, a habit, certain associations—and it might have been quite hard at the time. But as you look back at it now, my guess is it would seem insignificant to you. What you thought was so important to you at the time has no importance in retrospect. Yet at the time we're asked to surrender something, we often have to work at it.

Surrender is freedom. Seems like a contradiction, doesn't it? We're not talking about passivity here, we're talking about surrender. It is a demonstration of your faith in God and your trust that he will return to you that which he wants you to keep.

For many chelas the Surrender Rosary has been the last resort when everything else they've tried has failed. I suspect that most of us have come to that point at one time or another. We don't know what else to do, so we finally turn to the

Surrender Rosary. When I reached that point in the past and started giving the rosary on a regular basis, my problem didn't necessarily go away or resolve itself immediately, but I felt much more at peace and delivered from the sense of struggle.

Surrendering brings great peace. When you surrender you make yourself vulnerable to God. People can be afraid either of what God might ask them to do or what he might do to them, so they are a little guarded. Well, I think we can trust that our good Lord will bring nothing to us that is not his will. Allow yourself to surrender, and that's when the sense of struggle can be released and you receive the sense of peace and salvation.

Surrender is the most powerful action we can undertake. Mother Mary tells us:

> *Surrender! Surrender to this law within, all that which is anti-Mother, anti-God, anti-the-Real-Self—all of these schisms and divisions that are fabricated within the subconscious. Let go of everything! Give everything to God and understand that it's like carrying your dirty wash to the laundromat. You put it in, it comes out clean. You give to God everything that you are and he gives back to you everything cleaned and purified.* [94]

Mother in her commentary on this quote from Mother Mary explains:

> *If we can just open our hands and let go and let all of our energy, our life, our successes, our failures, our desires, our not-desires flow into the flame, then we will find that a great purge of the Holy Spirit will come upon us. We will be*

relieved of momentums of lifetime upon lifetime of incorrect consciousness.[95]

Think of that. As we surrender the patterns in our psyche that have gotten us into trouble lifetime after lifetime, we can be cleansed of them—they can be dissolved and removed forever!

Mother continues:

> *As God flows in, his energy flushes out the impurity and we find ourselves standing in the very midst of this central sun of being that is our own I AM Presence. The mystery of surrender is the moment of our dying unto unreality. It's the moment of letting go of each justification of the human ego—our false sense of responsibility, our false pride, our false humility, all of the burdens of sophistication with which we have cloaked the soul, the fad consciousness, the herd consciousness, which takes us farther and farther from the center of our own reality.*[96]

Mother Mary also tells us: "Let go of the things that you think you must have. Let go of the things that you think in your pride you will never do or the things that you think you will always do. Let go of all human attachments. Let go of every ambition except God's desiring within you to be God."[97]

That's pretty complete, isn't it? We've been holding back. Let us surrender a little more. Why do it? Because it is freedom. It's the only true freedom we will ever know—the freedom of non-attachment that the Buddha teaches. As soon as we let go of something, it returns to us—not as it was but as a purified version, the version we need to live our life according to the inner divine plan.

We need help. We have patterns in our psyche, in our human consciousness, in the folds of our garment that we don't even know are there, yet they are a hindrance to our path, our Christhood and our ascension. We need to acknowledge and surrender those things that perhaps we don't even know by name and ask God to take them and return to us only that which we can use in his service and for our progress. It's a ritual. It's something we need to do because it's a way of being cleansed and purified. Good intentions are not enough. It's wonderful to have good intentions, but unless we understand the details of our path to the ascension, unless we're attentive to those details, we can miss the boat in spite of our good intentions.

Mindset number 7: Every day I will work to surrender more than I did before.

Mindset Number 8:

I WILL FORGIVE EVERYONE AND EVERYTHING

About a week ago I was in Barnes and Noble and a book title caught my eye, *Forgiveness: 21 Days to Forgive Everyone for Everything*.[98] Doesn't that sound like something an ascended master might say? I didn't read the book, but I was intrigued by what the description on the Amazon website said, *"Forgiveness doesn't mean agreeing with, condoning or even liking what has happened. Forgiveness means letting go and knowing that—regardless of how challenging, frightening, or difficult an experience may seem—everything is just as it needs to be in order for you to grow and learn. When you focus on how things 'should' be, you deny the presence and power of love. Accept the events of the past, while being willing to change your perspective on them."* Of course, this author doesn't know about the violet flame and how it accelerates the

Path, but she clearly recognizes the importance of forgiveness in our lives.

Forgiveness is not a new mindset. Jesus spoke of forgiving seventy times seven.[99] Mother and the masters have frequently admonished us about the importance of it. We all know in our hearts that forgiveness is important, but for some of us it's quite hard to truly forgive. The slights, the misunderstandings, the physical harm, the emotional traumas that have come upon us because of what individuals have done to us are often not easy to forgive and let go of. But we know that we must do it for true soul freedom for ourselves and others. To forgive doesn't mean we are accepting that what someone did is okay. Rather, we forgive the soul—not forgive the action but forgive the soul—for what they did. God's law of karma, his mercy and justice will teach the soul what they need to learn.

I recently came across an incredible teaching from Mother on the violet flame and forgiveness. She explained that *every psychological disturbance within us began with our failure to forgive some part of life*. What a profound teaching! It is enlightened self-interest to *seize the violet flame*, call upon the law of forgiveness and cast all our burdens into the flame. Here is what Mother said:

> *So here is Sanat Kumara and there was Jesus Christ giving to all of us the greatest keys of all time and space. Every psychological sickness, Sanat Kumara is saying right now, every psychological disturbance in you, psychosis, neurosis, whatever it may be that you think you have, began with your failure to forgive some part of life. And that's the hang-up.... Unless you cast the whole thing into the flame, you will find yourself short and not being the instrument of this form of prayer.*

Forgiveness is the foundation of your healing of the mind and the subconscious. Leap! Run! Seize the violet flame! Call upon the law of forgiveness! Be purged of it! Tell God you forgive every part of the whole universe you have ever wronged or who has ever wronged you. Mean it! Feel it!

And every time you see someone that starts irritating you, forgive and forgive and forgive. Just pour oceans of violet flame on everyone you meet that even begins to have the slightest point of discord or agitation with you. It's no doubt a re-encounter of some karmic cycle or a duplication of some karmic cycle. There's no need to be superstitious that everyone you have an argument with you have karma with, but you've got karma with someone somewhere that you once argued with that's making you argue again.

So the whole thing goes into the flame. Let nothing bother you, nothing, and I mean nothing. Because when something bothers you, you get discordant and then you need forgiveness because you've wronged God and the part of the whole universal body in the earth. Someone is hurt when you are discordant. You can't be discordant if nothing bothers you.

That doesn't mean you become a noodle. You get very stern with human creation, but you have peace. It's not a sternness that proceeds out of an agitated solar plexus. It's a sternness that is a clear vortex for the white fire of God.[100]

We obviously can't go wrong by pouring violet flame and forgiveness into almost any situation. However, I think we would all admit that forgiveness is easy to talk about but not always easy to practice. Why do we not want to forgive? Well, we may have a human reason, but to get where we're going, we *do want* to forgive. We don't want anything to keep us from reaching our goal and having our victory; we don't want any weight tying us down.

How many people carry non-forgiveness from lifetime to lifetime? Who gets any good out of something like that? Certainly not the soul you haven't forgiven, certainly not you, and certainly not God.

Mindset number 8: I will forgive everyone and everything.

Mindset Number 9:

I WILL KEEP MY EYES ON THE PRIZE

Our mindset or perspective determines how we act and live. On Sunday mornings at our house we sometimes have deep talks around the breakfast table. We recently had one about the concept of perspective in a spiritual sense, and how people would behave differently if they knew the truth about who they really were, what the goal of life is, and how to get there.

And guess what? With the Teachings of the Ascended Masters we know the answers to those questions. Just think about it—we have been given the keys to the kingdom! We have the knowledge, the tools, and the opportunity for our eternal victory. We don't have to search for the Fountain of Youth; we've found it. We've found every answer that we've been looking for.

Many of us have been on this planet a very, very long time, longer than I think we could even comprehend or understand. We have meandered; we've gone here and there. Mother has taught that we've done everything there is to do on this planet. We've committed every sin and made many mistakes, some of them over and over again. And by God's grace, we've done a lot of good things and we have made progress. But now we have the circumstances, the time, the place and the knowledge all together, and we can use them to finally win our victory.

When the requirement for the ascension was still balancing 100 percent of our karma, I don't know what we thought between embodiments, but we might have felt a little discouraged, "God, are we ever going to get there?" Now we have the mercy of the dispensation of only having to balance 51 percent. Do we really comprehend the magnitude of this gift? We also have the violet flame, which has not been given in an outer way on this planet for thousands of years. We live in a country where they don't put us in jail because we believe something different from what others believe. We have had messengers and ascended masters take us by the hand and lead us. We have everything in place to win this victory *if* we have the will to walk this path.

If we see the truth, if we recognize that it is here, that this is a path we want to walk, how can we allow any thing, any person or any circumstance to come between us and the path God has put before us? At the same time, we know how hard the tests are, how difficult the karmas sometimes are, and the pain that comes upon us. We're at the point perhaps of the last bits of our unbalanced karma and the last negative momentums we haven't overcome, and they can be quite difficult. We know many of the repetitive patterns that limit our progress. While we need to recognize those things that we're seeing, we don't have to deal with all of them at once as that can be overwhelming. So we can work on identifying one thing at a time, one pattern we know God really doesn't want us to have, and tackle that.

Don't think because you're doing good things for God that your negative karma will be overlooked and you'll sort of slip in the back door. It doesn't work that way. We need to do good things for God; we need our service and our decrees to balance our karma and help the world. But we're not going to get in through the back door. We're going through the front door! And if that means dealing with the momentums that have kept us from our true love (which is the love of God), from our twin flames, and from our ascension, then we're going to face those momentums. We have the tools and the knowledge and God is ready to help us. If you think about it, he's really only asking a token from us. Think about all the mistakes and the karma we've made. Yet Saint Germain says that if you apply yourself you can make your ascension in this lifetime or the next. Isn't that extraordinary? Keep your eyes on the prize because when you allow yourself to be distracted by circumstances, people or weariness, then there's a danger you can lose this gift and this opportunity.

A saying goes, "If people knew better, they would do better." Well, we know better. We know what is before us. It's a one-day-at-a-time path. Work on one of these mindsets or on clearing one negative trait you see in yourself every day. Don't let the routines and patterns of life eat up your time and your life so that you never quite get around to doing those things that will earn you the prize.

Pay attention to details. The ascension is in the details of the Path. But we don't want to become immobilized, thinking that if we don't do this thing or that thing or the right thing each day, something bad is going to happen. While love is a key and balance is another key, we also need to pay attention to the details of *how* to overcome.

The prize is there. How many times have we stood before the Karmic Board at the end of an embodiment and said, "Well, it didn't quite work out the way I was planning and I'm really sorry about that, but this happened and that happened," and so forth? We don't want to be in that position again. We want to return to God everything he has given to us and more. We want to honor our messengers and our gurus by following their example and becoming the fullness of our Holy Christ Self. Nothing else is an acceptable offering.

It is good to acknowledge, "This is where I am in time and space and that is where I want to go. I'm not sure exactly where that road is going to take me, but I'm going to walk it every single day of my life. I'm going to be attentive to what the masters have taught us because that is key. I'm going to be in balance. I'm not going to be a fanatic. I'm not going to be passive, and I'm not going to feel sorry for myself. I'm going to recognize and acknowledge that I have karma and substance to deal with, but I know it's temporal. It's going to be gone. It will be no more." We are told God will remember our sins no more, so we should let go of them as well. Let us move on and be about our Father's business.

Opportunity is what Portia brought to us when she came out of nirvana in 1939—an extraordinary opportunity. Obviously, the knowledge of the Teachings of the Ascended Masters is no guarantee that we are going to ascend. That only comes with the assimilation of the teachings. In fact, knowledge not used is more karma for us. If this makes us squirm in our seats, that's okay. I want Morya to make me squirm a little bit, to wake me up from all the patterns and behaviors that have kept me from where I want to go, from my first love.

I love that old hymn that says, "When the roll is called up yonder I'll be there." We keep our eyes on the prize—returning to God, our first love. Our victory will be the greatest joy of our existence. We know about the via dolorosa, we know about the dark night of the soul, we know that pain leads to bliss.

But do you know what? There will come the day of the joy of self-mastery. It *is* possible to succeed!

Jesus said in the garden of Gethsemane, "*...this is your hour, and the power of darkness.*"[101] Well, the power of darkness has had its day. Now it's time for the power of light to have its day—if we choose it. We are on the stage. The angels and masters are in the amphitheater watching us with bated breath, hoping beyond hope that we will fulfill our fiery destiny.

You can be alone on that stage, and at times you *must* be alone. God places us alone on the stage in order to prove our mastery. So even though we have family and friends, we can feel very alone sometimes.

As I said, neither passivity nor fanaticism will get us where we want to go. Only love will—love of God, love of our souls, experiencing the joy of life by running with a dog or playing with a child or celebrating the beauty of the day—all the while remembering who we are and where we are going.

Mindset number 9: I will keep my eyes on the prize!

If any of these mindsets sound like something that would be helpful for you to work on, do it. No matter how small it is, accomplish something every day to help on your homeward path.

Let us be up and doing!

The wreath of victory awaits us.

THE POISON
OF PRIDE

The notions of pride are the most diabolical poison that the fallen angels have succeeded in sowing in almost every seat-of-the-soul chakra of every person on this planet. Think of this, beloved!... The disease of pride is the disease that can thwart the ascension of everyone on the path and there is no exception.

—SANAT KUMARA

SEVEN

The Poison of Pride

What is the pathway to sainthood? How do we follow in the footsteps of the saints? I believe the answer to those questions is a lifetime study. Our beloved messengers have taught us about the path of sainthood over and over, including the attributes of God that we must embody, the parts of the human consciousness that we must let go of, and the tests we will encounter as we walk that path. They have carefully prepared us, because *the path of sainthood is the path of our ascension.*

Many years ago when I was new in the teachings and learned about the violet flame and the ascension, I was so excited to find out that we can make our ascension *in this life!* It seemed that by doing our best, by doing violet flame and serving life, we were all going to get Home. And yet, even with the violet flame, even with the incredible dispensation that we only need to balance 51 percent of our karma to make our ascension, we must still walk the path of sainthood. We must still walk every part of the Path that Jesus Christ walked, including the initiations of the transfiguration, the crucifixion and the resurrection—not in the exact same way that Jesus did, but in the way best suited to our soul's needs.

It is of immense help to understand these initiations. We can't assume that by having knowledge of the Path and giving the violet flame and giving valiant service we will somehow avoid the more difficult initiations. The dark night of the soul and the dark night of the Spirit will come to each one of us at the appropriate point on our path to sainthood.

As I talk and share with people along the Path, it's clear that many of us are being stripped of inner and outer encumbrances. We are having more serious challenges than perhaps we have ever had before. As we are going through this, it helps to understand that it is part of the path of our personal sainthood, of becoming the Christ. Otherwise it's possible to become so overwhelmed with events in our lives that we forget that God is behind the events and there are spiritual lessons we need to learn.

Today we're going to look at something we *must* overcome along this path—pride. The messengers have taught about the pride of Lucifer, his arrogance, and the kind of boasting that led to his fall: "I'm not going to bow down before those sons of God. I'm better than they are. I know the secrets of the universe." While we may not manifest the type of boastful pride that Lucifer did, there are other subtle forms of pride that are so much a part of our consciousness that we don't even know they are there. And unless we ask God or our friends on the Path to point them out to us, we may not recognize that they are a block to us moving forward.

The Poison of Pride

In the dictation we're hearing today, Sanat Kumara teaches:

> *The notions of pride are the most diabolical poison that the fallen angels have succeeded in sowing in almost every seat-of-the-soul chakra of every person on this planet. Think of this, beloved! ... The disease of pride is the disease that can thwart the ascension of everyone on the Path, and there is no exception.*[102]

Sanat Kumara is warning us that we have the poison of pride in our seat-of-the-soul chakra that was sown there by the fallen angels. In other words, while we have our own momentums of pride, we also have implants of pride that we don't even know about that are affecting our behavior. He's telling us this so we can clear these things with our calls and decrees.

The God and Goddess Meru‡‡ once acknowledged our efforts at overcoming, but warned us of the pride that was polluting our being. They said:

> *You are overcoming, beloved! Each and every one of you is overcoming. But you must see that you move against those momentums of ancient pride that reek to such an extent that the angels must wear gas masks, as it were, to be free from the offense of the stench of the purging of that unconscious and the subconscious levels of being and of the carnal mind.*[103]

---

‡‡ The terms "god" and "goddess" denote that they are cosmic beings who ensoul the God consciousness of their spiritual office or role.

The stench of pride is not a very pleasant thought, is it? The angels even have to wear gas masks as we go through the purging of our pride! Perhaps if we could smell it, we'd have much more incentive to get rid of it! It has to come out and it has to go. This is rather like having a cavity, and when the dentist drills it there is often a bad smell. We endure it knowing that the cavity has to go. We endure unpleasant experiences as necessary in our physical life, and similarly we must go through unpleasant experiences in our spiritual life. And, by grace, the angels will graciously accompany us as we are going through them.

Continuing, the God and Goddess Meru tell us we must not only be free from pride, but also

> *...be willing to see yourself in need of total reformation. And that reformation is called "conversion," and it is the turning around of your being and it is the acceleration of the atoms until they throw off so much darkness that you pass through the dark night of the soul and the dark night of the Spirit and all seems darkness to you.*[104]

That is an amazing teaching! We usually think of the dark night of the soul and the dark night of the Spirit as initiations that God is putting us through. Yet the God and Goddess Meru tell us it is also our own misqualified substance coming out that causes our soul to pass through the dark night. That substance *must* come up and out, because if it doesn't, we can't become a saint, a Christed one. This understanding can give us a major incentive to free ourselves of pride and other negative momentums as quickly as possible with the tremendous gift of the violet flame and the other spiritual tools we have.

Isn't it interesting to see how karmically accountable we are for our state in life? We are still going to receive those initiations because they are part of the path of sainthood, but perhaps the time can be shortened as we rid ourselves of momentums of darkness.

A longtime chela once told me a story about an experience she had many years ago that relates to what we're talking about. I can't remember the exact dialogue, but here's the gist of it. Mark Prophet came into the room and she looked up and said, "Hello, Mark, how are you?" Mark got an expression on his face like a grimace, like an I-don't-even-want-to-look-at-you kind of expression. She was really surprised and asked, "Mark, what's the matter?" He replied, "Oh, the stuff that's coming out of you right now." Then she asked, "Well, what stuff, what stuff?" And he simply replied, "It's not your fault, but it's very unpleasant." She didn't know what to say. A minute later Mother walked in and made a face, almost turned away and said, "Oh, dear!" The chela told me, "I didn't know what to say. I didn't feel any different." The point was that something negative was coming up and out of her, was leaving her and being transmuted, but it was quite unpleasant for the messengers to look upon. And the experience was rather humbling for her. As we go through similar purges, we should remain humble and remember that it is the mercy and the grace of God that negative records do come up to be transmuted. This is our path to soul freedom!

Blind Spots

I think it's safe to assume that we all have the poison of pride in our being to a greater or lesser extent. I also believe that many of us are sincerely trying to overcome it. But as I mentioned earlier, the danger is that we can have blind spots hiding some of the subtler forms of pride. However, God has not left us comfortless in the midst of our karma. There are proven ways to overcome this poison and to free ourselves as the saints have done before us. The first step is to identify pride within ourselves. After all, how can you go after it if you don't know it's there?

In her book *Everything Is Energy*, Dr. Marilyn Barrick enumerates some of the major aspects of pride and how they manifest in our psychology. She writes:

> *Pride can be as simple as a person that refuses to wear a hearing aid, insisting that everyone else needs to speak up! Or a person with poor eyesight who rejects the indignity of eyeglasses. Or the person who begs to differ and has to have the last word. All of us can benefit from exploring and transmuting prideful attitudes and behavior in ourselves. We can ask ourselves, 'What kind of subtle prideful behavior do I indulge in?'*[105]

One pitfall we might fall prey to is a subtle sense of superiority coming from the thought that—because we are walking the Path and have devoted our lives to the service of the Brotherhood and the mission of our messengers—we are *special*. We might even think that "specialness" should somehow make up for our human substance and the negative energy in our electronic belt. But it does not! We cannot escape the need to wrestle with pride and all the other poisonous patterns and negative records until we are free of them.

Even though we may have worked very hard and faithfully used the violet flame, we cannot bypass the necessary inner work. We have the tools to go after these patterns and records in our electronic belt. Our devoted service allows God to show us these things in case we are blind to them. It is much better for us to face them and challenge them through prayers and calls and decrees *before* they manifest, before we do harm to other people or to God's plans. So let's go after pride and the substance in our electronic belt before it rears its ugly head as it is wont to do.

Many years ago the teaching was given that not a single one of us, *not a single one of us,* could be in this community without the sponsorship of an ascended master. So whatever attainment we may have in our causal body was apparently not enough by itself, perhaps because of our karma or some flaw in our consciousness. Therefore, as sponsored students of the ascended masters, we should be humble and grateful beyond words that God gives us the opportunity to walk this path because we realize we have much to overcome and much to do. We have to be careful that we don't somehow think, "We are going to save the planet. God has entrusted that task to us." The truth is that God has entrusted us with the knowledge of the Word and the tools that—by his grace and only by his grace—will save this planet and the solar system. *God is the doer.* Our human consciousness cannot save anything. It is not an acceptable offering. We have come to the point on the Path where it has got to go!

There are parts of our being that aren't of God that we are pretty attached to. We like them because they are part of our human personality, part of who we think we are. Maybe it's a sense of injustice you indulge, consciously or unconsciously thinking, "You know, I kind of like this sense of injustice. It gives me an excuse to complain about things that happen to me. It gives me something to lean on when I'm criticized." It's got to go; *it's got to go*. Pride and these other negative patterns in our being must go into the flame if we are going to make it Home.

The High Cost of Pride

I love the teaching about why Alpha is God over all. Omega told us that one of the reasons is because Alpha is the most humble being in the universe. Think about that. Isn't that amazing? The most humble being in the universe is the Lord God Almighty. Helps put our life in perspective, doesn't it? Helps us understand how, on the other end of the spectrum, pride is the beginning of sin, just as it was the beginning of the fall of Lucifer. Harboring pride has a very high cost spiritually.

The following is an excerpt from a dictation by beloved Djwal Kul given on March 27, 1970[§§] through our messenger Mark. It helps motivate us to be serious in our determination to root out the patterns of pride within us.

> *As I come to you, then, speaking of the inner light of the symbolic masonry of the Spirit, I am sure that you will recognize the great potential that exists in the deciphering of the hieroglyphs of the hierarchy. These experiences, of course, cannot be imparted to the neophyte, or the beginner. Yet he who is advanced will often say to himself, "I am a neophyte." Because he recognizes that the great peril to all advancement is human pride and ego.*
>
> *When individuals on the spiritual path begin to conceive of the idea that they are unique, that no one else is like them, what they have conceived of may be ever so true. But it must also be recognized that it is a point of danger to*

[§§] A short portion of this excerpt is included in the "Nine Mindsets for Your Soul's Victory, Part 1" sermon, p. 95.

overemphasize this unique quality of being. For when individuals become enamored with their own unique qualities, they are sometimes victims of a subtle pride that seems to set them apart and above their fellowmen.

This often occurs upon the spiritual path and has been the cause of the downfall of many who were almost avatars. And when I say the modifying word "almost," I am referencing souls who have come so far upon the Path that the crown of the avatar was actually held over their head and the hierophants were prepared to lower it when the pride of the individual was read as a part of the life record of that individual embodiment. And then the challenge was issued by the advocates.

And the advocates, in issuing their challenge, found that the judges could not help but deny the crown to the individual at the supreme moment of conferment, simply because the individual's pride would not permit the law of God to act and confer it. Thus, we understand that pride goeth before a fall and that God resisteth the proud but giveth grace unto the humble.[106]

I speak to you in this wise tonight because we have the life record before us of many who are known to you in the occult world. We choose, however—because of the strange juxtaposition in which the consciousness of man becomes placed when we name names—to avoid the naming of actual names. But we could draw from the life records, from akasha, the splendid life records of many who have made it all the way to their ascension and their victory. Yet, at the same time, others who also walked in their same class and were classmates of these great ones did not make it because of the subtleties of pride that had actually entered into their consciousness.

> Many times the laws of God will act upon man to restrain his pride. To prevent him from actually falling, God will permit a thorn to express itself momentarily in his flesh, in his consciousness. There will ride in some vibratory action which will cause him distress and he will stumble momentarily. This is not an act of God tempting man, for God does not tempt man. But it is an act of the hierarchy designed to prevent a soul that has performed a very meritorious service to life from losing his crown or becoming a castaway through this subtle quality of pride.[107]

Isn't that powerful imagery with a stunning message? The crown of the avatar is about to descend upon a soul, but is withdrawn at the last minute because pride is found within the individual! Such a person has obviously given very meritorious service. They have obviously worked hard to follow the Path—but not hard enough. They have left a vestige of pride within themselves. This tragedy is amplified by the fact that they don't even know that they were about to receive this crown and lost it because of pride unless God shows that to them.

It's a sobering thought because we all work so hard. We've striven not just in this lifetime but in many lifetimes for the opportunity to be here in this time and place, at this nexus in eternity that is so crucial to our own path and our ascension. Do we want to stumble on the pebble or the boulder of pride and fall before we reach our goal? It's something we all have to truly consider.

Recognizing Pride

So what are we going to do about this? Well, we have to call a spade a spade. We have to be honest enough to recognize pride within ourselves and name it. We have to name it so we can go after it and enlist the support of the ascended masters in dealing with it.

Mother and her staff compiled a list of sixty-two aspects of pride,[108] and some of them might surprise you. As we consider them now, it would be good to note which of these forms of pride might be manifesting within our being. Then as we make calls on the list, we can especially ask to be cut free from the ones we know we have.

Here are the aspects of pride:

1. Self-idolatry or idolatry of others
2. Putting people in a hierarchy of who is better than who, or more important, and then treating people differently depending on who they are in "hierarchy"
3. Prejudging people based on their grooming, dress, skin color, etc.
4. Changing the way you act depending on who you are talking to
5. Ignoring the "little people"
6. Pride of place or position
7. Thinking you are more important than someone else because of the kind of work you do
8. Thinking that you are better than others
9. Inordinate self-esteem
10. Putting yourself or someone else down
11. Disdainful attitude and demeanor
12. Nose in the air or looking down your nose at others
13. Patronizing or talking down to others
14. Using words you know someone doesn't understand
15. Manipulating others to get what you want
16. Controlling situations and not sharing responsibility

17. Thinking you have to do everything because no one else can do it better
18. Not giving others the opportunity to help or assist you
19. Being unwilling to share your knowledge, so that you can maintain control
20. Not being able to work with others, unable to compromise or give in
21. Refusing to change or to consider that you might need to change
22. Shouting or yelling in anger or aggravation
23. Pointing out others' mistakes in a blaming tone
24. Thinking a person "should know better" and using a demeaning tone of voice toward them or about them
25. Using a tone of voice that indicates irritation
26. Sarcasm
27. Always insisting you are right
28. Not admitting you are wrong
29. Having to have "the last word"
30. One-upmanship
31. Having a sense of self-importance
32. Being preoccupied with yourself
33. Always needing to be the center of attention
34. Drawing attention to yourself
35. Talking too much, or talking about yourself all the time
36. Thinking others are thinking or talking about you
37. Having a "What can you do for me?" attitude
38. Having a "My brother is my keeper" attitude
39. Thinking you are above the Law, or a "special" son or daughter of God
40. Being easily offended
41. Being overly sensitive or insensitive
42. Not forgiving yourself or others

43. Ingratitude
44. Thoughtlessness
45. Not realizing that you have pride or a problem (spiritual blindness)
46. Being dishonest with yourself and others
47. Taking credit when it is not due or for others' work or efforts
48. Bragging
49. Being vain, looking at yourself in the mirror a lot
50. Displaying your talents, clothes, money, looks
51. Being overconcerned with appearances and other people's opinions
52. Nonresolution with God
53. Nonsurrender to the will of God
54. Not trusting others, God, the messengers and the masters
55. Being a workaholic and wanting praise for all that you do, or accumulating so many tasks so that people think you're great because you do so much
56. Needing to rescue others from their problems
57. Overworking yourself, pushing yourself beyond what your body can handle
58. Not taking care of your physical body or inordinate concern about the care of the body
59. Not paying attention to your inner child
60. Lack of self-esteem
61. Feeling unworthy
62. Being insane or acting crazy

Looking at this list, I think we can all admit we have pride in one form or another. Some are easily identified, while others can be very subtle. It's important to know how various aspects of pride manifest so that we can recognize them and go to work on eliminating them. We may even notice different aspects of pride in ourselves or others that this list doesn't include.

There is also a prayer by Cardinal Merry del Val (1865–1930) called "The Litany of Humility" that clearly identifies some aspects of pride and some fears and wrong desires that may plague us. What I like about this prayer is that as we identify each thing, we immediately ask Jesus to deliver us from it, to assist us in overcoming. Then we have to roll up our sleeves, go to work, and get rid of our negative momentums. They're a block and hindrance on our path to sainthood. Moreover, we will feel a greater presence of God and a greater bliss in God as we free ourselves from these momentums and allow our Holy Christ Self and our I AM Presence to take their place in our being.

The Litany of Humility

O Jesus! meek and humble of heart, Hear me.
From the desire of being esteemed, Deliver me, O Jesus.
From the desire of being loved, Deliver me, O Jesus.
From the desire of being extolled, Deliver me, O Jesus.
From the desire of being honored, Deliver me, O Jesus.
From the desire of being praised, Deliver me, O Jesus.
From the desire of being preferred to others, Deliver me, O Jesus.
From the desire of being consulted, Deliver me, O Jesus.
From the desire of being approved, Deliver me, O Jesus.
From the fear of being humiliated, Deliver me, O Jesus.
From the fear of being despised, Deliver me, O Jesus.
From the fear of suffering rebukes, Deliver me, O Jesus.
From the fear of being calumniated, Deliver me, O Jesus.

From the fear of being forgotten, Deliver me, O Jesus.
From the fear of being ridiculed, Deliver me, O Jesus.
From the fear of being wronged, Deliver me, O Jesus.
From the fear of being suspected, Deliver me, O Jesus.
That others may be loved more than I, Jesus, grant me the grace to desire it.
That others may be esteemed more than I, Jesus, grant me the grace to desire it.
That, in the opinion of the world, others may increase and I may decrease, Jesus, grant me the grace to desire it.
That others may be chosen and I set aside, Jesus, grant me the grace to desire it.
That others may be praised and I go unnoticed, Jesus, grant me the grace to desire it.
That others may be preferred to me in everything, Jesus, grant me the grace to desire it.
That others may become holier than I, provided that I may become as holy as I should, Jesus, grant me the grace to desire it.

You may be thinking, "Wait a minute! This is too much! Who am I going to be after this?" You're going to be more of God than you ever have been. You will be freer from fear and the desire for anything other than God. That's a huge step forward on the path of sainthood.

The saints get so caught up in the bliss of God that they want nothing, absolutely nothing else in their worlds except to be with God and to serve him and to help others in pain. They don't need anything else.

There may have been a time when we have needed many things—or thought we needed them—but that time is receding. What we need now is the presence of God with us.

Where Do We Start?

So where do we start? We can begin by getting down on our knees, confessing our pride to God, and asking him to deliver us. We can ask for forgiveness for not seeing our pride and for allowing blind spots to develop. If we have trouble surrendering certain aspects of pride, we can ask God to infire us with the God-desire to be free from these momentums.

Then we go to work on ourselves. This is not just the wave of a magic wand and "poof" our pride is gone. This takes spiritual and psychological work. These aspects of pride are planted deep within us by Lucifer or other fallen ones or by our own wrong actions. They are interwoven into our consciousness and psychology, and some of them seem to be superglued in there.

The longer you are on the Path, the more you get down to rock-hard, solid substance that's not going to go without a fight. And when we cannot get rid of it ourselves, we must ask for God's help.

Here is an excellent call you can make to help deal with momentums of pride. You can use this prayer or one that you compose yourself.

In the name of the I AM THAT I AM, when I see an element of pride coming up in my personality, when I have prideful thoughts or prideful actions or words, I will say, "By the grace of God, I demand the binding of this pride, this portion of the dweller-on-the-threshold." Like a cosmic surgeon, I diagram pride on my cosmic clock, and as I see it, I call it, I name it and I surrender it so that it can be slain. I am determined, by the grace of God, to be rid of it, to no more have an expression of that pride.

And anytime that subtle or overt pride comes back, I will go after it and I will hit it hard. And I will say, "By the grace of God, I demand the cause and core of pride within me be bound! I demand the binding of the dweller-on-the-threshold within me of human pride, devil pride, fallen angel pride, every kind of pride there is. Burn through and bind it now!"

By my conscious will, I separate out from the beast of myself. I will watch it like a hawk. I will not allow that pride to be expressed through me again, by the grace of God. I will get rid of my prejudices and I will get rid of whatever way my pride manifests—pride in my ancestry, pride in my social status, pride in my education, pride that says I am better than somebody—the whole gamut of pride.[109]

We use the Science of the Spoken Word and the tools that God has given us, and we go after pride and other manifestations of the dweller-on-the-threshold. We *identify* the negative energy, we *name* it, and we *surrender* it. Surrendering it is key; we have to be willing to let go of it. We can't just pull it out and then put it back. We have to let go of it completely. Then we fill the vacuum with God's virtues, including humility and compassion.

We *can* be delivered from these momentums that have plagued us for eons, that have kept us separate from God. It is time for them to go, and we need to enlist God's help because these are strong momentums.

In a dictation, Durga, one of the manifestations of the Divine Mother in Hinduism, asked us if we had the courage to call for her to stand where we stand and deliver us from negative momentums. All the divine mothers in heaven and all the ascended masters and archangels are ready to perform this cosmic surgery on us. When we take our stand and make the calls, it gives them permission to come in and root out negative substance. As they help us slay these momentums, I like to imagine them coming in with their swords and literally cutting off a chunk of substance and throwing it into the sacred fire or dissolving it by the sheer intensity of their being. And as we do our part to work on these things, that allows the masters to do more, especially when we have the courage to ask for their help.

Then, of course, we have to be careful not to recreate those momentums. We may be delivered from something, but if we go out the next day and do the same thing, the momentum is going to come right back. Obviously, we may make mistakes because we are still human, so we have to be vigilant, ask for forgiveness, and keep on keeping on.

A chela on the path to sainthood needs to make intense calls on pride every day. Dweller calls are also an invaluable part of our daily service as we go after core pride, core anger, core rebellion, the implants of the fallen ones within us—you name it. We need the courage to stand and challenge all these things in the name of God—not in our own names, but in the name of God—for we must remember that God is the doer.

Thou the All, I the Nothing

Another key to overcoming pride is to emulate our beloved Mother in her embodiment as Catherine of Siena.

> *Jesus once appeared to Catherine as she was praying and said: "Do you know, daughter, who you are and who I am? If you knew these two things you would be blessed. You are that which is not; I am He who is. If you have this knowledge in your soul, the enemy can never deceive you; you will escape all his snares; you will never consent to anything contrary to my commandments; and without difficulty you will acquire every grace, every truth, every light."*[110]

Catherine would recite "*Thou the all, I the nothing*"—the nothing of the human consciousness. Sometimes I paraphrase this in my prayers and say, "O my Jesus, thou the all, I the nothing," or "Holy Christ Self, thou the all, I the nothing." I always feel better after saying those prayers. Try it sometime!

It takes a lot of effort to defend our egos and human consciousness, and it's wasted energy. When we finally stop defending our human consciousness and release these patterns into the flame, we will experience more of God's fire and energy. This leads to soul freedom, to the liberation of our soul from human bondage. Why would we want to defend our human consciousness, the human ego with its misqualified energy that has burdened us for so long?

Now that we can see it for what it is, we *don't* want to defend it, we want to get rid of it and accelerate our path. We want to be free of this darkness. We want to clean out the debris in our electronic belt. We want to shorten the dark night with God's help. And perhaps some manifestation of pride is the very thing preventing us from receiving the crown that Djwal Kul spoke about.

I'd like to close by reading an excerpt from *The Imitation of Christ*. We've heard many times from the masters how important this book is to our path. It's definitely a good one to keep by our bedside. Notice how the tone and vibration of this excerpt reflects the attitude "Thou the all, I the nothing." It is a recognition that our human consciousness is not good enough and never will be good enough and that only the presence of God within us is sufficient. This section is entitled "Of Humble Submission." I want to close with this because it gives such a vision of hope and joy and bliss in God for those who are humble before him.

> *Make no great account of who may be for you or against you, but mind and take care that God may be with you in everything you do. Have a good conscience, and God will adequately defend you, for he whom God will help no man's malice hurt. If you know only how to hold your peace and to endure, without doubt you will experience that the Lord will help you. He knows the time and the manner of your deliverance, and therefore you may resign yourself into his hands. It belongs to God to help us and to deliver us from all turmoil. Many times it is very useful to us for keeping us in greater humility that others know and reprimand our faults. When a man humbles himself for his faults, he then really pacifies others, and easily satisfies those who are angry with him. God protects and delivers the humble man. He loves and comforts the humble. To the humble he inclines himself. On the humble he bestows grace, and after he has been brought low, raises him up to glory. To the humble he reveals his secrets, and sweetly draws and invites him to Himself. The humble man, in the midst of reproach, remains in great peace, for he depends on God, and not on the world.*[111]

The reward for going after our pride and replacing it with humility in Christ and in God is the same joy and bliss of his presence, his sweetness, and his tenderness that the saints have experienced.

Padre Pio once said he would not give up his suffering for gold because his suffering brought him the sublime presence of God. Similarly, as we suffer in the surrender of our human consciousness, the bliss and joy of God can come to us as well. It is there waiting for us.

As we do our work, God will do his. And by his grace, as we move to free ourselves from pride, the planet will also be freed from a portion of pride. As we walk farther along our path to sainthood, as we begin to make calls on the darkness manifesting in ourselves and in the fallen ones manifesting pride, the victory of earth can be won. God can bring it forth. This is the work of the ages. It is the work that God is calling us to do now—and praised be his name for this opportunity.

Let God be the all in us, and the poison of pride will harm us no more.

A BUDDHA'S CHRISTMAS VOW

If you want the easy life, the world offers abundant opportunity for that way, the 'way that seemeth right'; but you know the end of that way is death and you have chosen life.

—**GODFRE**

EIGHT

A Buddha's Christmas Vow

Would he listen to the voice of reason or would he listen to the voice of God within? They are not always the same. Common sense and honest analysis told him that all was lost. For George Washington and the fight for freedom, Christmas 1776 was one of the darkest hours, if not *the* darkest hour, of the revolution. Yes, Saint Germain had a plan for America, a plan for freedom for the lightbearers of the planet; yes, he had his chelas in place; and yes, there was a plan for a golden age. But that did not make it inevitable. Many thought the Americans had essentially lost the war, and that it was just a matter of time before the Delaware River froze and the Hessian troops would walk over to Washington's camp and dictate the terms of surrender.

We all know the story of the American army crossing the Delaware, but we can only imagine what George Washington (who was becoming a Buddha) went through to make that decision. On November 17th of that year Washington's army was six thousand strong. On December 20th most enlistments for the year had expired and the number had dwindled to about two thousand. On New Year's Eve, almost everyone's term of service would expire and Washington would be left with an army of about twelve hundred. He wrote to John Hancock at the time, *"Ten more days will put an end to the existence of our Army."*[112] The voice of reason told him he could not win.

The movie *The Crossing* tells the story of Washington crossing the Delaware. It has a scene where General Gates—another American general who, shall we say, did not have the attainment of George Washington and viewed Washington with contempt—mocked Washington's plan to cross the Delaware. He explained with reason and logic why it wouldn't work. First, the superior Hessian army, the finest, most disciplined fighting force in the world, was approaching the American army comprised of a ragtag group of boys, one-third of them without shoes. Next, there was the difficulty of moving an army across the river undetected, given all the noise they would undoubtedly make. And, of course, when the army was in the river, they would be sitting ducks, totally vulnerable to Hessian cannon fire. Then, even if they got across the river, what were the chances of them actually surprising the Hessians? The voice of reason said there was no hope.

Benjamin Rush, a Philadelphia doctor and signer of the Declaration of Independence, visited Washington at his headquarters on December 23, 1776, just two days before Christmas, and found him quite discouraged. Washington sat at a writing desk, quill in hand, scratching the same phrase onto scraps of paper, a scarce commodity in camp. Rush wrote of this meeting, *"While I was talking to him, I observed him to play with his pen and ink upon several small pieces of paper. One of them by accident fell upon the floor near my feet. I was struck with the inscription upon it. It was 'Victory or Death.'"*[113]

That was a Buddha's Christmas vow.

For Washington, "Victory or Death" was not an empty phrase. Before his troops disbanded at the end of the year, he would either win a victory over the Hessian forces camped on the eastern bank of the Delaware or he would die. There was no middle ground.

It's an inspiring story for sure and one that clearly exemplifies the father of our country, who became the Ascended Master Godfre. *But what does it mean for us now, at Christmas this year?*

Washington was forced to choose: he could act or he could surrender. He had to do one or the other. When we look at how bad things are in the world today, do we feel the same compelling need to act? To take a vow that might not match Washington's words exactly, but would match his fire and determination for victory that goes against the voice of reason?

While we have shoes, many of us can feel a certain "battle fatigue." As "reasonable" men and women, can't we see the handwriting on the wall—that the earth seems to be slowly and inexorably headed not for the golden age, but more likely into a time of great darkness?

For many of Washington's soldiers who left him after their enlistment was up, it was a logical, reasonable and practical decision. After all, hadn't they done their duty? They had. While others simply awaited the outcome of the war, they had enlisted and fought for the cause. Didn't they need to go home to their families, to plant their crops, to tend to their livestock? Didn't they need to get on with their lives? Wasn't it time for others to do their part too? Many did reason this way and left, but fortunately not all.

We Can Do More, We Can Give More

Well, we're not going to desert Saint Germain and Godfre and the ascended hosts in this hour! Our presence here and our many years of service (even decades for a lot of you) is proof of that.

But has something held us back from the type of vow that George Washington took on that day? Have we not been quite desperate enough or felt enough fire to take our stand and make our vow at the level of intensity and commitment necessary for the victory of Saint Germain's golden age? For the fulfilling of the messengers' mission and the plan of God for this planet? We know that God will reinforce any vow that we take. Yet at some level, are we not quite ready to make that strong a vow? Are we fearful of what may come upon us if we take this ultimate stand?

After all, we can reason that if we keep doing our decrees and serving, we will balance our karma and make our ascension. And there is some truth to that. We've been working. We've been striving. We *are* balancing karma, by God's grace, and hopefully we will reach our goal. But is that all we want to do in this hour of greatest peril to the world and the precious souls of God? Mother once said that if we win our ascensions and do not save the planet it will be like ashes in our mouth. In other words, we will have failed to bring in the golden age as we desired to do.

I recall opening a *Pearls of Wisdom* volume when I was new to the teachings, and the words on a random page stood out that essentially said, "You can do more, you can give more." *You can do more, you can give more.* Intellectually, I think we can all agree that we can do more, that we're not maximizing our time. But emotionally, the thought of doing more may seem overwhelming.

How do we sustain the fervor and intensity necessary for the victory, month after month, year after year? For starters, we need to surrender the idea that our human consciousness is capable of doing that. It's not. Only the mind of God within us can do it. Mother admonished us to stop trying to be clever people. I love that. Whatever momentum we have in our mental bodies, forget it. It may be useful and it may be one way that we got this far. But ultimately we have to let go of it and let the Christ mind take its place. And of course, though we've been told to give up the sense of struggle, we all know that's easier said than done.

I remember a Sunday service at Camelot that illustrated this point. As usual, we were decreeing to set the forcefield for a dictation. We decreed and decreed and decreed and still Mother did not come out. I'm sure more than a few of us were thinking, "When is she going to come out? I'm getting tired, and I'm hungry too." When she eventually come out she basically said, "In case you were wondering why I haven't come out sooner, it is because I was waiting for you to clear the energy, which you have still not done." She went to the altar, made a brief, fiery call then turned around to face us and said that the energy was cleared so the service could continue.

What was the lesson there? It wasn't that we weren't working hard to clear the energy; we just weren't able to do it! Everyone was sincere in spite of our fatigue or our hunger. We really wanted to prepare the forcefield and clear all opposition to the dictation. So why could Mother do it with one brief call when several hundred of us couldn't do it in several hours? Oh, you say, "Well, she was the messenger," as though that explains everything. Perhaps in a way it does, but it's not an excuse for the rest of us. Mother was the embodiment of her Christ Self and she was able to contain so much light and fire in her being that the energy was cleared when she made the call.

If we, individually and collectively, are going to get the job done for Saint Germain and Godfre and the Brotherhood, there is no alternative to our Christhood. Nobody is going to disagree with that. We all agree we have to put on our Christhood. So what is holding us back?

Jesus' Call to Become the Christ

Many of you may remember when Jesus gave his landmark dictation in 1987 and said it was time to become the Christ.[114] I had been in the teachings for a number of years even at that point, and I remember saying to my wife, "I'm not sure how to do that. He said it's time, but I am not clear on what to do next." I guess it's a question of not seeing the forest for the trees because *all* the teachings of the ascended masters are about how to become the Christ!

Even so, over the last few years I've still been wondering, "What does the Christ look like?" We know what the Christ looked like in Mother, but do we recognize what it looks like in each other or in ourselves? If there's a fully Christed one in our midst, would we even know it? Many didn't even recognize Jesus. Can we recognize the Christ in each other? Hopefully we do.

We are aspiring to be the Buddhas in winter, even as Washington was. What is keeping us from the next step in surrender that will allow us to put on the level of Christhood or Buddhahood needed to secure this victory? God is not holding us back, our Holy Christ Self is not holding us back, Jesus is not holding us back. Who is holding us back? We are, of course.

Our family has a dog who has a lot of energy, and we have an invisible electric fence around our house to keep her in the yard. The way it works is that the dog wears a device on her collar, and if she goes near the buried wire, she gets a small zap. It's quite effective in keeping the dog inside the fence. Well, sometimes we take the collar off so she can go outside our yard. Yesterday we took it off to go sledding on a nearby hillside. But she wouldn't go because she didn't want to get zapped. She didn't realize the device was off, and she wouldn't budge past her normal boundary. Eventually I had to gently but firmly pull her across the boundary. She was not ready to trust that she was going to get through that electric fence without getting a shock.

I wonder if we're like that sometimes. We're so used to not wanting to cross the line of surrender, that even when God takes our hand, we are not sure we want to go. We can pray that God will pull us, but we have to cooperate a little bit. At a certain point, our dog did cooperate and she got beyond the electric fence. Then all of a sudden she realized she wasn't going to get zapped, and off she raced, joyous and happy. What is it going to take for us to get to the other side of our self-imposed "fence" to a joy and happiness of freedom greater than we know now? Will we trust our Lord to take our hand and guide us through that?

Washington wrote, "Victory or Death." We may not be facing physical defeat and death. But I think we would agree that we are facing the victory of the golden age or the loss of the dreams of Saint Germain and the Brotherhood for the Aquarian age.

We may not face a year-end deadline like Washington and his army did, and perhaps that is part of the problem. How long have we been postponing the day of reckoning with our human consciousness, our dweller? Yes, we do our dweller calls because we don't want to outpicture the dweller. But have we really taken the step to be totally done with it?

If you haven't seen the movie *Lincoln*, I strongly recommend it because it shows some of the hardships of Lincoln's life and what it took to preserve the union and America's destiny. As with Washington, few can imagine what he went through to do this, but this movie does an excellent job of portraying Lincoln's mastery and determination for the victory—no matter what it cost. While we know he ultimately paid the price with his life, it's absolutely inspiring to see how he lived and what he went through every day. It was messy and arduous.

The masters have said that they will never forget what Lincoln did for America. I also believe the masters will never forget what we do for America and the Great White Brotherhood, and that is a humbling thought. Though we may not be president or wield great earthly power, we know that the power of God within us is even greater. Let us pray that we do not shy away from the level of service that these two great souls demonstrated.

The Rules of the Game

In the dictation we're hearing today, the Ascended Master Godfre talks about the rules of the game. He says: "*We cannot make life easy for our chelas. If you want the easy life, the world offers abundant opportunity for that way, the 'way that seemeth right',*[115] *but you know the end of that way is death and you have chosen life.*"[116]

Whether Washington had won his Christmas victory or not, he had chosen the way of life by the decision he made. And even though Lincoln physically lost his life, he had also chosen the way of life.

We are told "Choose life!" That essentially means choosing to follow the Path toward Christhood and victory, just as Washington and Lincoln did. And when we bask in the light of the masters' dictations, all seems possible. We affirm, "Yes, I want to put on my Christhood and help win this victory for Saint Germain!" Then our tests come later, and the masters see how much light we have actually embodied, compared to how much we imagined we had embodied when we were sitting in the aura and light of the masters.

Godfre tells us the rules of the game are sweet in the mouth and bitter in the belly.[117] Let's not resist if the tests seem difficult. Let's learn the rules and take advantage of what we know. Yes, the Path may be hard at times, but it is not *too* hard!

Let us summon the courage to let go of those things we have been hiding in the folds of our garments, lest the Lord ask us to give them up. Don't we all have things tucked way back in our consciousness that we can't see? At a certain point the Lord will say something like "You may no longer keep that if you want me. You need to surrender it."

Our prayer at that time can be, "God, I surrender. Help me to surrender more." We have to ask God for the courage to go where our human consciousness does not want to go, lest we become uncomfortable. Pain is hard, but remember, it's temporal—when it is gone, it is gone. The via dolorosa does not last forever, and I think we can make it longer and harder by our refusal to surrender at a deeper level. As much as we would like to think we can continue forever to have one foot in heaven and one foot on earth—one part of us the Christ and one part of us the dweller—we cannot. We can no longer live the double life of Dr. Jekyll and Mr. Hyde.[118]

In his 1989 Thanksgiving address, Jesus said:

> *Embody the works, beloved, and be quickened by the Word. Be not satisfied in that state of consciousness that is somewhere between the astral and the mental body, somewhere around the six o'clock line [as you chart your Cosmic Clock], engulfed in a sea of indecision and self-pity and all that self-justification.*
>
> *Blessed hearts, I will show you how to get rid of self-justification. It is as simple as the nose upon your face. Simply get rid of the self! Then you may serve your life out justifying your Christ Self, justifying your I AM Presence, justifying their trust in you, their love in you, [you who are] that soul of Light cast into the sea as a glistening pearl. Fear not, beloved. Thou shalt be made whole. Let thy God descend!*
>
> *Therefore I would bring to you the vision, that you might see the filthy rags, the filthy rags that you still allow your self, [i.e., your soul,] to be wrapped in. I will allow you to see the dweller that is [also] thy self; [for it is] thy self-creation.*
>
> *I will allow you to see the ugliness [of the beast] that you might desire the beauty [of the Christ]...*[119]

If we vow this day to take a renewed stand to put on our Christhood, God will accelerate our testings, and that will include surfacing the parts of ourselves that we may not want to see—pockets of pride, resentment, hatred, and things we thought we were long free of but that still abide in our electronic belt. Remember, we're going after the dregs of our karma in this lifetime, clearing the very bottom of our electronic belt. By God's grace, we have transmuted many layers of karma, and now we're hitting the hard stuff. Although this substance is foreign to who we truly are in God, it does exist and Jesus said he is going to show us those "filthy rags."

It's humbling to see these things. Sometimes it can be so overwhelming that people condemn themselves. However, none of us should identify this negative substance as who we are. Taking accountability and clearing it is just part of the process. That's why Godfre reminds us to *"Know the rules of the game."*[120] Think about the karma that Lincoln bore—in a past life he was the Pharaoh who opposed Moses and had the firstborn sons of the Jews killed. In the succeeding embodiments of this soul that we know about, he lost his firstborn. Yet in the face of the heavy karma he bore, he was still willing to serve the cause of freedom, no matter what the cost.

Washington was quoted in *The Crossing* as saying the few soldiers that remained that Christmas would follow him into hell if he asked them to do so. Are we willing to follow our Lord into the hell of our human creation in order to defeat it once and for all? Washington's men trusted him. Do we trust our God, our Saviour, our Holy Christ Self enough to follow them into that darkness and, by God's grace, emerge victorious?

A Call to Love

This is actually a call to love more. As Mother Teresa counseled, *"Love until it hurts."*[121] Maybe that hurt will be the pain of our human substance being transmuted or maybe it will be the bliss of a love that is so great. We must be prepared for the temporal pain of seeming separation from God—the dark night of the soul and the dark night of the Spirit that are part of the rules of the game. Yet even knowing the rules doesn't make it easy to go through these initiations because the emptiness can feel so great.

The initiations of the dark night are intense; they are not comfortable. That's certainly not the direction the world is going, but it is where we really want to go. Let us move beyond merely studying the teachings and basking in the light of the masters and *become* the teachings. It is *our* hour.

Hearing Godfre's dictation today will fill us with light, determination and fire. But will we retain it come Monday morning or Thursday night or whenever the weight of karma returns upon us? Let us remember the rules of the game, study the lives of the saints, of Washington and Lincoln and those who gave their all for the victory. After we hear Godfre's dictation, the question we face is: Are we going to change something in our lives? Will we do anything different today or this week?

We have to start somewhere. We get into routines like everyone else, with our decrees and services and work and family and other responsibilities, and there's nothing wrong with that. But at some point on our spiritual journey, either events will interrupt that routine or we will interrupt it and say, "God, this is wonderful, but I want more. I am willing to give more and to do more." Though this is a path of joy, there comes a time when it is a path of tears and we must implore God to deliver us of our human substance, of whatever blocks our moving forward to a greater level of Christhood.

And while it's easy to pray to God and the ascended masters, do we continually talk and listen to our Christ Self as our greatest friend, our mentor, our protector? Do we have that intimate relationship with our Christ Self? We need to have that if we're going to put on more of our Christhood. We must know the voice of our Christ Self, and we won't know that voice if we don't listen.

We know that God does not want us to wait until we ascend to put on the fullness of our Christhood. Why do we tend to postpone that day? Maybe, like our dog, we're afraid to cross that line. Let us have the courage to work on our psychology, our fears, our hurts or whatever is blocking our spiritual progress.

Let us be delivered of self-justification and all the reasons why we can't do more or give more. This isn't to say that we're not busy people right now, and it doesn't mean that our hours of service have to increase. Remember the lesson of Mother clearing the energy in seconds while hundreds of people couldn't do it in hours. Feeling like we don't have enough spare time can become an impetus to do more in the time we have. Of course, we must also continually work to bind our dweller and its momentums, for those must decrease that the Christ might increase.

Let God deliver us from self-satisfaction and the subtle sense of smugness that we are God's chosen people and we're doing so much already. We are God's chosen people *only* if we choose to become the Christ.

The hour is late, not only in this year, but on this planet. However, it is not *too* late for us to accelerate on our path of personal Christhood. There is a price to be paid, and those who have gone before us have paid it. What if Mother had not made that choice? Where, God help us, would we be? And if *we* choose not to pay the price, what is going to happen to the beautiful souls of light on this planet who are either not ready for these teachings or their karma prevents them from having them in this hour? They are just as precious to Almighty God as we are or as Jesus is.

Are we at the point where the fire of love and determination to get on with our Christhood is greater than our fear of surrender? If we are not there, we need to ask God to help get us there. We have to start somewhere, with something. Padre Pio used to tell people to stop offending God. Good advice, don't you think? While we may not be offending God in obvious outer ways, given the knowledge and light that we have, I suspect we are offending our God in subtle ways. Though he is gracious to us, don't we want to change our ways and stop offending him?

This doesn't happen if we are on automatic pilot. Just because we decree and serve doesn't mean it happens. We have to actively engage with our Holy Christ Self, love our Christ Self, listen to our Christ Self, and obey our Christ Self. We have to step back and let our Christ Self go before us. Remember what Jesus said—we must get rid of the unreal self. This takes effort and work and prayer and sacrifice, but it is the ultimate solution to everything that faces each of us personally and the planet as a whole.

Is Christmas this year really so different from Christmas 1776? Isn't the choice really the same—victory or death? Living simply as a human or as a Christed one? And remember, this isn't just one battle. Washington fought for many years after that tremendous victory. We don't have to wait to be the fullness of our Christ Self. We just have to start somewhere.

This week do something different in your life than what you've done before to become closer to your Christ Self—maybe surrender a habit or sing a devotional song in the morning to your Holy Christ Self or write a letter to God or care for someone in need. If we start in earnest now, then a week or a month or a year from today we will have embodied more of our Christ Self; we will be that much closer to the fullness of our Christhood.

The war is on. The consequences are enormous. What would the world look like today if Washington hadn't crossed the Delaware that night? What will the world look like a hundred years from now if we don't put on our Christhood? Though by all "reasonable" accounts the battle on the world scene appears to be lost, we know it is *not* lost. But it can be lost if we are unwilling to pay the price individually and collectively. God will give us the courage, and we can call upon the ascended masters and their momentum for the victory. We have the tools to help us pass our tests. *God in us is able to win this victory.*

O God, we are ready to make a vow. Give us the strength to make it and to keep it. And if we falter, as does happen, we will not forget our vow. We will call upon the law of forgiveness and try again.

Washington made his Christmas vow. Thank God that he did.

Our Holy Christ Self is waiting, Jesus is waiting, God is waiting, and the precious children and souls on this planet are waiting. Haven't they waited long enough?

Isn't it time for us to make our Christmas vow?

WHO AM I
IN GOD?

We're going to have to get rid of most of our identity, point by point....Take it off. You take off one garment and God gives you something else to put on it its place. Do you see what I mean?

We take off the human to put on the garment of light, and that's beautiful. Who doesn't want to shed their troubles?

—**MARK PROPHET**

NINE

Who Am I in God?

When most of us ponder the question "Who am I?" we usually think in terms of what we are doing or what our profession is: I'm a student, a mom, a businessman, a grocer, and so forth. By contrast, if you were answering the question "Who am I in God?" you might respond, "I am a son or daughter of God. I have a Mighty I AM Presence, a Holy Christ Self, and a threefold flame in my heart. I am on the path of my ascension, working to balance my karma, put on my Christhood, and fulfill my divine plan."

Anything wrong with that response? No, it's all true.

But what if you were asked, "Who are you in God *today*?" Or to put it another way, "What have you realized of God in your outer awareness and attainment? How much of the Christ consciousness have you put on?" Those questions are not about what you will be in the future or what you already are at the spiritual core of your being; they are about what you have realized of God that you are manifesting right now, today.

So the real question is: "What portion of my Christhood have I realized?" But how can we know that? It has been said that no man can take a true measure of himself, and I think that's right. However, one way we can get an idea of our measure is through the tests that come our way, because as we get closer to the ascension the tests are harder and passing them requires greater mastery. If we can recognize and understand a test, then perhaps we can know where we are in following the footsteps that Jesus demonstrated in his life. For example, at some point on our spiritual path we will experience the tenth station of the cross—Jesus is stripped of his garments. While he was physically stripped of his garments, most of us will experience this initiation as being stripped of our false identity. When your false identity is taken from you what is left? What you have assimilated of your True Self, your God consciousness!

Many years ago, Mother told us the story of a Christian pastor who was putting on his Christhood and becoming a Buddha, even if he knew nothing about these things in his outer consciousness. The man was Pastor Richard Wurmbrand. He was a Romanian Jew who converted to Christianity along with his wife, Sabina, soon after they were married in 1936. Between 1945 and 1947 Richard smuggled Gospels into Russia and distributed one million of them to Russian troops, often disguising the books as Communist propaganda.

In 1947 Richard and Sabina attended the Congress of Cults organized by the Romanian Communist government. Most of the religious leaders of the country were there and came forward to praise Communism and to swear loyalty to the new regime. Sabina said, *"Richard, stand up and wash away this shame from the face of Christ."* Richard warned, *"If I do so, you'll lose your husband." "I don't wish to have a coward as a husband,"* she replied.[122] Then Richard declared to the four thousand delegates, whose speeches were broadcast to the whole nation, that their duty is to glorify God and Christ alone.

Because of his faith, Richard was imprisoned by the Nazis during World War II and later by the Communists when they took over Romania. On February 29, 1948, the secret police arrested him when he was on his way to church. They took him to their headquarters and locked him in a solitary cell and labeled him "Prisoner Number 1."[123]

Pastor Wurmbrand is best known for his book *Tortured for Christ*, which recounts his experiences during the fourteen years he spent in prison, including three years in solitary confinement. Mother used the experiences recounted in this book to teach about the path of becoming the Buddha. I highly recommend the book because it's an inspiring story of faith and of victory over unbelievable odds.

In one of his lesser-known books, *With God in Solitary Confinement*, Wurmbrand wrote:

> Out of fourteen years in jail under the Communists in Romania, I spent three years alone in a cell thirty feet below ground, never seeing sun, moon, or stars, flowers or snow, never seeing another man except for the guards and the interrogators who beat and tortured me. I seldom heard a noise in that prison. The guards had felt-soled shoes and I did not hear their approach. I had no Bible, nor any other book. I had no paper on which to write my thoughts. The only things we were expected to write were statements accusing ourselves and others.[124]

We'll learn more later about how he survived, not only physically but spiritually. But without question he was required—after everything was taken from him in an outer way—to answer the question, "Who am I in God?"

He was stripped of his garments at a level few of us can comprehend. And in pondering his description of his time in prison, we cannot help but wonder how we might react to a similar situation. Again, the answer lies in who we are in God. Yet who we think we are in God (or in any other way) may not be who we really are. In *The Chela and the Path* El Morya says, "*You are what you are regardless of what you think you are.*"[125]

True vs. False Identity

So who are you? In her lecture "The Victory Way of Life" given at Summit University, Mother taught, "*You have come to believe that the contents of your four lower bodies are actually your identity. We are obsessed with this belief to the point of self-hypnosis. We hypnotize ourselves to believe that the combination of substance in our four lower bodies is actually our identity.*"[126]

Equating our identity with our four lower bodies—etheric, mental, emotional and physical—seems natural to almost everyone. But it just doesn't happen to be true, as the messenger explains, "*So the key is, no matter what your sense of identity, give it up.*"[127] Why? Because it's not real. We think it's real. We use it every day. But it's not ultimately real.

Giving up who we think we are is easier said than done. We might be asking ourselves, "Well, then, who am I really? What will I be if I give up my sense of identity— my roles, my human personality, my habits, etc.? I use it to navigate the world, and that is how the world views me. What will take its place?" Those are pretty fair questions, and perhaps that is why so few of us are willing to take this step on our own.

Mother tells us that giving up our sense of identity is hard, that it:

> takes enormous courage, because what do you have but your sense of identity? It takes a very strong sense of identity to reject the sense of identity. However, the stronger the sense of identity, no matter what it relates to, the greater your ability to get rid of it. When you have no sense of identity, you have nothing to give up, nothing to empty; you have no sense of being full of substance and darkness.[128]

In other words, the fact that we have a strong sense of our false identity is actually good, because it gives us the strength to reject it. It gives us the courage. Mother and the masters have even taught that sometimes it's easier to convert a murderer than someone who is so wishy-washy that they've never accomplished much of value in their life.

We don't have to feel guilty that we have a strong sense of false identity, because it has served us well up to this time. But now we are at the point in our pursuit of Christhood where it can no longer serve us. Nevertheless, we got where we are today partly *because* of our false sense of identity. So it's been useful in some ways; it's simply that its time is up.

Much like other things on the spiritual path, it is easier to accept the idea of giving up our false identity as a goal than it is to actually do it. We may think, "I'm just about ready for this, and somewhere down the road I'm going to give up that identity. I'm getting there—not quite there yet, but I'm getting there." But if you are on the Path and keep putting it off, guess what? God will be sure that this stripping happens to you. Sometimes this initiation comes in increments and sometimes it comes as a floodtide, but come it will.

For most of us, having a false sense of identity is comfortable, even though we know that it's ultimately unreal. We rationalize to ourselves, "Yes, part of me is walking the spiritual path, but I also have this other part of me that I need to function in the world." And for a while, this split—having one foot in the world and one foot on the Path—does seem to work. However, if we get too comfortable in this pattern and compromise our spiritual path by accommodating our false identity, God may pull the rug out from under us so that we suddenly find ourselves sitting on the ground wondering what just happened.

Well, when that happens, God is sending us a message, telling us that because of our devotion and service, we are ready to be stripped of our garments. People often think of this initiation as a calamity, and indeed, it can have a tremendous impact. But in reality it's good to recognize that when we are ready, God brings us this test to free us from our unreal self. And we don't have just one part of our false identity to lose, we have many. So the biggest challenge comes when we lose many parts within a short time.

A few years ago I went through a series of tests of this nature, some more serious than others. A less serious instance occurred one Sunday when I was preparing for a service. I went to the sacristy where the ministerial robes are stored, and mine was gone! Despite all my searching and asking questions of other ministers, it never turned up; it just simply disappeared. I had to laugh because I was literally stripped of outer garments that I thought were such a key part of my identity!

This is not to make light of the initiation of being stripped. It can be devastating to the psyche if we're not ready. When parts of our false sense of identity are taken from us and we have not fully realized our identity in Christ, it can be quite disorienting, to say the least.

And what happens when this initiation is coupled with a period of feeling cut off from God? We may feel confused and bewildered, as if everything is lost, and cry out to God asking why he has forsaken us. We might wonder: "Has this been a game I've been playing—pretending to be a chela, doing all the right things? Has it been real?" When we feel rejected by God, what is left? That is when all we have left is what we have actually realized of God, of our Christhood, within our being.

I know of a woman who went through a series of tests like this after many years as a chela of the ascended masters. She got to the point where she questioned whether she should even be on the Path, not because she didn't believe, but because she felt rejected by God and the masters. The Path can be very lonely at times, and even though she was surrounded by people, she still felt quite lonely.

As she pondered who she really was in God, she could only come up with one thing that she absolutely knew to be real in her being—she loved God. Whatever else was going on in her world, whatever she felt she had lost, whether she was rejected by God or not, she knew in the deepest part of her being that she loved God. And that was enough.

It was enough for her to reaffirm who she was in God, to start letting go of her old identity and seeking her true identity. This didn't happen quickly for her. It has taken many years and required ongoing surrenders that have sometimes been painful. Yet after everything else seemed to have been taken, the one true thing she found in her being—her love of God—was the thing that gave her the strength to go on. It defined who she was in God.

Choosing Christ or the Dweller

The bottom line is that there are only two ways to go. The first is to continually strive, surrender your false identity, and love your way to your Christhood. The second is to give up the fight and embody your human creation, your dweller-on-the-threshold. When Pastor Wurmbrand was put into solitary confinement, he was forced to make the choice in order to survive physically and spiritually. He couldn't try to please both his Holy Christ Self (or Jesus) and his dweller (or the human consciousness) at the same time. We might think we can please them both and even try to do it for a while, but it cannot work forever. We cannot serve two masters. So why delay the day of reckoning? Let's decide to finally make the choice!

Now you may start wondering what to do when you have made the choice and you are being stripped of your false identity. One reaction is to rail against God, and unfortunately many people do this initially, "How could you do this to me, God, after all I have done for you?" That's obviously not the preferred reaction. So when this stripping happens to you, there are some things that can help you pass through this initiation victoriously.

> *Recognize that receiving this test is a sign that you are ready to pass it, and view it as the opportunity to move up higher spiritually.*

What most people miss is that when the stripping happens to one on the spiritual path, it is a reward not a punishment.

Don't be surprised if you feel disoriented and shaken about who you are or if you feel like you don't fit in anywhere.

In all probability you may feel that way because that's the nature of the initiation. Keeping daily rituals (such as devotions, quiet walks or songs to God) can help your soul navigate through this.

Humbly surrender what has already been taken from you.

Think about that for a moment. Don't we sometimes try to pull back the things God has taken from us—a part of our identity or a person or a possession or a job? We cry out, "No, no, give that back to me, God!" But after it's gone, if we know that it's God's will, we need to surrender it in order to restore peace in our being. By surrendering, we acknowledge that the stripping is according to God's purposes and is a good thing.

We may also need to surrender the results of what has happened to us through this stripping, along with any anger we might have toward God or others because of this initiation. Though this may take some time and prayer, it can bring peace to our soul even in the midst of the pain of grieving and letting go.

Trust and love the will of God for your life.

God either causes things to happen or he allows them, so both ways can serve the will of God. Rest in the knowledge that the will of God is good—period. Not 75 percent of the time, not 99.9 percent of the time, but 100 percent of the time. You can affirm this in your being and accept nothing in your life except God's will.

It's liberating to trust in God's will! You can call for it every day, "Not my will, not my will, not my will but thine be done!"

And when you say that, try not to mentally hold back, even a little. Try to let go and let God. When you do that, you can have the peace that the will of God affords us. Remembering Jesus' words: *"Fear not, little flock; for it is your Father's good pleasure to give you the kingdom,"*[129] you can let go of fear and anxiety about what may be coming next.

Embody an attitude of victory.

The Cosmic Being Victory tells us that this takes work because the world is wallowing in a sense of non-victory, believing: "All is lost. Nothing can save us now. People have made choices. What's the use in trying?" We have to challenge that mindset in ourselves and on this planet and embody the sense of victory.

We have pages and pages of Victory calls in our decree book to help us affirm, "Yes, I claim the victory!" We have to affirm it with all the might of our being, and maintain a sense of victory even when it doesn't appear like the victory is being won.

In another part of Mother's lecture "The Victory Way of Life," she admonishes us not to try to be a good or bad human being. She says:

> *Victory tells us not to get into the human consciousness of, "I don't think I am strong enough, but I'm going to get strong." He says that's not it at all; it's a question of accepting the strength we already have. There's a big difference here, because to conceive of yourself as a weak human being and then to decide that you're going to become a strong human being is not it. Forget it. God doesn't want you to be a good or a bad human being.*[130]

For instance, when God asked Moses to return to Egypt, Moses could have said, "Okay, God, I understand. Just give me a little time to prepare. I've got to go back, practice a few things, work on my speech patterns...." In fact, Moses did ask enough questions and raise enough concerns to make God rebuke him. God had a response to every objection Moses raised and basically told him, "Forget it!" God didn't want a good or bad orator; he wanted someone to be his instrument. Similarly, God doesn't want us to be humanly good in a relative way; he wants us to become the absolute good of our Christ Self. This stripping process is not about perfecting the human; it's about taking off the old man—the relative good and bad of our human identity—and putting on the new man, which is our Christ consciousness.

Mark Prophet in his lecture "Meeting Your Inner Master" tells us:

> *We get so mixed up about our identity. Somebody just told me that something I had said made him feel as if he no longer had an identity. Well, maybe that's a good thing because our identity—and we have mostly identity problems—is what gets us into trouble.*
>
> *We're going to have to get rid of most of our identity, point by point.... Take it off. You take off one garment and God gives you something else to put on in its place. Do you see what I mean?*
>
> *We take off the human to put on the garment of light, and that's beautiful. Who doesn't want to shed their troubles?*[131]

Know Yourself.

Jesus exposes another false sense of identity that often occurs in those who follow the ascended masters' teachings. In his dictation delivered on Easter 1993, he told us a story that is the reverse of the ugly duckling tale.

> Now, your situation is the reverse of that of the "ugly duckling"—the swan who thought he was a duck. You are like a duckling that believes he is a swan because he has lived all his life with swans, but he is still a duckling.
>
> You have not yet become that swan, that paramahansa. Yet you live among swans, the ascended masters, and so you take for granted that because you have studied their teachings you have the attainment of an ascended master, as if by osmosis and without soul labor. (Some of you will deny this, but I say it is so. And each one of you will have to ponder it in your own heart.) Yet when it comes to exercising that attainment, you behave like ducks because you are ducks—that is, you have the consciousness of ducks because you are ducks—that is, you have the consciousness of ducks, though the swan is your true inner identity.
>
> Now take yourself for what you are, and no more and no less. Then look in the mirror and say:
>
> "Quack, quack. I do not like myself the way I see myself. I do not like to hear my speech—quack, quack—all day long talking about nothing that amounts to anything, just making noise and getting attention and getting nothing done.
>
> "Therefore I will decide to be that swan. I will decide to be that paramahansa. Yes! I will be that one, for God in me

and Christ in me is that one. And I will go on a voice fast and I will pray and fast, and I will see the transforming light entering my body and I will know what it means to be a vessel for my Lord and Saviour Jesus Christ."

Blessed ones, I can save you only if you and I are one.[132]

What a powerful statement from our Lord and Saviour, "I can save you only if you and I are one." And what a motivation to let go of the false belief of being a swan before we have truly surrendered and become the Christ.

Do a voice fast, as Jesus suggests.

Use this time for inner study and reflection. And after your voice fast, use the power of the spoken Word to help you clear all that opposes you putting on your Christhood.

The Science of the Spoken Word is a tremendous tool that we can use. It's not the whole answer, but it's a very important part of it. Again, try giving Victory's calls in the decree book.

A number of years ago I wrote to Mother about something and I got an answer that didn't seem to respond to the question. She said, "Do Victory calls every morning." And I thought, "How does this relate to my question?" But as it turned out, it obviously did. So if we do Victory calls every morning, maybe our problems (or what we think are problems) will begin to disappear.

Pay attention to the details.

Over the years I have learned that as we move forward on the Path, paying attention to the details of our chelaship becomes more and more important. On each succeeding step, we need to pay attention at a level beyond what was required before. This is not fanaticism or a fear that if we make a mistake we are doomed. It is the recognition that tests can become more subtle and we can't be passive or laid-back in our chelaship as we strive to put on our Christ identity. As we get closer to the goal, our attention to detail—even a fastidiousness—is necessary because the risks associated with missing a step are greater.

Jesus forewarned us that we don't become swans just by hanging out around the teachings. So when a deep initiation comes to you, such as the stripping away of part of your false identity, embrace it as the very opportunity your soul needs the most. Recognize it as a reward for your striving. You can anticipate this test by striving to put on your true identity, bearing in mind that putting on your Christ identity does not happen by osmosis or just by attending three services a week.

We are in a war for the victory of our souls. As Jesus teaches us, this is our soul labor! Though we may be physically weary at times, we cannot weary of this battle. We have been told that we come back to the exact place in our initiations where we have failed before, though we may not know where that point is. We might have dug a rut of failure on this initiation of being stripped of our garments or possibly another initiation. So whenever you're struggling, feeling like you're running out of gas and can't go on, it's time to recharge yourself with the sense of victory and to determine, "This time, by God's grace, I am not going to fail!"

A few weeks ago we took our daughter to Washington, D.C., to see the sights—the Capitol and the many historical buildings and monuments there. The Smithsonian Museum has a display on Apollo 13, the lunar mission that some of you may remember. There was a small explosion on board and the astronauts told NASA ground control, "Houston, we've had a problem here." Although Apollo 13 was not able to land on the moon, the mission was considered a "successful failure" because of the experience gained in rescuing the crew. A movie was made about that mission, and it had a line that became famous: "Failure is not an option."

Failure is not an option—a great motto! For the true devotee, failure *cannot* be an option. This is not pretending that everything's fine when it isn't. It's honoring the depth of the initiations you are going through. It's affirming throughout this process that you will win your victory in God, that this time—no matter what—you're going to keep on until the fight for your soul is won because *failure is not an option.*

This journey is full of joy if you allow it: the joy of simple things, the joy of the altar, the joy of God, the joy of a sunrise, the joy of a child. Your pain may not necessarily go away as your celebrate joy, but if you invoke the fires of victory and lead a victory way of life even through the hardest tests, then you can make it.

Buddhic Tests

And what became of Pastor Wurmbrand on his spiritual journey? When we left him, he had just been put into solitary confinement. He spent three years there, never seeing the light of day or the sun or stars or a green plant. He never saw a woman, but only the guards and his torturers. He admits he had periods of doubt, of anger, of fear, of hopelessness. He even had times of apostasy when he questioned his belief in God: Was it real? Was it true? We might expect that he had all the reactions that anyone would have in that situation, including resentment, the sense of failure, and wondering what he had done to deserve it. It's natural to experience thoughts like these as part of such an intense initiation.

His tortures were beyond description. He said he could not even mention many of them, and the ones he did relay were horrible and degrading. His food consisted of one slice of bread a week and a weak soup each day. He got tuberculosis that was left untreated. The fact that he survived was a miracle in itself and proof that God had a mission for him. It's interesting that he described his time in prison as the making of a messenger. As I mentioned earlier, Mother taught about the Buddhic initiations he went through, even though he would never have referred to his experiences in those terms.

Pastor Wurmbrand knew he was not going to survive if he didn't put his house in order. In his book *With God in Solitary Confinement*, he explains how he organized his time to have a rhythm and something to mark the turning of the hours each day: "*During that time I rarely slept at night. I slept in the daytime. Every night I passed the hours in spiritual exercises and prayer. Every night I composed a sermon and delivered it. I had faint hope that one day I might be released. And so I tried to memorize the sermons. In order to do this, I put the main ideas into short rhymes.*"[133] Using this technique he memorized three hundred and fifty sermons, and a number of them are in his book.

Wasn't that ingenious? That was his Christhood at work. He found a way to survive without any sensory input except torture. Under those conditions many would have gone insane or simply given up and died. But something else happened to this pastor. He not only survived, he was *transformed*.

Here is an excerpt from his book *If Prison Walls Could Speak* about his experience in solitary confinement for three years. It clearly shows he had transcended identifying with his human condition.

> *Dear Brothers and Sisters*
> *To what shall I compare my solitary cell?*
> *It is like a wood full of the fragrance of flowers. No tree in the forest gives off a sweeter perfume than the one out of which crosses are made.*
> *To what else should I compare my cell?*
> *It is like a rich storehouse.... God, the angels, the devils, the saints, my forefathers, my friends, my enemies, all future generations, the whole universe and its Creator are here. There is no joy which I cannot experience by the simple method of rejoicing with those who rejoice. In the spirit, I can accompany others on wonderful journeys, I can share their emotions as they worship in church or enjoy a good meal. I can rejoice with mothers bending over the cots of their babes. I can play merrily with young children. I can weep with those that weep....*
> *But I would also liken my cell to the studio of a sculptor. Michelangelo looked at a block of marble, and saw an angel. All he had to do was to hew away the superfluous stone. I believe that these cells are places in which the great Sculptor shapes his future messengers.*[134]

Isn't that profound? He took some of the bleakest circumstances we could possibly imagine and turned it into a world full of God and light and love and joy and everything wonderful. Could he have done that by holding onto his old identity? Of course not. He had to strive to put on his Christhood. He had to strive to become a Buddha.

Wurmbrand had two choices in his solitary cell. He could bemoan his fate to the extent that he would give up and eventually die, or he could assume what Mighty Victory calls an "attitude of victory"[135] and use his desperate dilemma as the catalyst to his soul's victory. His incredible description of his cell clearly shows the choice he made to have an attitude of victory. He took the dire circumstances he was in and used them as the catalyst for changing himself, and that led to his victory.

You might say, "That was really a tremendous victory, but I'm not sure how I can relate to that situation today." Understandable, of course, since we are in far freer circumstances than he was in. Yet in terms of our soul the choices are the same: to assume an attitude of victory or to basically give up and not strive for our soul's victory. We also have what might be considered another choice in this hour, besides the two that Wurmbrand had. Since our situation is not so extreme, we can make the choice that many in the world have already made, as Mighty Victory puts it, *"to vegetate and let the energies of their life stagnate in pools of wrong habits, thoughts and feelings."*[136]

We can choose to lay back, take it easy, and have the attitude, "Well, I've worked so hard, I've done so much, and it didn't seem to make any difference; just look at my life." But to vegetate is really to die, isn't it? Letting one's life "stagnate in pools of wrong habits, thoughts and feelings" definitely seems like giving up and accepting the death consciousness. Making that choice also builds a greater momentum of failure, and it becomes harder and harder to win our victory. So if we make that choice, we may have to face this same test over and over again, perhaps even embody again, until finally, by God's grace, we pass it.

Why Not Go For It?

Why not go for it? Why not give our all to putting off the old man and putting on the new man? Why not surrender who we think we are and let our Christ Self occupy our four lower bodies? That does not mean being insensitive to what's going on in our life or the world around us. It means throwing off the shroud we have put on and habitually wear, thinking it's who we are. It's a shroud of non-identity, because we are what's hidden beneath it—our God-identity.

It's time to stop defending our unreal self. Let's be willing to accept and even embrace the stripping away of the old identity that is not real, that is not of God, and that prevents us from putting on the fullness of our Christhood. May we humbly recognize when we are being stripped, and embrace it by making fervent calls for the acceleration of our freedom from all that is unreal. Let's surrender and trust God during this process, even when we may feel totally alone and bereft. Those are the very moments when we need to affirm and know in our being that the will of God will not leave us in that place but will help us put on our Christhood.

This letting go of who we think we are must be real and not superficial. We can't pretend to do this. It must come from the depths of our soul that has accepted her reality in God at long last. Like Pastor Wurmbrand, let us willingly and lovingly go through this process of being stripped and become the Christ example that our community and the world need to see.

Let's go for it! Let's build a momentum of victory that will not let us rest in failure. The time is right. We're in the right place, with the right opportunity, the right knowledge, the right tools, and the right attitude. What else do we need, except the fire and determination of an attitude of victory?

Let us no longer allow the world or the conditions of our life or what happens around us to deny us our victory. Let us choose this day to be the Christ and to serve the Christ in all. If we do this, then we will not need to answer the question "Who Am I in God?" because we will *BE* the answer for all to see.

THE 49 PERCENT CHALLENGE

Therefore, heaven can wait for the aspiring ones who will tarry to finish the course that is set, to mark the 100 percent balance of karma.

—ARCHANGEL ZADKIEL

TEN

The 49 Percent Challenge

What appeared to be the "All-Seeing Eye of God" caught my attention. I was browsing in an antique store not really looking for anything in particular when I noticed it in a framed picture down another aisle. Intrigued, I went to look at it more closely. It was indeed the All-Seeing Eye of God at the top of what turned out to be an old 19th-century English poster titled "The Broad and Narrow Way." I was amazed to find that it quite accurately laid out the path to attaining our Christhood in pictures and Bible verses. Needless to say, I soon owned it, and it now graces the wall of my office at home.

The poster uses Matthew 7:13–14 as the starting point: *"Enter ye in at the strait gate: for wide is the gate, and broad is the way, that leadeth to destruction, and many there be which go in thereat: Because straight is the gate, and narrow is the way, which leadeth unto life, and few there be that find it."*

206 | PRACTICING SAINTHOOD

THE BROAD AND NARROW WAY.
Matthew VII, 13, 14.

(Personal collection of the author)

The poster shows the broad way on the left (the left-handed path), and the narrow way on the right. It's interesting that to enter the narrow way you have to bow in humility because the gate is small, depicting that the very first test you receive is a willingness to bend the knee. There is even a helpful directional sign outside the two gates with one pointing to "Death and Damnation" and the other to "Life and Salvation." Wouldn't it be great to have such clear signs all the time!

At the end of the left-handed path on the poster is hell, while the right-handed path leads to the Holy City, where all are under the All-Seeing Eye of God. One interesting feature is that even after the two paths diverge there are several points where it is possible to go from one path to the other (from the darkness to the light or from the light to the darkness). That offers hope for those who have chosen the broad way and caution for those who have chosen the narrow way. While in some ways the poster seems quaint today, it still holds some powerful messages for our spiritual path.

The Hour of the Greatest Trial

We have before us the goal of balancing 51 percent of our karma along with meeting the other requirements to gain the victory of our ascension. I remember when I first learned about the 51 percent dispensation, it sounded like a pretty good deal. Balancing 51 percent instead of 100 percent is obviously much more attainable, and adding the violet flame into the mix made our ascension seem very possible. I never really thought about what happens after balancing 51 percent, but just assumed that things would take care of themselves. After all, I would have secured my victory, right?

Ah, but things are not quite that simple. We know the 51 percent dispensation was given because so few were making it to 100 percent because the Path is even more demanding after

51 percent. Archangel Michael and Kuthumi explain, "*It is the dark night of the soul of personal and planetary karma of which I speak that all must face following the balancing of 51 percent of their karma if they would move on to the ascension after the 100 percent and then some.*"[137] One gets to "100 percent and then some" by balancing world karma. They go on to explain that the initiations get so difficult that souls who had won their ascension were later losing it because of the severity of the tests.

That gives one pause, doesn't it? The tests become so intense that people were losing their ascension after they had won it. We know that many of us had bonded with our Holy Christ Self and balanced over 51 percent of our karma on Atlantis, and yet we obviously fell back. Mother teaches in her lectures on the golden age of Atlantis that the opportunity we have to ascend is different today, not only because of the 51 percent dispensation, but because we also have knowledge and understanding of the steps on the Path, the violet flame, and other tools we can use. We still have to carefully prepare, because people who weren't prepared for what comes after the 51 percent weren't always able to sustain that level.

We have also been taught that Archangel Gabriel visits us when we reach 51 percent and gives us the option of taking our ascension at that time or choosing to stay in embodiment and balance as much karma as we can. By deduction, that means those of us here and around the world have either not yet balanced 51 percent of our karma or have made the choice to stay on. And perhaps people we consider to have met untimely deaths are actually souls who have chosen the option of taking their ascension when it was offered to them.

Choosing to stay or to leave is not a small decision. On *The Open Door* internet radio show several months ago, we had a program entitled "The 51 Percent Solution."[138] We played the following excerpt from a lecture Mother gave on discipleship:

> ...You have to realize that at 51 percent of your karma balanced, that is the hour of the greatest trial.... At that point you're on the six o'clock line and one point past it. Six o'clock, as you know, is the halfway point on the cosmic clock, and it also symbolizes halfway... if you're putting 25 percent in each of the four quadrants. So with that extra 1 percent balanced, you take the plunge into the astral plane. You either ascend right then, if you know what's good for you, or if you decide to go on, you are ready...[139]

That's the first time I ever heard her say it that way. Her comment seems to clearly indicate that for some it would be wise to ascend at the 51 percent mark because there is the danger of sliding backwards. However, we also know that it is harder to balance our karma from the ascended state. Another factor is whether you want to (or are destined to) continue spreading the message to other souls about what they can attain.

Setting the Goal:
Balance 100 Percent of Our Personal Karma

Some masters have even called us to balance 100 percent of our karma. In his dictation given on Palm Sunday 1979, Lanello said,

> I have come to you in the past to speak to you, my staff upon earth. And I have told you that though the requirement is 51 percent of the balance of your karma that that is not enough for those who would be initiates unto the fulfillment

> *of the victory. I have set before you, then, the goal of balancing 100 percent of your karma. And every one of you with us this day and hour, hour of victory has been hand-chosen by the Lord to be given the opportunity to make that goal his own. Do not look around you but look to yourself.*[140]

God knows what is best for each one of us, but if we decide to go past the 51 percent, we need to be prepared. First, we need to know that it can be done—even all the way to 100 percent! Lanello would not have put that goal before us if it were not possible. After all, who has the greatest teachings, the greatest opportunities and the violet flame? We do, of course, and we've been preparing for this, not just in this embodiment, but in many previous embodiments as well. If we decide to go on and we only make it to 65 or 75 percent, then at least we have a cushion in case we make more negative karma. We may think that once we make it to 51 percent we are home free, but that number can go down as well as up. Even if we balance 100 percent, we can still make new karma and fall below that percentage. One example that Lanello gave for how this can occur is by engaging in criticism, condemnation and judgment—an easy way to make negative karma, and something people just over 51 percent want to carefully avoid.

As I mentioned earlier, we have been taught that it's harder to balance our karma from heaven. We also know that the earth needs examples of souls who have balanced 100 percent of their karma. Furthermore, we know that heaven needs advanced souls and Christed ones in physical embodiment if the earth is to be saved.

There's an equation of light and darkness on this planet. Archangel Zadkiel said:

> Therefore, heaven can wait for the aspiring ones who will tarry to finish the course that is set, to mark the 100 percent balance of karma. Heaven can wait for the initiates of the sacred fire who will press forward with all diligence in the meeting of the basic requirement of the 51 percent and then pursue on to take that grade of mastery of the astral plane of dealing with the beasts of the human consciousness.[141]

In other words, God needs souls embodying light in the earth, embodying their Christhood to hold the balance for the removal of the darkness that exists here. It's like a cosmic balance scale: the more light there is on the planet, the more the masters are able to remove the darkness affecting the planet adversely.

Vanquish Every Challenger to Your Christhood

If we choose to stay, we need to be ready. We need to know what to expect and how to master it. We need to be aware of the plots of the fallen angels to take us from the Path. The more advanced the initiations are, the more subtle they can be. How do we ensure that we always know the right way since we do not have signs pointing to either "death and damnation" or "life and salvation" to guide us? It takes great attunement and great discernment to navigate and emerge victorious from the astral sea. To do this we have to be awake and alert through the remaining 49 percent of our karma because our souls are vulnerable, and with greater attainment come greater challenges. Others have made it, and by determination and God's grace, we can too.

One of the keys is to develop our heart and not rely on our mental body. As Saint Paul tells us, it is good to have the mind of God, the mind of Christ.[142] Instead, some people have concentrated on developing their mental bodies so that they can be successful in the world. They can have the job or the work they want, they can have abundance, they can have power. A well-developed human mind will carry someone a very long way on this planet. But it won't carry us to God. We can only reach him through the heart—through love.

Mother once remarked about an individual on staff that was very devout and sincere on his path, yet when she looked into his heart she saw how little attainment was there was because he relied so much on his mental body. We often admire people's minds, thinking how smart he or she is or how wonderful it is that they have an encyclopedic knowledge of the teachings. Of course, there is nothing wrong with someone being smart or having great knowledge. The danger is focusing too much on our mental body and not enough on our heart, because the mental body will never be sufficient to pass the higher tests on the Path. That takes attainment and an expanded threefold flame in our heart.

We need that attainment, since our most difficult karma comes up after we've balanced 51 percent of it. As Mother cautions, we should not underestimate the challenges we will face. We are prepared in many ways, but we do not know what records and karma will emerge from our unconscious or subconscious minds. We may have heavy karma that could go back to Atlantis or beyond that has to be transmuted, especially if this is to be our last embodiment. While we need to acknowledge the challenges these karmas bring, we do not fear them or shy away from them because we know our true self-worth is in God.

On Good Friday 1993, beloved Elohim Purity and Astrea instructed us:

> When you choose the high road of balancing 100 percent of your karma on earth, you must reckon with the aggressive challenges of the fallen angels who will seek to tear from you the self-mastery you gain with each new level of attainment. Knowing you will be challenged, you ought to put yourself in the mode of being in training to become Olympic champions, spiritually speaking....
>
> So you must put yourself in training and stay in training to be a champion son or daughter of God with a will to vanquish every challenger to your Christhood. You must increase your determination and your will to attain the mark of the high calling in Christ. You must seek empowerment from the source of empowerment, your own Holy Christ Self. Your life, then, will become a competition in the highest sport of all.
>
> Who will win? You or your challenger?[143]

Our Christhood is key to balancing all our karma and winning. Just how do we put on our Christhood? As you know, we don't perfect the human. We work to get rid of the human consciousness, we surrender it so that the Christ can take up residence in our being. We do our dweller calls, striving to create a vacuum—a place for our Holy Christ Self to reside. We make our life a living prayer so that our every thought, word and deed comes from our Holy Christ Self. Learning to do that and integrating our Christhood incrementally day by day will be our protection and will help us to win our victory.

Isn't this why we have followed the Path: to learn and demonstrate mastery? To be the fulfillment of all that the messengers and the masters have taught?

When we think of the investment the Brotherhood has put into releasing these teachings to the world and assisting us with our personal chelaship, we know there surely need to be living examples of Christhood who are proof that following this path works! God does not allow what he sends forth to return unto him void, and we can be the fruit, by God's grace, of these teachings. We want to bring our Christhood and our ascension to God at the conclusion of this life, to lay them upon the altar of his heart as the offering for all that has been given to us.

Now is not the time to take it easy or be satisfied with our achievements. In her lecture "Now Is the Time for Us to Make Our Ascension," Mother admonishes us not to take chances in making any more karma:

> *Please do not play games with the masters and say to yourself, "Well, if I do this little thing or do that little thing..." or "I break the rules sometimes but I'm really a good guy, you know. I'm working for the masters. I do a lot for them. They'll look the other way if I decide to just cross the line and do something I really want to do that I shouldn't be doing." This is really a very bad attitude, a very bad attitude.*
>
> *If you want the whole nine yards, if you want the victory, you have to come to that point of utter humility and realize that nothing is sound or secure in this world.*[144]

It really is true that nothing is sound or secure. Just think of the recent fires in northern California where some people had only one or two minutes to respond, to get out and save their lives. Things can change very quickly. Our readiness is not motivated by fear but by the awareness that things can change in a blink of the eye, not only in our personal lives but also in the world. We need to take this seriously, and I know we do. But this also requires a greater level of awareness of what we are dealing with—everything from personal karma and things arising from deep levels of our being, to fierce opposition to our souls and even to the victory of world affairs. Again, we have to be awake and alert when following this path.

Seeds of Spiritual Pride and Ambition: Peter and Loyola

Perhaps we are already careful about not making the "little" mistakes Mother spoke of, but what about things that are not so obvious? Our blind spots are where the going gets tough and becomes tricky—where there is a habit or something in us that we simply do not see. And we all have blind spots! Proverbs 16:25 says, *"There is a way that seemeth right unto a man, but the end thereof are the ways of death."* How do you determine whether what you're doing is right or only seems right? We have human patterns or ancient karmas that come up from our unconscious or subconscious mind that cause us to do things that seem right to us, but are in fact dangerous to our souls, our path and to other people. I have often thought about staying in my room for the rest of my embodiment, but I'm pretty sure El Morya wouldn't approve! We can't avoid life; we have to be part of it. Once more, the answer is attuning to our Christ Self moment by moment.

In "An Exposé of False Teachings" from 1976, Kuthumi and the Brothers of the Golden Robe gave us the example of how subconscious patterns in two saints of the Catholic Church allowed them to be used not as instruments of light, but as instruments of darkness—Peter, the apostle of Jesus, and Ignatius Loyola, one of the founders of the Society of Jesus (also known as the Jesuits).

Jesus knew Peter had the seeds of spiritual pride and spiritual ambition implanted in his heart, and he warned him,

"*Simon, Simon, behold Satan hath desired to have you, that he may sift you as wheat...*"[145] At one point Jesus even turned to Peter and said, "*Get thee behind me, Satan.....*"[146] Kuthumi explained the meaning behind Jesus' words in a profound teaching: "*.... any member of the false hierarchy can temporarily manifest through anyone, even the chosen devotee.*"[147]

When Peter denied his Lord three times the night Jesus was arrested, he failed his test of totally surrendering to God. He sought to save his life but ended up losing a profound opportunity; he did not ascend at the end of that life and has reincarnated to this day. Continuing to reveal the tragedy of Peter's human weaknesses, Kuthumi says, "*...the taint of Peter's consciousness has never been wholly removed from the structure of the Church...*"[148] He explains that Peter was also vulnerable to the "*Luciferian philosophy of the ends justifying the means.*"[149] As we shall see, Loyola also subscribed to that same false teaching.

Ignatius Loyola was a proud and ambitious man. Kuthumi tells us that Loyola, like Peter, had seeds of spiritual pride and spiritual ambition sown in his subconscious by the fallen ones during a previous embodiment. He was already vulnerable; he hadn't been on guard when these seeds were planted in him, and he did not challenge what happened. He was accountable because he allowed it to happen. As he carried these seeds of darkness from one embodiment to another, they grew. The danger increases as such seeds become embedded in subterranean levels of consciousness. That is why it is so important to go after our conscious, subconscious and unconscious patterns with our decrees and prayers.

Loyola claimed he had a vision where God the Father and Jesus appeared to him and God asked Jesus to "*take this man for your servant.*"[150] Kuthumi explains that it was actually the false hierarchy impostors of God and Jesus who came to Loyola, and he succumbed to the flattery of these fallen ones. He had not addressed pride as a point of vulnerability within himself and he became its victim.

I find it quite interesting that Loyola so liked what the false hierarchy told him that he repeated it over and over again until he convinced himself that his calling was real, *until the lie became his truth.* As Hitler taught, people will believe a big lie if you repeat it enough. If Loyola had any doubts about what he was doing, he convinced himself otherwise by repeating the lie over and over, like a form of self-hypnosis. You wonder if at some level he didn't really know something was wrong with the vision and his calling and that's why he wasn't willing to challenge or question it in the name of Jesus and find out the truth. Perhaps he really wanted it to be true, so by constantly repeating it to himself he made it his truth. There was no way he could have heard his Christ Self speaking to him after closing the door so tightly.

Kuthumi also explains that the *Spiritual Exercises* written by Loyola *"are replete with the doctrines of the Devil well woven into the true teachings of Christ,"*[151] and that the two cannot be separated until the end times. So how would an innocent reader, someone picking up those readings today, know what is truth and what is error? They would be inclined to think that, because Loyola is a saint in the Catholic Church, what he wrote must be good. Though some of it *is* good, some of it is not and is actually full of error and evil.

A Time for Maximum Alertness

We need to learn from the examples of Peter and Loyola. We need to watch for our weaknesses—pride or ambition or anything that pulls us away from our Christ Self. We need to be willing to name them and rebuke them, "Get thee behind me, Satan." If we allow ourselves to be vulnerable, darkness can come through us. We have to be aware of that and be prepared and vigilant for such tests that will come our way.

In the dictation we are hearing today, Mother Mary reminds us to be sure to keep our daily rituals, communing with the Holy Spirit and attuning to the Holy of Holies. If we allow ourselves to stray from that, we can become vulnerable to dark forces from the astral plane. She warns that we need to be careful that we are not distracted by worldly demands "*or mundane events that take you from your spiritual path.*"[152] We are all busy people, taking care of the details of our lives, our personal responsibilities, families, jobs and so on, while we are also serving the masters. But we can't allow our busyness, no matter how important or necessary it is, to interfere with our communion with God and our Holy Christ Self.

The carnal mind and karma can play tricks on us if we're not careful. We can be deluded not only by the things that keep us busy, but also by past patterns and the repetition of mistakes and failures at certain points of the Path. In other words, when we fail a test, it comes back to us; and when we keep failing it, we build a momentum on failing it, which makes it harder and harder to pass. That's why we are serious students of the ascended masters. We take their words and advice seriously. We're not robot chelas; we aren't perfect chelas; we make mistakes. But we are striving with the pure motive of our heart, and that allows grace to enter in and make the difference. Always remember the gift and grace of the violet flame.

God knows we're not going to be humanly perfect, but he also knows that we need to strive with a certain level of intensity in order to be victorious for our souls, for the Brotherhood and for this planet. We've been waiting a long, long time for this opportunity. Sometimes God has held our deep records, traumas, and karmas in abeyance because we were not ready to stand, face and conquer them. But now some who have striven for many years and decades on the Path *are* ready! Those of you who are new to the path don't have to worry that God will return these hard things to you right away. They will come to you only when you're ready, and perhaps you are more prepared than you know. Therefore it is a time to be joyous about the awesome opportunity we have! But it is also a time for maximum alertness, and a time to note what's going on in our life, our thoughts and our feelings.

I think we sometimes forget we're having tests. We are so busy that when some problem comes up we simply think about how we are going to solve it. We don't realize it is a test of our souls at some level. Of course we have to deal with things on the outer, yet at the same time we want to be attuned and alert to what's going on at inner levels. We want to recognize events as opportunities that are coming to us for a reason. If we lose our connection to God, then we become vulnerable, just as Peter and Loyola were vulnerable. Good intentions are not enough; they are wonderful, but *they are not enough*. We have to apply what we know.

Our soul is navigating and transmuting ancient records that reside in our subconscious and unconscious minds. The unconscious records are deeper and more often from past lives. Even though they are outside our conscious awareness, they definitely impact our thoughts, feelings, behavior, relationships, work—all aspects of our lives. They can cause us to follow the way that seemeth right but is not.

Clues to Ancient Records

There are clues that can help us discern when we are dealing with deeper, unconscious records. One example is unexpected, intense feelings or behaviors that erupt as if from nowhere and don't always match the circumstance. They are often feelings and behaviors that are not normal to our daily lives. Our reactions can be anywhere on the spectrum of rage or anger, panic, terror, extreme anxiety or grief. Such records may even show up as physical symptoms in our body.

We want to observe ourselves, not condemn ourselves. We want to be aware of our feelings, not repress them. We want to pay attention and note if our feelings are related to inner pain. We can ask ourselves questions like, "Why is this coming up for me now? What is the lesson here? What is the record that I need to transmute?"

It's not comfortable going through these records. And because it's uncomfortable, we may try to get comfortable by hiding a problem or shoving it away. We can subtly avoid pain with all sorts of tactics of our human ego: taking refuge in intellectually "knowing the teachings" in our mind but not our heart; staying busy; taking care of others in a co-dependent relationship; dismissing or rationalizing behavior; controlling circumstances or people; being sure we're "right;" staying stuck in sadness or any kind of repetitive habit or addiction—the list goes on.

As mentioned earlier, Loyola told himself over and over again that he was sent forth to conquer for Christ, and although it was the false hierarchy that sent him forth to do their bidding, he wanted to believe their lie. Why didn't he want to know the truth? One reason could be that he would have had to change. He would have had to do something different.

He might have been concerned he would lose his position of authority and prominence and that other people would think less of him. Knowing what happened to him can make us seriously consider what we value more: our position, our egos, our role in our life, or our relationship with God.

It would be good to ponder some of our patterns and be honest with ourselves and God about where we are in consciousness, then do the spiritual work and seek guidance and help where we need it. Sometimes confessing to God and forsaking a habit suffices. (God obviously knows our problems already.) Sometimes processing with a trusted friend can help. And the messengers and masters have recommended the help of a professional therapist in dealing with the most repetitive and troublesome records or emotions that arise within us, such as core anger.

As I said previously, in arranging our lives we don't want to be so busy with important matters that we do not spend time alone in communion with God each day. Sometimes people create God and the masters in their own image. They hang a picture of one of the masters on their wall and they talk to that picture. Then instead of really listening for a response from the master, they kind of give themselves the response. They want that master to be *their* master; they want that master to support the decisions *they* make. Unfortunately, that is the opposite of surrendering and submitting ourselves to God's will.

It is important to bend the knee before God and our I AM Presence, both symbolically and physically. The Maha Chohan spoke about this in his dictation given July 6, 1996:

> *Thus you understand why so many are left in incarnation—simply because they do not bend the knee. Blessed ones, it is very important to bend the knee and to do so*

swiftly. It is important to be humble. It is important to love and still love unto the fulfillment of your mission and your transition into the octaves of light.[153]

Saints are humble. They are not passive, but they're humble, and love is their motivation. What is our motivation? Let us surrender those things which are not done with love as our motivation. Let us purify our hearts and be humble before God and the Christ in our fellowmen. Loving kindness is the mark of Maitreya. Even if we have to occasionally use firm words when we're talking to people or working with them, we sustain the presence of kindness. It's the way we have been taught. It's the way of Maitreya and his Mystery School.

When we bend the knee in profound love of God and his will, we are willing to surrender all to him—all that we are or *think* we are—for nothing is more important than our relationship with God and the masters. We give everything to God: our service, our position, our egos, our plans, our rationalizations, everything.

The Gift of Discernment

We should also pray for that most important gift of the Holy Spirit—discernment. How can two people see the same thing and see it so differently, even spiritual things? The difference is discernment. Someone told me a story about being in Summit University and Mother came to class one day and asked the students how they knew she was the messenger. Good question, right? There were all types of answers: "You give dictations," "You teach us," "You've got the mantle," and so on. But all their answers were wrong. She responded that they knew she was the messenger *by vibration.*

How can two people hear the exact same words and have such a different interpretation? Discernment of vibration. Someone can say all the right words with a smile on their face, but if the vibration is not right, they are not right. That's where discernment comes in. Without the awareness that it gives us, we can be led astray.

We need to continually pray for the gift of discernment. It is not mental knowledge. Discernment is the Holy Spirit giving you an awareness in your heart of what's really going on. Some people don't want to know what's going on, because if they know then they are going to have to do something, and they really don't want to surrender or change. So if you want to know the truth, if you want discernment, then you have to ask for it; but don't be surprised if it requires action on your part when you receive it.

If we truly trust God, we *do* want to hear the truth and act on it. I have frequently prayed to God for absolute clarity on a decision or a course of action, and I often say, "God, you can't be subtle with me. The answer has to be really clear, otherwise I'm bound to miss it." I did this once many years ago when I was new on the Path and doing a novena to the Great Divine Director. I was convinced he wasn't responding quite fast enough, and I remember making a call to him one day: "Great Divine Director, I'm doing all these calls and I don't know if you're even hearing me. I need a tangible, physical sign that you are." Now, I don't think I'd make that call today, but when I was younger and new on the path, I thought it was okay. That night my wife came home with a gift for me. She had decided on a whim to go to a gift shop on her lunch hour, and ended up buying me a very heavy statue of Ganesha—the Hindu name for the Great Divine Director. I sheepishly said to the Great Divine Director, "Okay, I got the message."

Let's hope we don't need physical signs too often. Let's have faith and trust that God is hearing us, and that if the answer doesn't manifest as quickly as we might think it should, there are reasons for that. Let's be sure we do not drown out the voice of our Holy Christ Self, as Loyola did, so we cannot hear it. If we do that, the voice of conscience will stop speaking to us.

Let's draw our Holy Christ Self closer and closer. Mother taught us to obey immediately. Mother Teresa said she had the gift of obedience, and we need the gift of obedience to the voice of our Holy Christ Self. When we hear it we need to act on it, once we have made sure it's our Holy Christ Self. We learn to recognize that voice through our daily devotions and spending time alone with God, praying and listening.

The Equation of Victory

Be aware. Pray for attunement and discernment. Don't do all the talking; let God do some of the talking too. Attune to what you are feeling and what your heart tells you regarding the truth of things. Don't condemn yourself for making mistakes because God does not condemn any of us. We can make it with God's help. If we strive and work, we'll learn our lessons and we'll pass our tests.

We are center stage and God, the angels, and the masters are waiting and watching to see how we will do—perhaps even holding their breath, so to speak, to see if we will finally have our victory. If we are willing to give God permission to do what is needed to ensure we stay on the straight and narrow path no matter the cost, then he will correct us when we are off course. We don't want to let ourselves, our souls and our God down. Therefore, we are willing to strive and work in humility, surrender our egos, give up the human desires that are not of God, and be satisfied with the divine succor that God gives us.

The masters have told us that we have come very close to our ascension before and not made it. We have fallen short in the past, and we don't want that to happen again! Knowing that nothing could be more important than our ascension—not relationships, not jobs, not anything—we need to ask ourselves, "What am I willing to do to really make it all the way Home this time?" That doesn't mean we will turn away from our responsibilities, but we will keep co-measurement as to what is the greatest need of the hour. We will be mindful of our path and our service to life and to God.

We are doing many things that the masters and God need to have done on this planet. We can do that to a greater extent if we prepare ourselves to be chalices of light, hold the light in harmony, and acknowledge that God is the doer of *all* good things. God is the center of everything. It's not about our ego or human consciousness; it's about our identity in God and our ability to hold light. We can hold more and more light as we pay attention to our karmas, work to balance and correct them with the violet flame and other spiritual tools, enlist support from the heavenly hosts, and pass our tests.

Winning our victory has requirements; it is an equation. We know the equation; we've been taught it and we can follow it. Let us not stumble because we don't have the messenger in embodiment encouraging us and goading us on. It's our time to demonstrate Christ-mastery, and we have to be attentive in order to do that. "There's many a slip 'twixt the cup and the lip" is an old proverb similar in meaning to "Don't count your chickens before they're hatched." To keep moving forward, we have to be chelas who are awake, who are attentive to what's going on in our lives and in the world around us.

Let us not forget that making it to 51 percent balanced karma is a great victory! It's a huge victory, and if we can maintain that percentage, we'll move on to higher realms in our service. Perhaps there are some who should take their ascension at that time, but, personally, I can't imagine leaving before we have done everything possible for Saint Germain and the establishment of the golden age on planet Earth.

Whether we have or have not yet balanced 51 percent of our karma, we need to be ready. We do not know when our hardest test will come to us. Even if it is upon us now, we might not recognize it. We need to know that we can win our victory! We need to ensure that we hear the voice of God—the still small voice within us. We want to listen for the message from God that may come to us from others; as Morya said, *"If the messenger be an ant, heed him."*[154] We need to pray that we have the discernment to recognize darkness, no what matter what form it takes, no matter if it's within us or outside us.

We must try to have time for God every day. Not two or three times a week, but *every day* we have to find some time to be alone with God; not just in decrees and services, but in holy communion—calling for the Holy Spirit, surrendering our all to God, pleading for illumination and the surety of God's will to guide us.

Mark Prophet spent hours and hours on his knees in his attic as a young boy praying for the gifts of the Holy Spirit. Do we want it that much? Are we willing to give all of ourselves to receive it? Do we want to love God, love his will, love our neighbors more than we love our human consciousness, our pride, our egos? That sounds like the path to sainthood, doesn't it? The path to becoming one with our Christ Self and balancing 100 percent of our karma.

Whether our tests are obvious or subtle, they are tests that will allow us to demonstrate the mastery we have striven to acquire. We are indeed on the stage; let us make it our final role before we return Home to God. Along the way, let us, with Gautama Buddha, be awake, lest Mara (the Hindu demon who tested him) catch us off guard.

Praise be to God, we have found the narrow way. With God's help, *nothing* need take us from this path. The Holy City and our ascension await us, and the narrow way will take us there.

SEVEN WAYS TO BRING LIGHT TO THE DARK NIGHT

You will become such a whirling sacred fire of diamond light as my diamond heart is superimposed upon you that you will literally charge through that dark night of the soul and charge through the initiations of the dark night of the Spirit....

Go through it. Get it over with. Become the master of your life.

—**EL MORYA**

ELEVEN

Seven Ways to Bring Light to the Dark Night

The dark night is an extraordinary and difficult experience for our soul. Listen to the souls of three individuals cry out in the midst of their dark night. The first is from the book of Job, chapter 30, verses 16 through 28 in the *New Jerusalem Bible*:

> And now the life in me trickles away, days of grief have gripped me.
> At night-time sickness saps my bones I am gnawed by wounds that never sleep.
> Violently, he has caught me by my clothes, has gripped me by the collar of my coat.
> He has thrown me into the mud; I am no more than dust and ashes.
>
> I cry to you, and you give me no answer; I stand before you, but you take no notice.
> You have grown cruel to me, and your strong hand torments me unmercifully.

You carry me away astride the wind and blow me to pieces in a tempest.
Yes, I know that you are taking me towards death, to the common meeting-place of all the living.

Yet have I ever laid a hand on the poor when they cried out for justice in calamity?
Have I not wept for those whose life is hard, felt pity for the penniless?
I hoped for happiness, but sorrow came; I looked for light, but there was darkness.
My stomach seethes, is never still, days of suffering have struck me.
Somber I go, yet no one comforts me.

The next piercing cry is from Jesus in his dark night of the Spirit: "*My God, my God, why hast thou forsaken me?*"[155]

And the final cry is: "*I am bereft of every peaceful moment, wearied to death all day with a variety of perplexing circumstances. (I have lost) all comfort and happiness. (I have never been) in such an unhappy…state…Such is my situation that if I were to wish the bitterest curse to an enemy on this side of the grave, I should put him in my stead with my feelings.*"[156] Any ideas who said that? George Washington in 1775.

After hearing these readings, some of you might be wishing you had skipped this morning's service! But I chose this topic because of what I see going on in people's lives right now. Many souls, including longtime students of the ascended masters, are having the most extraordinary and demanding initiations that are challenging them more than anything else they have encountered on the Path. And if you consider yourself a candidate for the ascension, then similar initiations or dark nights will come to you at some point, if they haven't already.

I think we've all identified with Job and his miseries at one time or another. Perhaps we haven't rent our garments, but have we not cried out to God for mercy in our darkest hours? Job said, *"I hoped for happiness, but sorrow came."* Isn't that a powerful statement? Can't you feel the heart of Job? He doesn't know what to make of this. He doesn't know why this has happened to him. He doesn't know the reason for it, and he cries out, *"I hoped for happiness, but sorrow came."*

The mature chela of the ascended masters understands that pain and suffering are part of the spiritual path, and as Mother has said, they lead to bliss. Yet when they come it can be so overwhelming that our academic understanding of the Path dissolves and we are left, as were Job and others, lamenting our lot in life and searching for answers. Knowing that our Lord cried out on the cross asking why God had forsaken him helps us to understand that we too must pass through these tests on our path, because *"the servant is not greater than his Lord."*[157]

Now, what if we had a spiritual understanding of what we were experiencing and what we could do to help us be victorious over these profound challenges? I think we can agree that it would make a tremendous difference. Fortunately, we have been given that understanding.

Passing Through the Dark Night

Saint John of the Cross was the first to specifically identify two initiations that everyone on the path of their Christhood must experience: the dark night of the soul and the dark night of the Spirit. Here is a succinct definition of these two initiations: "The dark night of the soul is the test of the soul's encounter with the return of personal karma, which, if she has not kept her lamps (chakras) trimmed with light, may eclipse the light (Christ consciousness) of the soul and therefore its discipleship under the Son of God. It precedes the dark night of the Spirit, the supreme test of Christhood, when the soul is, as it were, cut off from the I AM Presence and must survive solely on the light (Christ consciousness) garnered in the heart, while holding the balance for planetary karma."[158]

Mother gave many lectures on these initiations in the album *The Living Flame of Love*, which contains essential teachings for the path of the ascension. She further describes the dark night of the soul in a teaching she gave to Summit University in 1986:

> When you have said, "I want to ascend to God. I want to return home. I want to be the bride of Christ," that is the moment when God begins accelerating the return of your karma so that it will not take forever. And you have agreed to that at inner levels. The karma descends upon you just like night falls, like a very dark night with no stars and no moon. It comes down as a blanket and you cannot see. It is called the dark night of the soul and the soul passes through the dark night, through the path that we have, which has been the path of the saints and mystics of all ages.... So when you pass through the dark night of the soul, you have passed through the third quadrant of the karmic clock... The dark night is over when you have gone through 75 percent of your karma and balanced it.[159]

Saint John of the Cross said that during the dark night of the Spirit the soul feels that "God has abandoned her, and, in his abhorrence of her, has flung her into darkness." The soul feels "chastised *and cast out, and unworthy of Him.... She feels, too, that all creatures have forsaken her...."* He further described the dark night of the Spirit as an *"inflow of God into the soul...purging the soul, annihilating her, emptying her or consuming in her...all the affections and imperfect habits which she has contracted in her whole life.... God greatly humbles the soul in order that He may afterwards greatly exalt her."*[160]

Anyone feeling a little overwhelmed? Well, the good news is we have the illumination to traverse these testings. If we are prepared and understand what is happening and what we can do to be victorious, then it becomes an initiation that we are ready to take because of our love of God and our desire to partake of the whole loaf of Christhood.

In a *Pearl of Wisdom* dated May 3, 1992, Jesus outlined what we need to do:

> *Therefore, in preparation for the dark night of the Spirit, you must become balanced in body and soul and in mind and in heart. Not one of these can be missed. And the spirit itself, the spirit of a man, a woman and a child, must be strengthened, infired and emboldened. You must be ready for any challenge, any adversary, any condemnation and any burden, then, of Darkness that does seem as a dark, dark night where there are no rays of light.*[161]

Your Christhood Book

When Darkness descends we tend to forget who we are, what we have experienced, and what we're here to do. Knowing this, Lanello advised us to keep a book of our Christhood that lists our victories so that we could refer to it when the Darkness envelops us.

Along that same line, when I was going through a particularly difficult time in my life, I used to read the Bible and quote scripture to God, especially the Psalms. Obviously, God didn't need me to quote scripture to him, but *I* needed to do it because it was an affirmation that God would not forsake me, would not leave me comfortless, would provide for the needs of myself and my family. Affirming he would do that did help reassure me.

Other than rending our garments and crying out for mercy, as the Israelites used to do, it is good to consider what are some things we can do to help us bring light to the dark night. The purpose of pondering this is not to help us avoid the dark nights, for they are part of the Path. We must go through them. And we can rest assured that—no matter how prepared we are—the dark night will not be over until we have passed our tests. We might wonder how long that will take, but it really depends on us.

For some of us, passing these tests may be a struggle. Don't be discouraged if you are having a hard time. Hard times can lead us to draw on a place of inner strength we didn't even know we had. I think for most of us these tests are going to require all that we have, including great love in our hearts and steadfast devotion, in order to pass through them victoriously. Some people may have less difficulty, but I think many of us have to be prepared for the going to be challenging because we understand what may be required of us.

I was considering the dark night and wrote down some actions that I thought might be helpful when we are going through these tests. Obviously there are many more helpful things and your list might be quite different; but these are a few ways we can be proactive. It is important to remember that we cannot be passive. Even when we wait upon the Lord, we are active in waiting. We must be actively engaged in all that we do, and passing these tests is definitely not just getting up in the morning and going through the motions of the day.

Number 1:
Have Courage!

It is not a given that we accept these tests. In the same *Pearl of Wisdom* I quoted earlier, Jesus taught:

> *For there are those who when seeing the abyss of their own human creation and the abyss of planet Earth and beholding Death and Hell itself will step back and say, "I will not take the initiation of the dark night of the soul this day or this week or this month or this year, but I will tarry in my level of comfortability and insulate myself from these true initiations of the saints."*[162]

I think the fear of an initiation is sometimes much worse than the initiation! We keep putting if off again and again, and all the while we are somehow tormented. It's as if we have avoided it so often that we push it away automatically. I wonder how many times we have come to this place and said, "Hmm, I'm not so sure; I'm not so sure I want to do this." Well, we don't have to wait. Let's get on with it. Let's do it!

Will we ever be better prepared than we are right now? I wonder. We have time and space and understanding—precious commodities. And not only is our Christhood at stake, but indeed the future of the planet. What impact will the one or the many who pass these tests have on the victory of planet Earth?

El Morya believes we can do it. In his dictation given on April 19, 1992 he said:

> *Yes, beloved, loving the will of God and his law, which is truly the law of profound love and wisdom, you shall then take heart—take courage to take on the path of the dark night of the soul and the dark night of the Spirit. And you will become such a whirling sacred fire of diamond light as my diamond heart is superimposed upon you that you will literally charge through that dark night of the soul and charge through the initiations of the dark night of the Spirit....*
>
> *Go through it. Get it over with. Become the master of your life.*[163]

Just think about his words: "You will become such a whirling sacred fire of diamond light *as my diamond heart is superimposed upon you...*" That is a key right there, isn't it? If every day we ask El Morya to superimpose his diamond heart on our heart, then we will have the promise fulfilled of charging through the initiations of the dark night of the soul and Spirit.

I remember in the late 1990s when the board of directors of our Church was meeting in Chicago and making some crucial decisions about the future of the organization. Mother called us on the phone and gave us a stunning message. She said, "Don't be wimps!" Very clear meaning, wasn't it? Very clear.

The same is true for the dark night. We can't be wimps. We have to have courage. It doesn't mean we aren't nervous or concerned or wondering what it's going to be like. Those thoughts and feelings may arise, but we must have the courage to go forward in spite of them. Each one of us can have that courage because we trust and we know that God in us can do it.

Number 2:
Get Right with God and with Others

Do you talk to God and listen to him? God knows us better than we can ever know ourselves. So can't we be honest with him about our pains, our sorrows, our striving, and even our failures? Be honest with God. Acknowledge where you need help. Start with something you know you need to correct and ask for help with that.

Asking for help and grace is part of our devotion on the Path. Can we go a single day without devout and sincere prayer on our knees before our God? God loves us and cares for us and wants us to be free. He doesn't expect us to be perfect but he expects us to do what we can to resolve problems, not only within ourselves, but also with others.

We can humble ourselves before our God and before the Christ in all. Ephesians 4:26 says, "*let not the sun go down upon your wrath.*" Some of us have allowed problems with others to persist for many suns and we must resolve this "wrath." We need to do it with a sense of urgency, so that we do not leave this life until we have made the effort to resolve it. We cannot control what the other person does, but we can control what we do.

The messengers and masters have taught the importance of confession so that we can be forgiven and go forward with the intent to sin no more. We must be able to face our God knowing that we have done what we can do to make amends for something that we know is not right. If there is something between you and a brother or sister on the path, do what you can to bring it to resolution. That's a basic teaching. But what happens is we tend to push these difficult things aside, thinking that somehow our work and other things we do will make up for it.

While we know and understand that God wants to forgive us and wants us to be able to move on, we need to be accountable, to confess our errors and make amends as best we can. That opens up the way for the light and mercy to pour in. Confession may be a silent prayer to God or your Christ Self. It may be spoken aloud to the one you have wronged or to a friend or minister. It may be a letter you write to God and then burn. The point is to acknowledge your error and ask for forgiveness.

Catherine Marshall (the wife of Peter Marshall, the Chaplain of the U.S. Senate in the 1950s) was once quite ill and was not getting better. She didn't know why she was not getting better, so she prayed and prayed and prayed. Then she got the inspiration to write to every person in her life she could think of and ask for forgiveness for anything she may have done to hurt them. Interesting thought, isn't it? She did just that and then she got better.

As we get ready for the dark night, we want to be free in God, free of everything that is an encumbrance to surrendering totally unto him. So we must get right with God and with others.

Number 3:
Have Perspective

I recently read a *Pearl of Wisdom* by Archangel Raphael in which he said that he had known us *"for ten thousand times ten thousand years."*[64] That means he's known us for a hundred million years! Rather hard to comprehend, isn't it? It puts things in perspective.

Many of us know we must be about our Father's business, while simultaneously balancing our karma, going through the initiations of the dark night, and forging our Christhood. The remaining years of our lives are but a *millisecond* in our cosmic history, and yet what we do in that millisecond is the key to our immortality and the victory of planet Earth. If we let this millisecond slip through our hands this time, how long will it be before the opportunity comes again? What will be the price to our souls, to God and to the planet if we are not willing to go all the way this time?

I understand it's fine to wax poetic about perspective and milliseconds in history, but when you are going through hard times, such platitudes don't necessarily help. When you've got a bad toothache, it's hard to put things in perspective. Interestingly, I have had a long history of painful dental work, and I have found a technique that has helped me cope with the sometimes extreme discomfort. To get through it, I mentally give praise to Jesus and to God, and I ask God to use my pain to help others. It doesn't take the pain away, but it gives me an inner purpose for experiencing it. If we feel that the purpose behind our pain is that others are helped, even great pain takes on a different light and becomes bearable.

It's true that when we go through the dark night it can be disorienting and seem that all is lost. That's the common thread that we hear from Job and others: "My God, my God, why have you forsaken me?" I can't tell you the number of people who have told me something to the effect that they don't feel like they are as far along the Path today as they were ten or twenty years ago. They wonder about that because they have done what they knew they needed to do, and yet they don't feel like they have made much progress. And, of course, no man or woman can take a measure of themselves or their progress, but our souls have an inner understanding of what it will take to get where we need to go.

The cloud hiding the sun of our I AM Presence will dissolve. It's not going to be there forever. Victory is in sight for each one of us. Our souls have been around for a hundred million years at least, and now is our time. It's a time to keep on keeping on, to rejoice and to prepare ourselves so that the winds of misfortune do not take us from our path.

Mother Mary has told us, *"Remember, this life is an endurance test,"* and *"the purging must come."*[65] The purging *must* come. We cannot be free until we are purged of whatever within us keeps us from our Christhood. It's common sense—the human cannot put on the divine; we must be freed of it. And we don't have to gulp when we hear that, because there will be a new freedom for our souls and our service if we endure the purging.

The eternal question of the chela is, "How long, O Lord?" The answer is simple, "As long as is needed." But that's not *too* long when you have the perspective of who we are, where we have been, where we are going, and that there is a purpose to our pain.

Don't think you have failed because you are experiencing pain or loss. When calamity comes upon us, what's one of the first things we think of as devout chelas? "I must have done something wrong. I must have terrible karma. Oh, can you imagine what I must have done to have this karma descend upon me? Look at me—I know the teachings, I know the truth, and yet these things come upon me. I'm not worthy to walk this path." That is a lie and we must challenge that lie!

As we walk in devotion to God and the will of God, yes, our karma will come upon us, but it's finite and it's for a purpose. As I have mentioned before, Mark and Elizabeth Prophet came into this life with less than 50 percent of their karma balanced.

They had to balance their karma and we have to balance ours. We would probably not repeat the things that brought this karma upon us today because we are different people. So we are just working to clean it up.

The number one book on the best sellers list today is *The Life-Changing Magic of Tidying Up: The Japanese Art of Decluttering and Organizing*. The number one best seller! Well, that's exactly what we're doing—we're tidying up our karma. While we feel the pain of returning karma and are sorry for what we have done to other people and to God, we know it is not who we are. Our karma does not define us. Our Christ consciousness defines who we are, along with the light of all the wonderful things we have done in this and previous embodiments that is stored in the magnificent causal body we each have.

We acknowledge our sin, our karma, but we do not identify with it. We do not see it as a point of failure but rather as a motivator toward victory because we are taking accountability for it and we're going to overcome it. So don't believe the lie that because bad things happen to you, you're a terrible person. Besides, the karma might be world karma, and bearing world karma is a privilege and an acknowledgement that God loves us and trusts us. Again, the bottom line is that we don't pretend that karma doesn't exist or that we haven't made mistakes, but we don't identify with them because it is not who we are. We're going to balance our karma and move on.

Although we remember "This too shall pass," we also know that God may not fix everything in our lives. For example, we know the apostle Paul had some infirmity of the body and he said he prayed to Jesus three times to be healed. And do you remember what Jesus' answer was? He simply said, *"My grace is sufficient for thee: for my strength is made perfect in weakness."*[166] Paul was not healed and retained that thorn in his side.

Everything in our life may not be perfect, in fact, it usually isn't. But if God is with us, if our Lord and Saviour is with us, then we know what happens is for the good of our souls. So if we can affirm with Paul that Jesus' grace is sufficient for us, then we have proper perspective.

I was recently rereading *The Autobiography of a Yogi* by Yogananda. He talks about meeting his guru for the first time, how excited he was, and how his guru told him that he loved him unconditionally. Then Yogananda shared that he would have to wait twenty-five years to hear those words again. Isn't that stunning? He talks about how his guru chastised him, brought down spiritual fire to deliver him of his human consciousness, and how we must understand the love of the guru-chela relationship.

God does not coddle us. He expects us to know who we are, where we're going, and that we will not receive waves of praise and glory every day. They will come, but they don't come often, and we should understand that. It's the way of the Path. It relates back to understanding that life is an endurance test and we must be purged.

Number 4:
Practice Holiness

One extremely effective antidote to darkness is holiness. The Ascended Lady Master Kristine said, "*O blessed hearts, I pray that you enter in to the very glory and sanctity of God.*"[167] Isn't that a beautiful thought? The sanctity of God—the glory, holiness, and purity of God. And Isaiah had a vision of the seraphim above the throne of God, "*And one cried unto another, and said, Holy, holy, holy, is the LORD of hosts: the whole earth is full of his glory.*"[168] The *whole* earth.

It seems we spend most of our time with God petitioning him and his angels for help. Of course, that is a vital part of our spiritual path and service. Yet there should be times when, like the seraphim, we simply love God and celebrate his presence, his sanctity, his holiness, and his creation. That allows us to enter into the bliss of God. We haven't forgotten our karma; we realize we haven't reached our goal and that there are still plenty of problems on planet Earth. But for a moment, for a space in time, we put that aside and celebrate the holiness of our God.

You can do this by simply looking around at the beauty and magnificence of God's creation. How many of you saw the sunset last night? It was so wondrous it drew me outside. It is hard not to praise God when you see that kind of beauty and magnificence and power. Each of us can start someplace to find something of God and his glory. You might want to use the refrain in decree 30.03, "O, God You Are So Magnificent!" to fire up the spirit of devotion and holiness in your heart. Doing this even when you don't feel any holiness can help prime the pump of the flow between you and God. God is holy and he deserves our praise.

The Maha Chohan told us,

> *Say unto God, as the priesthood of Israel did say: "Holiness unto the Lord! Holiness unto the Lord! Holiness unto the Lord!" Each time you recite the mantra "Holiness unto the Lord," you weave a stronger tie to the Lord God, confirming his holiness where you are, sending to him that holiness which he has given to you, multiplied many times over.*[169]

And Archangel Michael gave us this key, "*The consciousness of holiness is an aura of protection and it keeps you apart from those who would lead you astray.*"[170] There is much darkness on this planet, and we need to affirm the holiness of God, even in the darkest places. Remember holiness is an antidote to darkness.

Someone recently told me how he had been overcome by the darkness enfolding our planet. The pain of children and the people of God had become too much for him, and he didn't know what to do to enable himself to help bear that pain. When that happens to us, the temptation is to escape, to go away. And yes, we need to have balance in our lives; nevertheless, we will not turn a deaf ear to the pain of the people of this planet. So he thought, "What can I do to relieve this pain?" And he thought of Christmas carols—yes, Christmas carols in July. He played the songs "O Holy Night" and "The New Jerusalem" over and over again and allowed his devotion and love of God to flow through him in these songs. He said the light became so intense around him that it gave him the strength to bear this pain in a very different way. He said honoring the holiness of God brought tears and healing to him, and at that point he knew he could keep on.

The holiness of God must be celebrated by someone somewhere on this dark planet. Many monasteries in the Middle East have even been destroyed recently. There was an article in the *Wall Street Journal* last year about the churches in Europe and what they're being used for now. There was even a picture on the front page showing a beautiful cathedral that had been converted to a skateboard park with a young man riding a skateboard up and down inside this cathedral.

While some have turned from God, those of us who love God can rejoice and celebrate the holiness of God, the honor of God. And as we celebrate it, just as with the gentleman I told you about, the holiness of God can surround us with light and give us the strength to go on.

We celebrate the holiness of God, for he is worthy.

Number 5:
Give of Yourself to Others

Many have taught that the secret of happiness is to be of service to others. Serving others displaces loneliness and discouragement as it turns our focus away from ourselves toward others. When we are out doing something for someone else, whether a child or an animal or anyone we see who has a need, we can't be engulfed in self-pity. It just can't happen.

Mother Teresa experienced a forty-year period of the dark night of the soul and Spirit—forty years! Yet look what she accomplished in her service to the poor. Hers was an example of embodying the love of Jesus, and others never knew what she was going through. She never told them. Even in the midst of the pain of the dark night, she was full of fun and enjoyed everything that went on. That is mastery! So we can't use the dark night of the soul or the Spirit as a reason for not giving to others. We can give at some level, if only by praying for them. When we give of ourselves to others during our dark night, it will help us get through it.

The joy of service will help you in a way that you might not imagine. Have you ever looked into the room in the cafeteria at the Ranch where they wash the pots and pans? We know what hard work that is, don't we? So I asked one of the men who was working there one day, "You know, I see you here during every conference. Why do you keep doing it?" He got a smile on his face and said, "I love it." Isn't that interesting? It wasn't drudgery for him, it was service—a service to souls and the beloved chelas of the ascended masters.

Someone, somewhere, needs the service and help you can give them. And you don't have to look very far to find them. There is joy in service whether or not you are in the midst of the dark night. And, of course, when you serve others you are balancing karma and moving one step closer to your victory.

We can also help those who are going through their dark nights by showing compassion and giving heartfelt encouragement. While we must not interfere with someone's initiation by doing what they should be doing themselves, we can be a voice of love when they can hardly remember what love feels like. How many times have we been there ourselves? We've forgotten the light and the blessings we have received in our lives and the incredible experiences we've had, as if they are all gone. All we feel is darkness and bleakness and sorrow, and we may also be sick and in pain. During such times, it's nice to hear someone say, "I believe in you. I believe that you will endure and pass these tests God has brought you. And I am here as your friend, to stand with you, pray with you and witness as you go forward to your victory." Encouragement, true encouragement can help a soul keep on keeping on.

But in our desire to help, let us not become like Job's comforters. I looked up "Job's comforters" in the dictionary, and the definition is "A person, who, in trying to offer help or advice, says something that simply adds to the distress." Regarding such comforters, the book of Job, chapter 16, verses 1–3 in the *New Jerusalem Bible* says, "*Job spoke next. He said: 'How often have I heard all this before! What sorry comforters you are! When will these windy arguments be over?'*"

Here's a small, somewhat humorous example from my life of what having such comforters can be like. A number of years ago I received a rather public chastisement from Mother. There was a man that heard it who didn't live here in Montana but who came to every conference. For a number of years after that, every time he saw me he would remind me of that initiation. He always held me in that old matrix, while I definitely hoped I had moved on!

I pray that none of us would be like Job's comforters.

Number 6:
Surrender

Did not our Lord surrender to God when he said, "*...Father, if thou be willing, remove this cup from me: nevertheless not my will, but thine, be done,*"[171] and also later when he was on the cross, "*And when Jesus had cried with a loud voice, he said, Father, into thy hands I commend my spirit*"?[172] We receive encouragement and inspiration from knowing that even Jesus surrendered.

The Fourteenth Rosary dictated to Mother by Mother Mary is "The Mystery of Surrender." This rosary is indispensable for every chela of the ascended masters, every person who is going through the dark night. It must be a part of our lives if we're going to get through that test and pass it.

In the introduction to the Surrender Rosary, Mother explains, "*...the Blessed Mother has come to teach us how to surrender, how to let go of a false identity fabricated in Matter...how to release into the fires of the Holy Spirit the struggle and the sense of struggle...*"[173] She tells us that Mother Mary says:

> *Give all to God and let him give back to you that which he desires you to keep.... Take the mystery of surrender and let it commemorate the moment of your dying unto reality— the moment of the letting-go of each justification of the*

human ego, of a false sense of responsibility wherein you think friends and family and loved ones are dependent upon you instead of upon God. Let go of the things that you think you must have. Let go of the things that you think in your pride you will never do or the things that you think you will always do. Let go of all human attachments. Let go of every ambition except God's desiring within you to be God.[174]

Now, of course, the part about the false sense of responsibility wherein your friends and family and loved ones are dependent upon you instead of God doesn't mean we abandon our families or friends. It means that God may use us to fulfill their needs or he may use someone else, but first and foremost we should rely on him. In other words, knowing God will care for them doesn't mean we forsake our care for loved ones, but that we acknowledge that God is the doer and God is the one who provides all needs.

Surrender is freedom and power. It is not passive; it is very active. If you can't give the whole rosary, doing the "I Surrender" prayer [included at the end of this sermon] is quite powerful. It is full of liberating teachings. For example, it says, "In the name I AM THAT I AM, the Almighty One, I surrender all identity apart from the blessed Son of God,"—all identity other than our Christhood.

You know, we've been living as part human and part divine for too long. It's time we lived as our Christ Self, and we get there by surrendering our attachments to our human identity and thinking, "This is my identity, and this is how I want other people to see me because this is what I like." Well, if your identity is not centered in God, you're going to lose it. And praise God that you're going to lose it because it's keeping you from identifying with your Christ Self and reaching your ultimate goal!

Mother has explained that you go back and forth between your human self and your Christ Self. Back and forth—sometimes you are your Christ Self, then for a while you're back to your human self, then your Christ Self—back and forth. And the goal is to have the back and forth go faster and faster and faster until, boom! You *are* your Christ Self. That is how we put on our Christhood. But we have to be willing to let go.

So what does it take for us to really reach the point of surrendering our human consciousness? We like it in some ways, don't we? It's been comfortable for us. After all, we created it, right? It's been around with us for a long, long time, probably far more millennia than we would like to admit. There's a reluctance to let go of our human self because we think, "It's who I am, and I've built my life around it," and on and on. Well, we can live that way but it will *never* get us where we want to go.

If you don't know the next steps to take to become the Christ, you can begin with surrender. Take the surrender prayer and make affirmations out of it. Ask God to deliver you from whatever prevents you from being your Christ Self in action. It happens incrementally, but we must make an effort and be willing to surrender those lesser parts of ourselves. It begins with trusting God and his will, knowing he will take only those things that hinder you on your path. The Surrender Rosary will help you get to the point where you feel great peace and love and can say, "Yes, Lord, I want to be free of my human creation."

I have usually been driven to the Surrender Rosary when nothing else I tried seemed to work. It's been the court of last resort, but maybe it should be our court of first resort. I have found that when I have a particular problem that needs resolution, giving the Surrender Rosary doesn't necessarily resolve it, but I always end up feeling a certain inner peace. I always feel like God is with me and I can be at peace because—whatever the direction of the initiation—God is there. It's trust in God, trust in the Divine Mother, and sweet surrender to our holy vow.

Aren't you tired of struggling? I am. It's liberating to give ourselves to God, surrender unto his will, then take what comes and work to be free. If we do not make the effort, we will not put on our Christhood. It is not automatic.

There is power in surrender, great power. Use it.

Number 7:
Affirm Your God-Victory

I think we've all found that sometimes it's hard not to feel a little bit sorry for ourselves. We try so hard, we're so sincere, and yet often victory seems elusive or farther away than it was years ago. We must determine that *we cannot* and *we will not* give up, even if it means just putting one foot in front of the other. We must decide that we will challenge the projection of failure, affirm our victory, and believe in it!

In the dictation we will hear today, Mighty Victory says, "*I come to proclaim your victory in the Dark Cycle and in the dark night of the soul.*"[75] We must proclaim that victory with him. Do you know that there are thirty-six pages of Victory calls in our decree book? *Thirty-six pages!* Does the sheer volume of this tell us something? Of course it does—we need to be giving the words and fiats of Mighty Victory, even a paragraph a day or a page a day. Try that for a month and see if you feel differently.

Not only are these calls a declaration of victory, but they push back all doubt and fear and self-pity and self-condemnation—every force of anti-victory that assails us. Victory is a vibration. It is a challenge to the forces of darkness and it can help us through the dark night. This is not a cheerleading, superficial sense of victory. It is a deep commitment and understanding that our victory can be won and it *will* be won, with God's help, if we apply ourselves.

If Mighty Victory were here today and asked, "Do you believe in your victory?" wouldn't we say "Yes!" Well, he is here today asking us that question, but we have to believe in our victory to the extent that it moves us to action. And it won't be a victory unless we *take that action*. Saying "yes" is the first step, but it is not enough. We must proclaim our victory not once, but many times over as we follow the path our Lord takes us on. No one else can walk the Path for you—not your husband, your wife, your child, your friend—*no one else*. And what a blessing, because when you put forth the effort to walk the Path all the way to your victory, the crown of victory will be yours alone and no one can take it from you.

Mighty Victory has no doubts about victory. Do you want to tell him he is wrong? Probably not. Compose your own words of victory—make fiats affirming who you are in God and that you are on the way Home. Give a fiat to the universe: "I AM a son/a daughter of God and I AM determined to be free of this human consciousness in this lifetime and to return to God through the ritual of the ascension, so help me God!" It's a declaration to the world of your intent; it's a fiat to roll back the condemnation that is upon every one of us. It's an affirmation of who we are and who we can be. We are not yet perfected in Christ, but Christ is the essence of our being and we can affirm that because we're walking this path.

There comes a time when all must take a stand for victory. James McPherson, the editor of David Fisher's book

Washington's Crossing, commented, "No single day in history was more decisive for the creation of the United States than Christmas 1776."[176] As I shared in the sermon "A Buddha's Christmas Vow," it was that night that Washington and his army crossed the Delaware River and secured a pivotal victory that kept the Revolution alive. As he deliberated that night, Washington wrote on a piece of paper, "Victory or Death!"[¶¶] He made his choice—he was going to risk everything for victory. We have the same choice before us, and the choice for victory takes determination. His victory that night was not the end of the war or of his troubles, but no one doubted where he stood after that. The ascended masters and the universe did not doubt his determination.

Our declaration of victory can be the wind in our sails to help us through the darkest night. We've been at this point before. Now is not the time to falter. It's not the time to turn back. It's the time to pray to God for strength and determination to keep on. All we have to do is put one foot in front of the other each day, and God will lead us.

It is our time to pass the ultimate tests of our Christhood. We have the tools. We have the examples. We have the fire of determination to finally become who we are in God. And if we're willing to surrender our identity outside of God, then he will replace that with our Christ consciousness. Be willing to experience the pain of surrendering the unreal self to get to the joy that follows.

We have a deep soul conviction that, come what may, this time we will not come up short. We *will* pass our tests. We will not take our victory for granted, and we will not let down our guard until that victory is sealed forevermore.

¶¶ See "A Buddha's Christmas Vow," page 165.

We *will* encourage each other and pray for each other and celebrate each victory together. We will love enough to pay the price for ourselves and others. *We will love enough to pay the price for ourselves and others.*

We *will not* be surprised by the pain or the purging. We will find peace in surrendering our unreal self and all that we had thought our own.

We *will* trust in the process and trust in the Guru. Have you looked into the eyes of El Morya and said with your greatest devotion, "I trust you." It's a powerful statement—"I trust you." Not, "I trust you, Morya, but I think you need to understand the whole picture. It's been a while since you were on earth and you may not remember exactly what it's like down here." No. Rather, "El Morya, I trust you. I trust the will of God. I am open. I am willing. Show me the way." And remember, we can call to his diamond heart to be over our hearts and charge through our initiations. Try doing that and see how you feel.

See how it feels to get on your knees before God, to surrender, to let go, to affirm that this time is going to be different, that you are willing to pay the price. Yes, there will be tears. But one day, as we've been told, there will be no more tears save the tears of joy.

Mighty Victory closes the dictation we're hearing today with the inspiring fiats: *"I AM Victory! I proclaim victory for you and for all mankind! Invictus, we are one!"*[177] "Invictus" is a Latin adjective that means unconquered, unsubdued, invincible. So let us proclaim with Mighty Victory in the depths of our soul, "Invictus, we are one!"

The Surrender Prayer from *The Fourteenth Rosary, The Mystery of Surrender*

I Surrender

In the name of the Father and of the Mother
and of the Son and of the Holy Spirit,
Amen.

In the name of the I AM THAT I AM, the one true God,
  I surrender all that is less
  than the Christ consciousness within me!

In the name of Jesus the Christ,
  I surrender all that is less
  than the manifest perfection of my being!

In the name of the Holy Spirit,
  I surrender all misuses of the sacred fire
  within my four lower bodies!

In the name of the Holy of Holies,
  I invoke the flame of the Holy Spirit
  upon the altar of my heart
  and I declare this temple
  to be the temple of the living God!

In the name of the Christ,
  the only begotten Son of the Father, full of grace and truth,
  I surrender all mortal consciousness and mortality,
  all struggle and the sense of struggle,
  all sin, disease and death!

In the name of the Divine Mother
  and in the name of the Immaculate Heart of Mary,
  I surrender all that is less
  than the purity of the Cosmic Virgin!

In the name of the I AM Presence of all life,
  I AM THAT I AM!

In the name of the Father-Mother God,
  I surrender the spirals of all selfishness and self-love,
  all self-pity, self-justification and self-condemnation—
  all self-awareness apart from the flame of Life!

In the name of the one true God, my own Real Self, I declare:
  I AM this day a son of God!
  I AM the blazing reality of the noonday!
  I AM the living presence of love!
  I AM the Word incarnate!
  I AM the threefold flame of love, wisdom, and power!
  I AM a son of God!

By the authority of the flame of immortal Truth which I AM,
  I surrender all human consciousness—
  the human ego, the human will, the human pride,
  the human intellect and all human momentums less than
  the fullness of the Christ Presence which I AM!

In the name of the I AM THAT I AM, the Almighty One,
  I surrender all identity apart from the blessed Son of God!

I AM THAT I AM!

I AM the full and perfect manifestation
   of the immaculate conception of divinity
   held in the Sacred Heart of Mary the Mother!

I AM the fullness of the presence of living Truth!

I AM the Holy Comforter!

I AM THAT I AM!

In the name of Jesus the Christ,
   I surrender all manifestations of evil,
   all indulgence in error!

I surrender, by the flame of God-Reality,
   all unreality and the dweller-on-the-threshold!

In the name of Jesus the Christ,
   I call to Michael the Archangel
   to descend into the forcefield of this God flame!

And by the authority of the I AM Presence,
   I demand the binding of the carnal mind, the antichrist,
   all luciferian, satanic and temporal power
   that has ever manifested in or through
   my four lower bodies and my soul consciousness!

In the name of Jesus the Christ,
   I call for the twelve legions of angels
   from the heart of the Father-Mother God
   to descend into this forcefield in time and space
   to consecrate the flame
   of the Cosmic Christ consciousness within me!

In the name of Jesus the Christ,
  in the name of my own Christ Self
  and the I AM Presence, the Beloved One,
  I surrender the not-self, the fallen one and the
  consciousness of sin, disease and death!

I surrender the spirals of disintegration and
  I invoke the spirals of integration where I am!

I AM THAT I AM!

In the name of Jesus the Christ
  and by the authority of the two witnesses, in the name
  and by the authority of the entire Spirit of the
  Great White Brotherhood and the World Mother,
  I surrender unto Almighty God this day
  all manifestations and incarnations of evil
  throughout the Macrocosm and the microcosm
  of my own self-awareness:

I surrender the carnal mind, the Antichrist, the Devil and Satan!
  I surrender unto the Lord the fallen ones,
  the rebellious spirits, all demons and discarnates and
  the archdeceivers of mankind!

I AM THAT I AM!

In the name of the living God, I surrender unto the Lord
  the dragon who stood before the Woman
  who was ready to be delivered,
  to devour her child as soon as it was born
  and who went to make war with the remnant of her seed!

In the name of Jesus Christ, I AM THAT I AM!

I AM Alpha and Omega,
   the beginning and the ending, saith the Lord, which is and
   which was and which is to come, the Almighty!

I AM THAT I AM!

In the name of the living God,
   I surrender the beast that rose up out of the sea
   and the dragon who gave him his power
   and his seat and great authority!

I surrender all that would usurp the consciousness
   of the Christ within the Macrocosm
   and the microcosm of my own self-awareness!

Lo, I AM THAT I AM!

I AM Alpha and Omega, the beginning and the ending!

In the name of Jesus the Christ,
   I surrender the beast that came up out of the earth!

I surrender the beast, the image of the beast,
   the mark of the beast and the number of his name!
In the name of Jesus the Christ,
   the King of kings and Lord of lords,
   in the name of the Faithful and True and the armies
   of the Lord, in the name of the Lamb
   and the hundred forty and four thousand,
   in the name of the Woman clothed with the Sun,

in the name of the Divine Manchild,
who liveth forevermore,
and the saints that overcame the dragon
by the blood of the Lamb
and by the word of their testimony,
I AM THAT I AM!

I surrender the dragon and the Antichrist, the beast,
the false prophet and the great whore
within the microcosm and the Macrocosm
of my own self-awareness!

> In the name of the Father and of the Mother
> and of the Son and of the Holy Spirit,
> Amen.

(You can give your personal prayer of surrender here.)

SWEET SURRENDER

It is not necessary to be human any longer. You are not the 'hewn' man. You are made in the image and likeness of God.

Cease your strutting about to be good humans doing good works, always busying yourself to reinforce your self-image as a good human being. Cease all of this. Become zero that God may become the one-hundred percent of Being where you are.

—EL MORYA

TWELVE

Sweet Surrender

"It is not necessary to be human any longer."[178]

Think about that. It is *not necessary* to be human any longer—a simple but extremely profound statement by El Morya. It implies that at one point it was necessary to be human, but *now* it is no longer necessary.

This is such a profound statement for our psyche that we must ponder it deeply in order to realize its powerful meaning for our life and our spiritual path. How long have we been on this path in this lifetime and others? How long have we believed that our oneness with God would happen sometime in the future, and until we got there we would do the best we could? How long have we thought that we needed a human consciousness, a human personality to help us navigate the world and walk the Path? A *long* time.

El Morya is telling us our human consciousness is not necessary any longer:

> *You are not the 'hewn' man. You are made in the image and likeness of God.*
>
> *Cease your strutting about to be good humans doing good works, always busying yourself to reinforce your self-image as a good human being. Cease all of this. Become zero that God may become the one-hundred percent of Being where you are.*[179]

As El Morya points out, we have been "strutting" around on this planet for a long time, doing some good things and some not-so-good things. It is the time and the hour for that to end. In fact, it's been such a perpetual struggle that we haven't recognized it for what it is.

I can hear the wheels turning: "You mean I am not supposed to defend the human self that I have so carefully constructed and nurtured, that I have thought to be my true self, that I have considered my true identity? But I need that identity! I've got to navigate the world. I have to relate to people, and my identity needs to be there so they can relate to me. If I truly surrender it, who will I be?"

Well, the ascended masters have not lost their identity or even the strength of their unique personalities. Mark Prophet didn't lose his sense of humor or genuine concern for each individual when he ascended. He and all the masters retain the special essence of their being. Perhaps we have feared that we would lose those parts of ourselves that are very near and dear to us. Many of us have been students of the ascended masters for years or even decades. We've worked very hard. We've surrendered a lot of things—but not everything.

The wheels are starting to turn again: "I need to keep parts of my identity so that I can serve the masters, right? I need something to put on the altar so that I can do things for them.

That's not so wrong, is it? After all, the masters have given us much to do, and I have to do my best to follow what they've told us and to do God's work on earth. Maybe it would be better if I wait until after I ascend to become the zero Morya talked about."

Becoming Zero

Becoming zero. It's probably safe to assume that there are not many people in the world who wake up in the morning and say, "God, help me to become zero." What does it means to be zero? It means to be who we are in the truest sense—which is to be our God Self.

Yes, we've worked very hard and been very busy with the masters' work—important work, vital work. We've given countless hours of decrees and violet flame. Wasn't that the deal: We do the masters' work, we balance our karma through service and decrees, and then we get to ascend? That's what I *thought* the deal was. Well, that *was* the deal. But that's only *part* of the deal. There is a requirement beyond the giving of our time and energy. *The requirement is the dissolution of our human self and the putting on of our Christ Self.*

This is not a halfway measure. In this lifetime, many of us have been walking around part human and part divine. It's been like a juggling act, trying to put on our divinity without giving up too much of our human self. But we can't continue juggling indefinitely—it doesn't work! We must eventually choose one or the other. So do we want to keep pushing that choice into the future or do we want to make it today?

The question to ask ourselves is, "Do I really want to walk the earth as a Christed one?" Oh, it may be easy to say "yes," but do we want it badly enough that we are willing to become zero? As we call for the dissolution of our human consciousness, do we trust God enough to believe that he will replace it with something much greater and much better? That we will indeed become one with our Christ Self? If we trust and believe that, then let us be willing to walk that path all the way.

Yet Morya counsels that we have not given our all:

> *Beloved hearts, I have come to take a collection. And my angels who serve with me in Darjeeling who have been in council chambers with me this morning are fully prepared and apprised that they now come with baskets in hand, which baskets they shall send up and down the rows of this congregation. You have withheld! And therefore I demand the givingness of all within you or the least portion, if you will have it, of that substance which has resisted the perfect will of God for your life.*
>
> *I will tell you why you sometimes tarry and dally in reserving for yourself that nebulous state of consciousness which is neither the will of God made perfect nor resistance to that will but a neutral zone where there is no catching you in any act of disobedience—but neither is there any finding you in any act of manifest grace or thrusting for a purpose! Ho!*
>
> *Thus, you see, in the withholding there is also the self-manipulative techniques of the carnal mind that would have you believe that you are doing nothing wrong. Well, it may be so. But the question is: Are you doing anything right?*[180]

We must admit that it's tempting and easy to posture ourselves and rationalize what we've done or haven't done. Yes, we believe in the teachings, we want to do the right thing. We know the rules (or most of them). We know what's good and not so good and we even self-correct when we find ourselves in violation of that. But is that enough? Have we been on our knees imploring God to fill us with the Holy Spirit, with our Christ consciousness? Have we gone after that something within us that resists doing that? Are we afraid it may change us, change our lives, and shake our comfortability? Are we succumbing to a weariness in well-doing and wondering how much more God wants of us? He wants all of us! He is a jealous God. Therefore, it's up to us to decide how much we really want of God.

The Cave of Human Creation

We are walking the most challenging path on this planet for the greatest prize. And whether we're sixteen or sixty, this is not the first lifetime we've done this. Our souls have been on this journey a long time. So who is the limiting factor in how much God consciousness we have embodied? We can all raise our hand; we have done it to ourselves.

Morya tells us, *"Thus in the comfortability of the aura of the Great White Brotherhood you have slackened your pace, you have withheld your giving, you have not reached down deep into your pockets to pull out the last coin—and in this case the coin is the last withholding of your will to do God's will!"*[181]

It can be easy to say, "Thy will be done, O God" or "Not my will but thine be done." Yet perhaps somewhere in our psyche and consciousness has been the word—"BUT." This slippery withholding goes something like, "Not my will but yours be done, O God. *However,* I just want to be sure you truly understand my situation, my needs, my responsibilities. So, yes I want your will, *but* could we keep it within these parameters because that's what works nicely for me right now. I really do want your will, *though*, and I want you to know that." This withholding is not so subtle when we look at it that way, is it?

Morya continues, *"And you cannot rest in a comfortable niche, for there are no comfortable niches for those who are the eagles—the eagle Mother, as Sanat Kumara—those who are the sons and daughters of God who embody the very body of Christ."*[182] This is our amazing calling—to embody the very body of Christ. It's a high calling, and because it is so high, it is demanding. And we are here because we want a demanding path. Our soul wants this. Our soul is weary of wandering around the planet and wandering through the ages. Our soul is ready to go Home.

Even so, we tend to rest in our human creation because it is familiar. In her lecture "Discipleship: The Five Steps of Initiation under the Living Word," Mother tells the story of an individual and the world he created:

> *One day I was counseling a particular individual, whose needs I had been meditating on for some time, and this chela brought up the issue of the friend. And I have seen that on the inner, this chela (having been able to navigate for a long time on the intellect and psychic ability) has very little Christ consciousness that is realized in the flesh as attainment, as the mind that works in him on a day-to-day basis, as the mind that is the present mind.*
>
> *So I said, "Why is this so?" And then El Morya showed me that above the head of this person—as he is standing, let us say, in the electronic belt, in the chamber of his being—it's like the roof of a cave. It's like dark solid rock, and that stands between him and his Holy Christ Self.*
>
> *So the cave is hollowed out. The cave is comfortable. It's a place of accommodation, a place one can live. It's as if the*

cave hollowed out represents the world, getting along just fine down here.

Now comes the day of reckoning. By not having developed the Christ mind, here is this solid rock of human creation, karma, and the dweller. And this individual is going to have to take picks, axes, dynamite, everything he can think of to blast this granite over his head to get through that electronic belt to the secret chamber of the heart...[183]

Pretty sobering teaching, isn't it, especially considering that we've all probably done something similar in this life or other lifetimes. We've worked hard to accommodate our dweller and what we thought were our human needs, and in doing so we shut out God and our Holy Christ Self. We've worked hard to create our own cave and to defend it. Yet when the guru came, as Mother did with the sacred fire and the Word, it shook our worlds. It startled us, shook us up, and showed us where we were vulnerable. We were no longer totally comfortable in that cave. We wanted more than temporal comfort because our soul recognized that the day of reckoning will come.

Being Vulnerable to God

Yet some of us have still not allowed ourselves to become vulnerable to God. In fact, ironically at some level we've worked hard to *not* be vulnerable to him because we're afraid of what might happen to us. We might even think we have good reasons why we haven't surrendered. After all, we aren't like Mother Teresa or Padre Pio, living in a monastery or a convent; we're in the world! We've got responsibilities and things to do. Nevertheless, at some level we know we can't continue living in our cave of comfortability indefinitely, half-human and half-God. Look around the world and you'll see that the vast majority of people have chosen to embody their dweller. It's an easy path to follow. And those who have chosen their dweller don't necessarily have psychological problems, because they've already made their choice. The lightbearers are different. We have chosen to be all of God, yet we have withheld some portion of ourselves, and that has created fear and tension in our psyche.

So how do we overcome our fear? How do we come to the point of surrendering the rest of ourselves? Don't we all want to become the Christ? Of course we do; we *do* want to walk this path. That's why we're here, that's why we've chosen to do what we do, and why we've devoted so many years of our lives to it. But we often seem to put our Christhood somewhere in the future by thinking, "Eventually I'm going to get there, but I need to pace myself."

Haven't we "paced" ourselves long enough? It's very easy to stay busy in this world, and we've been staying busy for probably hundreds or thousands of embodiments. Staying busy can be a distraction from our goal. We need to take the final stand for our Christhood. It's time to take a step back from all this busyness and decide, "Enough is enough. I am done with my human creation. I want to be who I AM. I want to embody my Christ Self!"

When are we going to decide that we can no longer bear to be separated from God? When will we reach the point where the pain of separation from Him is greater than our resistance to total surrender? How long until we become tired of not being God?

Here's an illustration of the dilemma of resistance and surrender. Oliver Cromwell was the leader of the English revolution. There's a story that after the revolution was over and the king had been deposed and Cromwell was ensconced in power, he went to a clergyman as he was quite troubled, wondering if as a Christian he should continue to wear a sword or not. The clergyman wisely told him to carry the sword until he could no longer bear to carry it because he felt like it was separating him from the presence of God.

I think many of us are at a point similar to Cromwell's. As chelas we don't want to keep being human because it's obviously not the highest path; but at the same time, we're not sure we are quite ready to let go of our humanness and become one with God.

Pain as the Portal to Bliss

I remember when Mother introduced us to the concept that pain is the portal to bliss. I was a little troubled by that. I didn't know why you had to go through pain to get to bliss because they seem contradictory. I'm sure there are many aspects to that concept, but I think one understanding is that when we experience the pain of feeling separated from the presence of God within us, it brings us to the point where we want to surrender. Surrendering is accompanied by the pain of separating out from our human creation and letting go of it, which is a necessary pain that frees us to become the Christ, become God, and experience the bliss of that elevated consciousness.

Personally, I have been surprised how much pain it has taken for me to arrive at the point where I'm willing to let go of my comfortability and the identity that I thought was the true me, including the things in my world that have propped me up and seemed so necessary—my job, my career, whatever. It has taken a lot of pain to get to the point where I can say, "God, it's not worth it any longer. It's too hard. I can't defend this human consciousness. I'm weary of it and I'm weary of the pain that it brings." Of course, I'm still in the process of surrendering, but I can testify to the grace of God's help along the way.

Morya teaches:

> *And you realize that all of your strength and heart and love and mind and will must go into this final spurt to the finish line where you come in, not second or third but first—each and every one of you, first as champions of Life....*
>
> *We cannot be tied to the yo-yo of the chela's consciousness who wants light, wants the assimilation of healing, comfort, joy, wisdom, and all sorts of talents and powers and yet who does not desire—with the fervent desire of the very soul itself—self-dissolution.*
>
> *It is the principle of the extinguishing of the candle of the lesser self. It is the intense desire to be God and the corresponding desire not to be. Therefore the riddle "to be or not to be" becomes most clear: to be God and not to be the human self.*
>
> *Thus the decision must be made in both directions.*[184]

El Morya makes it clear that it's not enough to do dweller calls on our human creation and it's not enough to say, "I want to be God." It takes both. It entails a willingness to surrender as well as the dissolving of the human self. I did a search on the word "surrender" in the *Pearls of Wisdom* online***, and I was amazed at how many times "surrender" was preceded by the word "sweet." Not "bitter" or "sacrificial," although I guess surrender might be considered sacrificial. The word "surrender" wasn't preceded by anything negative. Just "sweet"—sweet

---

*** online access to published dictations and lectures

surrender. Doesn't that sound good? Doesn't that feel good when you say it? Sweet surrender.

However, we cannot pretend that the dissolution of our human self will occur without pain. After all, there is a price to be paid for our Christhood. But I think many of us are nearing the point where we are willing to take God's hand and truly, truly surrender. When we reach that point of surrender, we can do it with love, not only for our own soul but also for the planet and her people.

Mother and the masters have taught that God is in pain on this planet; he's in pain in his sons and daughters and children of light. We sometimes become numb to what's going on in the world because of the sheer rapidity of events and the horrible things that are happening daily. Though in one sense we must keep our boundaries in order to function, we cannot avoid the pain on this planet. We cannot avoid the pain of our children and youth. So when facing these things, it helps to remember that what we do matters—not just for ourselves but also for others; our choices are key to our path and our soul's survival, but they are also key to the survival of other souls on this planet. Therefore, if we are willing to pay the price to put on our Christhood—willing to endure the lumps of our karma; willing to take the pummeling of our Holy Christ Self and the masters that will shake us up and separate us out from the human consciousness—we will indeed be different and this planet will be different!

Let us be willing to pay the price. We cannot look around for someone else to become the Christ. It's not your husband, your wife, your brother, your sister, your friend. It's you individually. It's me individually. We cannot look to anybody else but ourselves. And we cannot keep God waiting any longer. There are souls being lost and what we do *can* make a difference.

God knows we need to keep our balance, so this is not a call to fanaticism. This is a call to love and surrender—surrender to the sweetness of your true being, your Christ Self.

A Call to Sweet Surrender

El Morya's dictation that we're hearing today was given thirty years ago. Perhaps some of you heard it. I know I did, which makes me wonder how long I am going to dilly-dally around—thirty years is long enough! It really doesn't matter if you've followed these teachings thirty years or three months; this is the hour for each of us to move forward. Trusting in God, we can let go of fear, take his hand and hold it every step of the way.

At the same time, it helps to be aware and understand what we're going through. Understanding won't take away the pain because the dark nights our soul must go through are very real and intense. Each of us will have to go through them, just as the saints have done before us. It will be hard and there will be pain as we feel the temporal separation from God and a loss of human identity. But we are blessed and armed with key teachings the masters have given us regarding what we will go through. We will understand what's happening, so we won't lose our perspective. We also have friends, ministers and professionals we can talk with, who can help us if we need it.

Let's persevere and be willing to experience the pain and pass through it, knowing that there's a divine purpose and plan. If we give ourselves to God—whether we totally surrender or give whatever portion we can give today—God will honor our offering by doing what we ask. That will move us closer to the divine and farther from the human, which is the purpose of the Path. There are rocks and challenges and initiations along the way, but that happens in the world anyway. So why not be willing to accelerate dealing with our karma, accepting the things that come to us, and taking these initiations as a faster way to unite with God and get Home?

As we are going through this process, let's not forget that we can pray for the people around the world who are in pain. That is also something the saints did. Padre Pio's biggest mission and the biggest thrust in his life was to help alleviate the pain in people's lives. He loved so much that he was willing to bear the stigmata and the constant twenty-four-hour-a-day pain so that others might be helped. By God's grace, we have the gift of the violet flame, so perhaps we may not have to bear pain in that same way. But we do need devotion like his.

We're not looking to be martyrs. We're striving to be people who are willing to take God at his word and to do those things necessary to become the fullness of who we are meant to be. The time is no longer in the future—it is now. We have to begin somewhere. When Morya passes his collection plate during the dictation today, we need to have something to put in—at least a portion of ourselves; and hopefully for some of us, the all.

Mother taught that Guy Ballard reached a point on his path where he decided he'd had enough of his human creation. Did his life become easy after that? No. But he won his victory and became the Ascended Master Godfre. Mother also proved it could be done. She surrendered her all to God and walked the earth as the Christ. Was her life easy? Hardly! Yet she loved enough to bear the weight of world karma and the light of the Christ simultaneously.

It's a serious decision and a serious commitment that lies before us, but we have been preparing for this for eons. God has taken our hand and brought us to this point. It is the time and the hour when we can give to our God those things which we have previously withheld. We must trust him and know that he loves us and will not let us down. Though at times we may feel bereft and lonely and cut off from God, and we may lose things that seem important to us, we must trust that this is all for a purpose, that all things *do* work together for good for those who love God and choose to follow his purposes.[185]

And do you know what? When we surrender, God gives us back *everything* that we need to have to fulfill our divine plan. For example, when I found the teachings, I was a bit afraid that I would have to be a monk. I didn't want to be a monk; I wanted to get married. But I was willing to surrender, and I made the promise, "God, if that's what you want me to do, I will be a monk." I wasn't happy about it, but I was willing to do it. It wasn't too long after I made that surrender that God brought me the woman I was to marry, and I have remained happily married to this day.

Morya encourages us:

> *You need only whisper to me in the still small voice of your heart:*
>
> *Morya, I desire—*
> *With the deepest desiring of my soul—*
> *To be free this day*
> *From all within me*
> *That assails your holy purpose.*
>
> *When you come to the hour when this prayer is given without the dividing in your members, without a pulling in this direction and that, when you are truly sincere and determined and willing to pay the price—whatever it may*

be—for that point of surrender, you will find that in the twinkling of my own eye that substance can come under submission to your God Self and never raise its head again. And as the days and months proceed, you will, section by section, dissolve that beast.[186]

Let us follow the example of Mother and the saints who have gone before us. Let us surrender a greater increment of our being so that others might find the Truth, the Path, and the salvation of our God in the ascension.

Now is the time and the hour. Let us ponder what we are going to put in Morya's collection plate so that we might take a leap forward on our journey back to God. Yesterday's offering is no longer acceptable. Today is a new day of joy. Today is the day of our salvation. Today is the day of our sweet surrender.

A WALK WITH THE BUDDHA

It is Wesak, beloved. I ask you to celebrate my day by taking upon yourself the portion of world pain that is meet for you, the portion you can bear....

I ask you to pray for those who are discouraged, as you well know that discouragement is the devil's best tool.

—GAUTAMA BUDDHA

THIRTEEN

A Walk with the Buddha

O ur reading today is from the gospel of Luke, chapter 24:

> And, behold, two of them went that same day to a village called Emmaus, which was from Jerusalem about threescore furlongs. And they talked together of all these things which had happened. And it came to pass, that, while they communed together and reasoned, Jesus himself drew near, and went with them. But their eyes were holden that they should not know him....
>
> And they drew nigh unto the village, whither they went: and he made as though he would have gone further. But they constrained him, saying, Abide with us: for it is toward evening, and the day is far spent. And he went in to tarry with them. And it came to pass, as he sat at meat with them, he took bread, and blessed it, and brake, and gave to them. And their eyes were opened, and they knew him; and he vanished out of their sight. And they said one to another, Did not our heart burn within us, while he talked with us by the way, and while he opened to us the scriptures?[187]

The vision of walking and talking with our Lord is a compelling one. To walk as friends on the way and share such intimacy is a comforting thought, isn't it? And surely we have done this, perhaps physically in other embodiments, but certainly in this life with the messengers and also during dictations. Saint Germain even said that when he spoke through the messenger in a dictation given in 1977 that he also recorded on another track, "*a very specific dictation directed to you personally and to your soul directly from my heart.*"[188] Isn't that astounding? Every one of us got a personal dictation from the master!

The masters have been as dearest friends to our souls, and like Abraham who was the friend of God, we also aspire to be their friends. As we know, friendship is a two-way relationship. One of the great benefits of community is that we may call upon our friends for their prayers and physical support in our time of need. What a joy to be able to support each other in our most challenging initiations and karmic returns! And what a joy to be able to support and help the ascended masters and the angels as they seek to help the evolutions of earth!

We may not know the full benefit of our personal calls and service, but we do get glimpses of how thin the razor's edge of victory can be. For example, on the day of the recent massive earthquake in Nepal, the twenty-three-year-old daughter of a member of our community was working as a journalist at the base camp on Mount Everest. The quake triggered an avalanche that killed thirty-nine people at that base camp, but her daughter was saved at the last minute by a Sherpa who pulled her out of the way of the rockslide. While we don't know the equation of karma that day on the mountain, we do know people were praying for this dear woman and she was protected and saved. And we just heard today that through a series of semi-miraculous events, she was able to get off the mountain to a place where they were staging some seriously injured people to be airlifted to safety. She was able to board the same helicopter and is now safe in Katmandu.

This is why we pray for each other and for lightbearers in general. Mother once told us that if we could see the results of our calls we would never want to stop decreeing. Sometimes it's hard to see or know results, so it helps to be reminded of how thin that razor's edge is between victory and defeat, between a soul making it or not making it.

As I've been meditating on this, I've come to a much greater appreciation for the difficulties that the masters face in trying to help a planet and a wayward people that have become so dense that they can hardly hear the still small voice within, let alone the call of the masters. We may think the masters can just intercede and make things right, but the law of octaves and the law of free will reign supreme. If the people of this planet have put up a barrier to the intercession of the masters and the angels, then they cannot cross it. They cannot intercede unless we call them.

In the dictation we're hearing today, Gautama Buddha tells us that he is here on a rescue mission and that he is "*continually moving up and down the streets of the major cities, in the capitals of the nations and in out-of-the-way places.*"[189] That is quite a different image than the one I often hold of the Buddha as a great being of light in silent meditation, perhaps meditating on the Divine Mother.

When I think back to Gautama's midnight dictations on New Year's Eve in the Chapel of the Holy Grail at Camelot,[†††] the feeling I remember was something like a beautiful flower unfolding. The presence of the Buddha was so peaceful and unique that it was hard to grasp its fullness. And when we

---
††† The Summit Lighthouse headquarters in Malibu, California, from 1978-1987.

think of being in his presence, we may see ourselves as silent or speaking in a very soft voice lest we disturb his inner work. However, while his equanimity seems all-pervasive, it is only part of his great being. For in spite of what many in the world think, the Buddha is not passive. In fact, I read in another dictation that when he is in meditation he must maintain a point of perfect peace *because he holds the entire world in his aura.* Think about that: maintaining a point of perfect peace even as he feels in his aura every single thing that happens on this planet—every birth, every death, every joy, every war, every shock, everything! In his office as Lord of the World, Gautama sustains this planet by maintaining perfect peace. That is *not* a passive Buddha. That is a very active Buddha.

So we know, as he tells us, he's walking the streets, profoundly concerned for the many great souls that are slain and taken out of embodiment again and again because they do not have *"the wherewithal to defend themselves by sacred fire or to invoke angelic guardians of their mission."*[190] How then shall these souls be saved and protected? What does the master do when by cosmic law his intercession is limited because of the free will of the people?

Look Through the Eyes of the Lord of the World

As we yearn to walk with the Buddha, perhaps in all humility we can ask him if we can accompany him and talk with him on the rounds of his rescue mission. Let us be willing to answer the call he makes in this dictation to *"look through the eyes of the Lord of the World this day."*[191] It's not a small request for us to see what the Buddha sees. Because if we are willing to see what he sees or even a portion of it, we will be changed forever. What we can see and bear is a measure of how much love we can contain, for only love can bear to see what the Buddha sees.

As we celebrate Wesak we are celebrating Gautama's presence with us. It is interesting to note how Gautama describes Wesak as *"a type of Christmas, beloved. It is a Christmas when I bring gifts of my causal body and I deposit them in your causal bodies and the causal bodies of my disciples throughout the world."*[192] He brings us gifts of blessings!

Perhaps as children we thought only of ourselves at Christmas and what Santa might bring to us. But as Paul wrote in Corinthians, *"When I was a child, I spake as a child, I understood as a child, I thought as a child: but when I became a man, I put away childish things."*[193] Similarly, there was a time when we were children on the spiritual path, but now we are sons and daughters of God ready to put aside the childish tendency to think mostly of ourselves and what gifts Santa or the Buddha may bring us. Of course we welcome and embrace the gifts of Gautama's causal body on Wesak, but we also welcome and embrace the idea of giving back to one who has given so much for so long.

Gautama makes the following plea for us to help him on his rescue mission:

> We have sent many souls to earth who have come solely to serve mankind on the path of the Bodhisattva. They have placed themselves on the front lines of battle in every field; but for want of spiritual protection, they have been slain and taken out of embodiment again and again.
>
> I therefore seek from among you those who will identify yourselves as rescuers, those who will rescue the lightbearers who have come with a mantle yet have no backing from the world, no protection, no practical theology that they can apply. Blessed ones, these are the lonely ones.[194]

Some of us may feel like we're barely holding on as it is, and wonder how the masters can ask us to take on more. While some of us may truly be bearing all we can in this hour, perhaps some of us or even most of us are able to do more and give more. Almost every dictation has a call or plea for us to come up higher, to hold more light in harmony, to accelerate our personal path and our service. We have heard these things many times, and we may wonder how we can rise one more time.

There is a weariness that can set in after many years on the Path, and the masters understand this. In his dictation given at the Freedom conference in 1987, the Ascended Master Godfre told the story of being called to appear before the Karmic Board and questioned regarding his assessment of the lightbearers' willingness to respond to yet another call for action.

> *Blessed hearts, their question to me was: "Beloved Godfre, how many more times do you think the lightbearers can bear to hear this message and respond when they have been the watchmen of the night year in and year out and some of them embodiment after embodiment?"*
>
> *And I said to that august body, "I do understand, O Blessed Ones who are our sponsors, that they may be weary and even bowed down by this responsibility. But I tell you, I know their hearts, and I know that in their hearts they will not fail and they shall respond this time to the measure required by Lord Gautama Buddha."*[95]

Therefore, in spite of our weariness we must ask ourselves, "Can I summon the love and the fire and the renewed determination to walk with Gautama and allow him to show me what he wants me to see?"

I had an interesting experience this week involving seeing and not seeing. I recently bought some noise-canceling headphones to wear at the gym so I wouldn't have to listen to the rock music that's played there. I was getting ready to go to the gym and was looking for the soft black travel case the headphones came in. I knew it was somewhere in my office, and I looked and looked and looked but couldn't find it. It didn't make any sense, and finally in desperation I called out, "Holy Christ Self, open my eyes!" It wasn't really a prayer, it was one of those fiats that just comes out. And there was the case, right in front of me on a shelf in my closet. I had put it back in the shipping box it had come in. I was so sure about what I was looking for that it prevented me from actually seeing it! I think "Holy Christ Self, open my eyes!" is a call I need to make more often.

To See or Not to See

Seeing or not seeing can also be a matter of choice. Do you ever reach a point when you're looking at the news and you see a headline or you see an article on the internet and it looks so horrible that you can't bear to open it up? Sometimes I do that and think to myself, "I can't take on more negative energy right now. It's too much. I have to keep my balance." It is not easy to look upon the raw pain and suffering of the world, yet in one sense that is what Gautama is asking us to do. He's not asking us to be out of balance, but he's asking us to open our eyes that we might see more. Even so, I don't believe the Lord of the World, Gautama Buddha, will show us more than we can bear.

In his 1993 Pentecost address, the Maha Chohan talked about seeing and bearing pain:

> *This is why the ascended masters are serious about their Father's business. We see life and death daily. Sometimes we shield ourselves as the World Mother shields herself in a gossamer garment and veil of light. At other times we allow ourselves to feel pricking our bodies, as it were, a million needle points so that we might enter the life and death and coming and going and thought and feeling and anguish and cry and disease of all five and a half billion souls in embodiment and many more waiting to enter the wings of life.*[196]

We may not be ready to see what the Buddha and the masters see, but I believe we are ready to see more than we do now. What we see can propel us to intensify the fire of love in our hearts and reorder our lives and priorities so that more souls may be rescued and allowed to fulfill their missions.

You may be thinking, "I *have* tried to order my life so that I can fulfill not only the responsibilities of my day-to-day life but also the mandates and calls of the masters." And we have done that. But the time comes when we have to move forward even more, whether it's one step up the ladder of initiation or one increment in consciousness. And though we may not be able to do much more physically, we may be able to do much more spiritually. Let's consider what we can do today to move higher than we were yesterday so that we might bear a greater light and a greater weight while still doing all the things we need to do in our daily lives.

And here is an exciting thought: answering the call of Gautama will do much more than rescue souls that would otherwise be lost, because as we fulfill this sacred labor we will be profoundly and permanently changed ourselves. While this is not our primary motive, the willingness to bear more pain, even the pain of intense love in sacrificial service, could very well be the key to balancing our personal karma and making our ascension. Is it a coincidence that the work our Lord has given us to do can also be the key to our salvation? The Maha Chohan teaches, "*...the balancing of the karma of the centuries in service to the ascended masters has been the great device that Sanat Kumara has given to us.*"[197]

We have a need to do this not just out of the love of our hearts for the Buddha and for these precious souls, but *we* need to do it for ourselves. How else are we going to come up higher? I ask myself this question: "God, what do I need to do? What am I missing here? What am I not seeing that's right in front of my eyes so that I might take the next step?" And have we not been called to become the Buddha, even as we have been called to become the Christ?

If you're like me, you've wondered, "How do I become the Buddha?" The Maha Chohan gives us this key: "*So you see, beloved, when you allow yourself to see all things and know all things, you must be well on your way to being the Buddha in manifestation.*"[198] I'll say that again: "when you allow yourself to see all things and know all things, you must be well on your way to being the Buddha in manifestation." The Maha Chohan continues, "*Never mind whether the Buddha is in manifestation in your causal body; see that the Buddha is incarnating within you daily.*"[199]

Some people may believe that ignorance is bliss but we know that's not true. We also know that seeing everything and knowing everything *can* be bliss, but it comes with the responsibility of being able to hold everything in light and in harmony.

A Portion of World Pain

We can ask Gautama Buddha to open our eyes that we might truly see what is the equation of our victory and the victory of planet Earth. I believe the two go hand in hand and can't really be separated. It won't work to say, "Well, I just want to win my victory, so I better go do this with the Buddha." That's not a motivation of love. God is in pain on this planet. Aligning ourselves with the Buddha's love leads us to ask what we can do to ease the pain of God on earth, what we can do to comfort a single soul.

Gautama opens our eyes and our awareness even to the plight of the angels and lightbearers who have vowed to stand for the light. He says:

> *I ask you to pray for those who are discouraged, as you well know that discouragement is the devil's best tool. Pray for all in the earth who are discouraged; and pray for the protection of those mighty angels who have taken embodiment and moved among the people and laid down their lives to save others again and again.*
>
> *When angels who have taken on human form come before me and the Lords of Karma for an audience at the conclusion of a lifetime, many of them plead to be allowed to reincarnate immediately so that they might resume their efforts to defend the mankind of earth against the wiles of the wicked. I say to you, beloved, there are many angels in embodiment, untold millions, who live only to serve and to help others. They are on the front lines, caring for others who are dying on the battlefields. And they themselves are often lost in the battle, for there is no end to their courage.*[200]

It's humbling, isn't it, to hear about these angels and their unselfishness and their willingness to go forth again and again.

So what is Gautama's plan for rescuing the precious souls he talks about in this dictation? It is simple yet profound as revealed in his request:

> *It is Wesak, beloved. I ask you to celebrate my day by taking upon yourself the portion of world pain that is meet for you, the portion you can bear. And I ask you again to pray for those whom God has sent to assist mankind who have no support or reinforcements for their mission.*[201]

As we are walking with the Buddha, it does not need to be an awkward moment for us when he asks us to take on more world pain, because when we trust God and the masters, we trust that they would not ask us to do anything that we cannot do if we are willing and will make the effort. The key is in the words "the portion of world pain that is meet for you, the portion you can bear." That is the fine print that allows us to be at peace with this holy calling.

That doesn't mean it will be easy, for the pain is real and the weight is real. But let us also remember that pain is the portal to bliss. That portion of pain will most likely look and feel differently for each of us since we are at different levels of attainment and of embodying love. Gautama is not asking us to individually hold the balance for the world as the messengers were required to do, and I don't believe that he is asking us to become "victim souls" like many of the Catholic saints who seemed to be forever tormented and covered with boils or what not. Instead, we have the violet flame—the miracle potion that transmutes pain and karma.

Jesus taught that when we fast we should keep it hidden from the world, washing our faces and not going around with a mournful look. Similarly, Gautama is not calling us to martyrdom! He is calling us to take the tools we have been given and apply them in a *balanced and focused* effort to rescue souls, knowing all the while that *God is the doer*. And of course, that's the mystery—it's not our human self that is the doer; God is the doer!

We position ourselves and order our lives to allow us to give the maximum possible while still keeping our balance. For those new to the Path this may mean a commitment to do the "Heart, Head and Hand" decrees daily. For others it may require a greater attention to our daily violet flame, rosaries and other rituals and increasing our ability to hold more light in harmony. While doing this, we mustn't allow ourselves to be overwhelmed by the magnitude of the needs on earth or to doubt that what we do individually matters. If each one of us does our part, then the planet and many, many souls can be saved. Remember Igor, the Russian peasant boy whose pure prayers allowed God to save millions during the Russian revolution.

In striving to do our part, it's good to watch out for the "what's the use" syndrome that murmurs: "The world is so dark. Everything is going wrong. Just look at our culture and society and all the wars and terrorism. We fought the good fight but can we really turn it around?" *God* can turn it around! We have to roll back the projection that what we do does not matter and won't make a difference. While we don't know the final outcome of the battle of Armageddon on planet Earth, we know that the victory is already won at the etheric level. Therefore, while we don't know what is going to happen physically, we do know that if we do our part, the victory *can* be won here below!

Love Motivates Us to Help Save Souls

Godfre has reminded us, "*You are not called to go to war, to go into battle where you may lose your life or even give your life in honor and nobility.*"[202] While I think we are all grateful for that, one of the challenges we do face is keeping a true perspective of the urgent need for our daily calls. We're almost drowned by the noise of the world and a culture that celebrates self-indulgence and an "eat, drink and be merry" attitude: "You work so hard. Be good to yourself. You need this; you need that; you need a vacation." Obviously we need a break sometimes, but be careful of the voice that says, "Just be like everybody else. Go easy on yourself." In some ways, living in the so-called "normal" world is harder than being on the front lines because when we don't have the reality of life and death in front of us, it is harder to keep a proper perspective.

Living in a culture that extols an attitude of selfishness and not worrying about others, it is a challenge to maintain the point of focus and intensity that is the spiritual requirement of the hour. We have to find creative ways to do that: to stay in balance in our physical, mental and emotional bodies; to have time for recreation and meeting obligations; to order our lives in a way that allows us to maximize the spiritual work we are doing. Such discipline and order in our lives can make the difference for many, as it did for the young girl on Mount Everest who was pulled out of harm's way at the last second. We want to be like the Buddha—awake! Therefore we must determine that the sweet song of death this culture produces will not put us to sleep.

As we celebrate Wesak in this hour, knowing that Gautama comes with gifts from his causal body, what are we going to give the Buddha in return? Wouldn't the best gift be to answer his call to join him in rescuing lost souls? Then what can motivate us to do this? What can motivate us to allow God to open our eyes and see things that are painful and hard? What can motivate us to order our lives that we might help bear a greater portion of world pain? Of course the answer is love—love for God and his creation; love of light in hearts that are burdened; love that will ease the discouragement of so many on earth, the lonely ones who do not have the hope of salvation that we have or the spiritual tools that can help them.

I'm not going to ask for a show of hands, but does anyone in this room or on the broadcast ever get discouraged? Of course we do! But look what we have! Think of souls who don't have the knowledge we have that there is a way out of our personal and planetary dilemma. Let us pray for the angels to whisper in their ears how important they are.

The path we're walking is not the way of the world, but it is *our* way. It can be as simple as remembering to make hourly calls to Sanat Kumara as he has asked us to do. It can be following Gautama's recommendation to *"Use your odd moments and travel time to give decrees for protection, not only for yourselves but also for every soul of light who holds the line at the battlefront..."*[203]

When I went to Summit University a student asked the teaching assistant, "If we're out running errands, do we have to give decree 6.05 for traveling protection every time we get back in the car?" I think the answer to that may be to do it if you feel the need to do it. I also think that when we're making the calls for traveling protection, even if we don't think *we* need it, there are certainly souls somewhere on earth who do need those calls. So maybe you don't personally need traveling protection every time you stop at a store and then get back into your car, but maybe someone else does. Those are moments that are not being taken away from something else; since you're already in the car and you're not doing anything else, you might as well take advantage of the time.

The Details of Chelaship

One of the things I learned after many years on the Path is that at a certain stage being more attentive to the details of my chelaship and service became essential. I felt I was being held to a higher standard, and in order to meet it I had to be much more attentive than before to all aspects of my life, my thoughts, my feelings and my actions. This is also true in how we respond to the call of the master; it is indeed the seemingly little things that will make a difference. While it is important to hear the call of the master and respond in the affirmative, it is more important to consciously *do something different* from what we have been doing. If we don't change what we are doing, we may stay in the same place or even go backwards on the Path. If we are going to become the Christ or the Buddha in manifestation, we know *something* has to change. With fiery love we have to do more and give more, not just in terms of hours or devotion, but in terms of internalizing and becoming God's light.

God needs us in embodiment, holding the quotient of light as well as the burden that is appropriate for us. We don't live in monasteries or convents and we have many responsibilities to families, jobs, et cetera. We can always make the calls that whatever portion we bear will not compromise our daily responsibilities to others. That portion might be various aches and pains that test our ability to stay harmonious while fulfilling our responsibilities. Some of the saints used to wear hair shirts to see if they could keep their harmony while being constantly irritated. Well, we don't have to wear hair shirts because we can receive these same tests in our daily lives, and when we recognize them as tests we can pass them more easily.

Something as mundane as a canker sore can be an instrument of bearing world pain when we keep our harmony and consecrate our pain to allow God to help others. I remember El Morya gave a message to a soul who had just been diagnosed with cancer. Along with his comfort, the gist of the message was for this person to make the calls for other people to be helped through the pain and suffering that they were going through.

When we make the call to bear world pain at a greater level, we shouldn't be surprised or concerned when something happens. Instead, we need to be mindful and remember our offer when something comes our way. We can see it as an honor and an opportunity for mastery, knowing it could even come in seemingly mundane things that happen in our daily lives. If you feel you have more than you can bear in harmony, you can call for it to be adjusted. Work with God and the angels to find your place of balance.

Walk With Joy

As we walk with Gautama and see in part what he sees and feel a portion of the pain he feels, he reminds us that the ascended masters do not walk in the fullness of joy because they also bear the burden of world pain. Yet Gautama has intense love for each soul and his musical keynote is the "Ode to Joy." In walking with him, we must also strive to have a portion of joy because joy is inherent in God's nature and not dependent on outer circumstances. When we experience pain and suffering—whether it's personal or planetary karma—we make the effort to embody joy at the same time. If we don't embody true joy, who will? We're not talking about the frivolous happiness many people are seeking, but the intense and powerful *joy of God.*

The Maha Chohan teaches us about the path of joy amidst the suffering of the world: *"You say, 'How can I be joyous when I see suffering around me?' You can rejoice that the law is good, that the law is just, and that all suffering shall be turned to light, shall be turned to God-victory when mankind no longer have the need to suffer."*[204]

And then there is the joy that you are answering the call of the master and that God in you is making a difference. It brings joy just knowing, "I can do something. I can make myself available to God. I know that God in me is the doer, and I am willing to position myself whatever way is best—mentally, physically, spiritually, emotionally—so that God may use this body temple and may use the light I invoke to help others. There is a purpose for my life. There is a reason to get up in the morning and go do something. Even if I have to see the pain of the world, I know that someone somewhere will be helped."

The Maha Chohan teaches when you are *"...willing to suffer for a little while the condemnation of this world that you might enter the realms of glory and your great home of light...you will bring literally millions of souls with you."*[205]

Millions! Can we do that at a human level? I can hardly get myself out of bed some mornings, so how can I help get millions of souls to heaven? Well, I can't, but God can! God can save millions by the power of our Mighty I AM Presence and through the light we invoke. He can do it through our willingness to discipline ourselves on the path of initiation, to order our lives, to see what the Buddha wants us to see, and to bear with joy that portion of pain that God wants us to bear. Perhaps we will not see the fullness of what he sees. However, aren't we willing to see more now without letting the pain of what we see overwhelm us, but instead using what we are shown to make a call or invocation? When we put our love for God and his precious souls into action, we can draw down more light and more violet flame to help hold the balance for these souls.

This is our high and holy calling. It is a sacred trust that reflects the unbreakable bond of the guru-chela relationship. Even with that bond there are times that this can feel like a lonely path, when the masters seem far away and perhaps unaware of our trials. Have you ever asked, "God, are you there? Are you listening? Do you hear me? Can you see what's happening to me?" You might say it in a more polite way, but isn't that sometimes the feeling we have? The truth is that such times can often push us to demonstrate our own mastery.

God is not simply a genie in a bottle who comes and does things at our beckoning. Yes, he does respond to our calls, but if we are working to put on our Christhood and become the Buddha, we will be tested to develop and demonstrate our mastery. Sometimes that seems like a lonely path. But the Maha Chohan comforts us by sharing the masters' perspective, *"Nor can you know how we know your sorrows and how we know your testings and how we know and laud your victories."*[206]

The sometimes seeming absence of God or the masters in our lives doesn't mean that they aren't there. It doesn't mean that they aren't intimately involved in and aware of what we're going through and have compassion for us. Rather they are holding us to the standard that will allow us to progress on our own spiritual path and help to save others. We can be saved because we have knowledge, the truth, and the violet flame, but the masters are concerned with those who do not have this knowledge or the ability to even use it if they had it.

Will we respond one more time to another call to action? The answer is a resounding "Yes!" And we will keep responding as God gives us the strength to do so.

Gautama must hold perfect peace in his being in order to hold the balance for every soul on this planet. He feels the pain of all, even the cry of a single child that has lost his mother. If we can't comprehend the needs and suffering of the billions as he does, then we can start by thinking of one person, one soul who will open the floodgates of compassion in our hearts.

If we are to walk with the Buddha, then let us walk with him not only as our Guru and Lord, but also as a friend. And let us bear with peace whatever portion is meet for us to bear. Let this be the gift that we give to Gautama on Wesak.

This is not the way of the world, but it is our way. Whether we are in the garden with our Lord in peace and communion or in places of great pain, *this* is our way.

CLAIM YOUR ADEPTSHIP!

Blessed ones, speak as Christ would speak and Christ will speak through you.... Think as Christ would think and Christ will think through you and the mind of God will become congruent with the physical vessel.

—ARCHANGEL JOPHIEL AND ARCHEIA HOPE

FOURTEEN

Claim Your Adeptship!

I was recently shopping on the internet, looking for religious books, and one of the recommended books caught my eye, *The Imitation of Mary* by Thomas à Kempis. Since his book *The Imitation of Christ* has so many keys for the path to sainthood, I was excited to learn there was another book by him and I ordered it right away. Actually, he didn't write it as a book; someone else went through all his writings and compiled everything that he said about Mary.

This reading is from chapter 8 of the book titled "Mary, Mediatrix of All Grace."

> *Dear Brothers, be faithful servants of Jesus Christ and loving devotees of His most holy Mother, the Virgin Mary, if you desire to be forever happy with them in heaven.*
>
> *You will be dear to God and His blessed Mother if you are humble of heart and chaste of body; if you are moderate in speech, prudent, conscientious, and self-controlled; and do not become for anyone an occasion of scandal or legitimate complaint.*

> It is greatly helpful for your salvation, for the honor of God, and for the praise of the Blessed Virgin, that you be devoted to prayer, committed to study and work, meek when rebuked, temperate in eating, chaste in the use of your eyes, and straight-forward in all your behavior.
>
> Therefore, if you desire worthily to praise and properly to venerate the Blessed Virgin, act as children of God: with simplicity, without malice or spite, and without lying, becoming angry, quarreling, complaining or being suspicious. Rather for the sake of Jesus and Mary endure every adversity with fraternal charity, humility, and patience in imitation of the lives of the Saints; do this for the sake of your own peace and for the edification of others, but above all do it that you may enjoy the glory of the Holy Trinity.[207]

If someone asked you to characterize what these words portray, what would you say? My first thought was that it described a holy life, one that a monk or a nun or a serious chela of the ascended masters might aspire too—a life of devotion, peacefulness, gentleness and humility. But how many of us would consider it the description of an adept?

When I think of an adept, I think of Mark Prophet who could control the weather or precipitate a hundred dollar bill if needed. I think of the masters in the East who have complete mastery of the body, some needing neither food nor drink. I think of Padre Pio who could bi-locate and minister to those in need in two places at once. And when I think of an adept in those terms, I never really considered that I would accomplish such things in my lifetime; it seemed far more advanced than any attainment I perceive in myself. Yet in the dictation we are hearing today, Mother Mary tells us to claim our reward, and that reward is adeptship!

Considering Mother Mary's teaching we can rethink our attitude toward adeptship and begin to see it as attainable, even as we need to see our Christhood as being attainable. In truth, the path of Christhood is not separate from the path of becoming an adept. So, for the sake of believability, it seems we need to stop thinking of adeptship just as physical phenomena—turning water into wine, walking on water, precipitating things, and so on. It seems we need to look at it in the terms described in our reading today. If we keep our harmony and live a holy life day in and day out then perhaps, by God's grace, we will attain part or all of the adeptship of the saints.

It's striking that Mother Mary asks in her dictation we're hearing today, *"Why, who among you has the greatest power of all? It is the little child. It is the little child! ... So, except ye be converted and become as little children, ye shall in no wise enter into the kingdom, the consciousness of God."*[208]

Note her use of the word "converted." How are we converted to become as a little child? Could it be that the way we think and the way we perceive ourselves need to change? The ego almost invariably chimes in, "You think I need to be converted to become as a little child? That might sound well and good, but I have responsibilities; I have duties, you know. I'm an adult. I need to do adult things." But do we? It's easy to wonder if we are talking about the same thing. How does becoming as a little child relate to becoming an adept? It may seem like a mystery, but perhaps it isn't.

Become as a Little Child

We do not attain adeptship by the length of time we spend studying and practicing these teachings or serving on the staff of the Church. Neither do we attain it because we have great knowledge of the teachings; having a well-developed mental body can even be a hindrance on the Path. While it might be tempting to equate mental acuity and knowledge with spiritual attainment, Mother Mary says, "*...those who are dependent on the human mind cannot let go and let God work through them. What a pity! What a sorrowful state to have that human mind be the only mind that you depend upon!*"[209]

She also tells us:

> *It is good to be the little child for a season, for some hours, even once a day throughout the year, to feel your helplessness and to know when you place your hand in mine or in the hand of Saint Germain or El Morya that everything will come full circle, all will come to resolution and you will know that sense of freedom as if you were free-falling, knowing that we will catch you.*
>
> *Thus, by this exercise of love and devotion, you let go of being the responsible one, the one that must take care of everything and everyone.*[210]

Brother Lawrence gives us similar advice in his book *The Practice of the Presence of God* (which I recommend as a great companion to *The Imitation of Christ*):

> *We must give ourselves entirely and in complete abandonment to God, both in temporal and in spiritual matters. We must find our contentment in the execution of His will, whether He leads us by sufferings or by consolations, so that everything should seem the same to a person who has truly abandoned himself.*[211]

Being totally abandoned and content with sufferings, the same as with consolations, sounds very Buddhic, or perhaps like one who has the attainment of an adept, don't you think?

I remember being so sick once that I couldn't do anything for myself or anyone else. When you feel that weak and that incapable of doing anything, it's a perfect time to be like a child as Mother Mary said, to accept that we can do nothing but trust in God and let go of everything else. It was easy for me to do that when I was that sick; it was really a wonderful, peaceful feeling. Unfortunately, when I got better, I once again started thinking that I was the doer and had much to do.

It's like a Zen koan. We know we have responsibilities and must fulfill them because others are dependent upon us. At the same time, we must surrender the idea that we are doing them, and remember that God is the doer. We must allow our Christ Self to be the doer.

Ah, perhaps we are getting somewhere in understanding adeptship.

Mother Mary continues:

> *Pause for a moment and remember who is the doer within you and who is the liberator and how it is the sense of struggle that makes the struggle. And if you would be a hero or a heroine or a knight in shining armour, remember that only God can work the work through you. Therefore self-effacement is empowerment.*[212]

Self-Effacement Is Empowerment

Ponder that: "Self-effacement is empowerment." What a transformative concept! Does self-effacement mean that we go around with our heads down, meek and lowly? Maybe in some cases that would be good for us. Or does self-effacement mean stepping aside—being converted from the consciousness that somehow we're separate from God and we are the doer who has to do all these things for all these people—and allowing God to be the doer within us. When we do that, we do become as a little child, don't we? We wait for our Father-Mother God to show us the way, we give them the glory for each accomplishment and we recognize there is no separation. Jesus said it so eloquently, *"Believest thou not that I am in the Father, and the Father in me? the words that I speak unto you I speak not of myself: but the Father that dwelleth in me, he doeth the works."*[213]

It is our perception of separation that keeps us separate, and I'm not sure just acknowledging that is going to change it overnight. Nevertheless, it's an awareness that we need in order to convert ourselves from our perception of who we think we are to being who we truly are.

Some of us might have a nagging concern somewhere in our consciousness: "If I let God do everything through me and he gets all the glory, well then, who am I?" Each one of our souls is unique, and our oneness with our Holy Christ Self does not take that uniqueness away. Yes, it's true that the same Christ consciousness that was in Jesus is also in our Christ Self, but we don't become a non-person when we become that Christ. Instead, we become all that we are intended to be. Think of the differences between the ascended masters. Think of El Morya on one hand and Mother Mary on the other. Are they both the Christ? Yes! Are they both ascended masters? Yes! Are they each unique in all of cosmos? Yes! So we need to let go of the concept or mindset that we are separated from God, that somehow we are entirely different from him; we need to consider that perhaps the difference is simply our human consciousness, and we need to let go of it.

As Catherine of Sienna did when she recited the words Jesus had given her, *"Thou the all, I the nothing,"* we become the All with a capital A when we know we are nothing. This same message is in *The Imitation of Christ*, but for some reason, we may have a hard time letting that message sink into the deepest level of our being so that it truly transforms us.

Mother Mary says:

> To be an adept means to have a certain mastery for the holding of light...you are moved neither to the right nor to the left, neither up nor down by circumstances, by whatever negative is hurled at you. Adeptship is to be unmoved, to be in the center of the T'ai Chi, to know oneself supremely as God but never as a human god—for God has displaced the human.[214]

How profound: When one becomes an adept, God has displaced the human.

As I have shared before, there is a danger that when people study these teachings and gain an intellectual knowledge of them, they want to merge that intellectual knowledge with their human consciousness in order to be well-thought-of by men. Not to give God the glory, but to glorify themselves because they know so much. At that point, they become a false teacher, whether that was their desire or not. We have to be wary of that pitfall. While we know it's important to study and understand the teachings, it's a sidetrack to believe that an intellectual knowledge of the teachings will get us Home; it won't.

I was thinking the other day how symbolic kneeling in prayer is. Getting on our knees to pray to our Father-Mother God, to our Holy Christ Self, is an act of submission. We are affirming that our human self is the lesser and God is the greater. Some nights we may not feel like getting down on our knees because it's too cold in our room or we're too tired or sore or whatever. "Oh, I'll just say my prayers lying in bed." Well, that's fine sometimes, but it's important that we daily acknowledge God and his supremacy in our being by submission. When we kneel before our God, we are submitting to him, and submission or surrender is a crucial step in our Christhood, our adeptship.

Let's briefly recap what we've covered: It seems quite obvious that we need to expand our definition of adeptship beyond simply having mastery over the physical world, for even black magicians who misuse light and energy can have that. Our definition of adeptship needs to include becoming like a little child, knowing that God is the doer, and being unmoved by any circumstance.

Pursue the Path of the Imitation of Christ

Knowing that God is the doer is key to putting on our Christhood; and putting on our Christhood certainly implies adeptship. Archangel Gabriel says that the person *"who will claim his Christhood and call forth the Father and the Son to take up their abode in his temple, that one may displace the Darkness of ten thousand-times-ten thousand individuals."*[215] One person displacing the darkness of a hundred million—wow! I think we all agree that our human consciousness is not able to do that; it's not even able to displace the darkness of one! We need to remember that "I of myself can do nothing," but God in me—as I call for my Christ Self and I AM Presence to occupy my entire consciousness, being and world—can do that.

Mother gave a lecture titled "The Path of Personal Christhood" that is so clear and so practical that every one of us can follow her advice from today onward until we have achieved our goal. In that lecture, Mother tells us that Archangel Jophiel and Archeia Hope explain that putting on our Christhood *"is a very gradual process. It doesn't happen overnight and that is why you have to be attentive day by day."*[216] Notice the word "attentive." We need to be attentive to how we speak, how we act and react, and note whether we are allowing our Christ Self to manifest within us moment by moment.

We might wonder how we can tell when we are the vessel of our Christ Self. Jophiel and Hope tell us:

> *When you hear yourself saying things that you know your Holy Christ Self would not say, then you know that that Holy Christ Self has ascended far above you and cannot enter in. When you say things with a tone of voice of condescension, with criticism, with burden or depression, sarcasm or the vibration of gossip, then you will know your Holy Christ Self cannot enter; for it is the law of God.*[217]

It is the law of God that your Holy Christ Self cannot be where you are when you engage in those things. Therefore we must pursue the path of the imitation of Christ. It takes a humble heart and a determination to imitate Christ, to follow the path of Christhood. Daily reading from *The Imitation of Christ* helps remind us of what it is to walk in Christ's footprints.

Jophiel and Hope give more instructions:

> *Speak as you know or believe Christ would speak, with love but firmness, sternness where required, mercy when it is due, soft-spoken when needed, in the intensity of the sacred fire when you would awake a soul who will not be awakened.*

> *Blessed ones, speak as Christ would speak and Christ will speak through you.... Think as Christ would think and Christ will think through you and the mind of God will become congruent with the physical vessel.... When you think thoughts impure, unkind, critical, intolerant, blessed hearts, the mind of Christ is not in you.*[218]

In the moment when you catch yourself doing something untoward, you apologize to someone, you make things right, you give your calls to the violet flame, and you get right back into communion with God with ever more alertness to see to it that you are in control of thought, feeling, and spoken word.

It's not easy to be unmoved by any circumstance, and God does not ask us to repress or deny our feelings of happiness or pain or sorrow or whatever it is that may come upon us. Of course we have these feelings. But in the midst of whatever comes our way, we can affirm the Christ within us and stand on that rock of Christ. It is a matter of not being moved from our commitment to our Christhood.

Here are a couple more tips Mother gave during her lecture, "*When you have feelings that are not feelings of the compassionate Christ, then you know Christ is not in you.*"[219] When that happens, you ask yourself, "Well, why do I have those feelings?" You get out your books on psychology, you read about the inner child, you go to work with those workbooks, and you get to the bottom of why you have those feelings so that you will be made whole. "*...Finally, beloved, perform deeds that you know Christ would perform and shun those which Christ would not engage in.*"[220]

WWJD? Do you remember that from a few years ago? "What would Jesus do?" The Christians who asked themselves that question were on to something. It may not always be as hard as you think. We really do know in most cases what the right thing to do is, but we often rationalize not doing it for some reason or another.

Keeping Our Harmony

As we imitate Christ, Mother tells us that others will imitate us—not necessarily just those around us, but also souls around the world who tune in to what we are doing. Isn't that amazing? People take a soul reading of us, and what we do they will do. It is truly a sacred responsibility to live that which we have been taught. The ego inevitably revs up excuses why not to continually strive to imitate Christ. "You know, I'm a human being. I've got to give myself a little slack sometimes." Is that the path of the saints? Obviously it isn't. Saints pay attention to detail. We don't want to engage in fanaticism, thinking we're going to fulfill everything by following the letter of the law. But we do want to pay attention to the teachings we have been given, because following them matters to our personal Christhood. Our becoming the Christ in turn affects the other sons and daughters of God and children of the light on this planet.

Is adeptship our goal? I think every one of us would answer "Yes!" But what if our next lesson in adeptship is keeping our harmony? While we might do a pretty good job of keeping our harmony compared to many in the world, that isn't the standard by which we measure ourselves. Mother's lecture "Imperil" exposed how serious irritation, mild dislike, fear and other negative energies can be breaches of harmony. She definitely put our momentum on harmony in perspective! For instance, how often do we get irritated with someone or use a tone of voice that we know is not Christlike? We need to watch ourselves and begin to demonstrate the adeptship that we are claiming as our reward. And when we do come up short, let's own it, let's work on it, let's apologize when needed, put it in the violet flame, and pray to receive that test again.

Anger is an obvious rift in harmony. In "The Path of Personal Christhood," Mother explains two types of vortices of anger we can get caught in: the first comes from a source you can't see, and the other is the in-your-face type of anger. The first occurs when we are feeling angry and don't know why. If we can't figure out the source of the anger, we usually assume, "Well, it must be a pocket of anger coming up from my subconscious mind, my electronic belt," and in fact, it could be that. But it can also be coming from an unknown source. Mother said it could simply be the *"the force of Antichrist attacking the path of our personal Christhood."*[221] If we are not careful, it is easy to allow that anger to express through our words and feelings. Recognizing when we are under this energy and responding appropriately is an opportunity to demonstrate our adeptship. So the key is to recognize it, don't identify with it, and don't express it. If we slip, we step back, rebuke the energy, and reclaim our harmony.

In some ways, it might be easier to be impersonal when confronted with unknown energy, but what about instances where you know the source? How often have we had an argument or a strong difference of opinion when we felt we were totally right and the other person was wrong. As Mother points out, we may be feeling quite self-righteous at that point: "Well, after all, I'm right, aren't I?" But there are always different perspectives.

We have a little ritual at our house that we follow most weeknights. After dinner, the dishes and homework, we watch an old sitcom from the fifties or sixties on Netflix, since the older shows seem the best ones for a family to watch these days. One night we were watching an old episode of *The Dick Van*

Dyke Show. For those of you who don't remember this show, it centers around Dick Van Dyke, his wife and young son. This particular episode started out with a fight between him and his TV wife over a very trivial matter. Sounds familiar, doesn't it? It got to be quite a fight, at least by 1960's standards, and ended with Dick's character storming out the door. The rest of the episode portrayed he and his wife telling others about the fight from their perspective. Since the viewers had seen the fight, the plot was to show how the person's perception compared to the reality of what happened. It was pretty funny to see how differently each one perceived the fight, and how they misrepresented their own actions and made the other person the cause of the whole mess. Of course, it was exaggerated to make it funny, but it really portrayed a point of human nature: "Humph! Well, it was all her (or his) fault, and I was really right."

Does this ring a bell in your life? We all probably have that tendency at times. And so we have to remember to allow God to be harmonious in us. We can never be a true adept if "being right" is more important than being harmonious! That's a hard lesson sometimes. Mother says:

> *Maybe you really are right but being right is not the ultimate point. And so, if you are right and someone else is not going to admit that, what you have to be concerned about is making peace with your God.*
>
> *So if it is love that you want and God's love flowing through you, you have to disconnect—from that feeling of being right. You have to be silent, either allow them to go on in a tirade or excuse yourself by and by. But whatever it is, serve the Christ in that person.*[222]

Isn't that interesting? She didn't say make peace with the other person. She said you have to make peace with God. The reason we must make peace with God is because harboring an inharmonious vibration does not allow our Holy Christ Self to be present in our temple. Naturally, we need to make peace with the other person to the best of our ability, but making peace with God is the most important thing. Then you can serve the Christ in that person, regardless of what their human consciousness is saying or doing.

Priming the Pump of Love and Devotion

I have confidence that if we ask God to give us tests of adeptship this week, we will receive them. If you don't believe that, try asking God for tests of humility and see what happens! We are all preparing for the final exams that will get us Home, and that requires passing our tests, both great and small. We know about the dark night of the soul and the dark night of the Spirit. If we prepare in humility and devotion, we can pass these tests. In the meantime, being willing to take lesser tests now will strengthen us for passing bigger ones. This is nothing new, but sometimes we forget how exacting the Path is. Also, we don't always recognize tests when they come our way, because some are so subtle and seemingly minor that we dismiss them.

Mother Mary helps us understand some keys that the saints found to passing tests and becoming adepts:

> *You have the Teachings, beloved, but you must understand that it is in the depths of your heart in holy prayer and deep communion that you find the keys that all saints have found. You may read a sequence of sentences and paragraphs in the* Pearls of Wisdom *directed to you. But their*

purpose is to lead you to the point of entering in to the starry space and nonspace where you alone know God, without words, unspoken, yet you have touched the hem of the garment of your own immortality.[223]

We are very devoted to studying the teachings and giving our decrees, and rightly so. However, in addition to that, we need to find time to be alone with God—to love God with an unspoken love, to feel the joy of his presence, to experience moments of bliss in God. If we don't feel love for God then we are limiting the return current of his love to us over the figure-eight flow. We have to prime the pump by giving our love and devotion. Look at the beauty of God's creation; look at the beauty and innocence in the face of a child; sing God's praises, as we have been taught to do.

The saints did not have easy lives. They often had some kind of disease in their bodies or they were persecuted by other people, including those in their own community; yet they had the bliss of God. They didn't mind bearing the hard things because they seemed trivial next to the joy and bliss of God that was within them. Their lives can help motivate us if we are feeling stagnant and wondering, "What am I doing? Where am I on the long path Home?" That's when we need to prime the pump of love and devotion and become as a little child like the saints did.

As aspirants on the spiritual path we become increasingly more aware of our human substance; we're uncomfortable with it, and we work to the best of our ability to get rid of it. Since we know it's not who we are, it's good to take the time and space to say, "I know I've got substance and I'll attend to my karma, God. But for a moment I just want to open my heart up to you and love you. I want to tell you how grateful I am for your blessings and light and love. I want to experience your Presence and bask in your glory. I want to open myself up as a free-falling soul, trusting that you will catch me. I want to feel the joy that a child feels in its mother's arms, complete peace and trust, knowing you love me for who I really am." That is opening ourselves up to the bliss of God and, as Mother Mary teaches, it is a key to becoming an adept.

We don't have to wait until all our karma is balanced to do this. We're not denying our karma or the fact that we have to bind our dweller and do the spiritual work required for our path. We are simply acknowledging who we truly are. We're allowing the light and bliss and joy of God to be present in our temple. We can savor those moments, and they will carry us through our trials, as they did for the saints before us.

In order to do this, find a time in your day when you can be alone with God, when you can open up your heart and do nothing but love God and experience that communion. Remember that Mother Mary told us we will find the keys to our personal Christhood in that aloneness.

We Are Living a Mystery

In the dictation we will be hearing, Mother Mary also gives us a prayer that outlines the final stage of becoming an adept: *"Now, O Lord, I have assimilated thy Word. Now I would assimilate thy Being. Now I would become Thyself. Receive me."*[224]

"I would become Thyself." We have heard the Word of God and studied it. Now it is time to assimilate his Being by becoming one with our Christ Self. We cannot do this through our human self. We can only do it by becoming that which we already are—the Christ Self that God bestowed upon us in the beginning.

We truly are living a mystery because putting on our Christhood is much more than just displacing the human, it's becoming "Thyself"—becoming God. Why did the saints pant after God? Because they wanted that union; they had experienced it, if only for a moment, and they wanted more. They were willing to give up the lesser self to attain that oneness. That is the same price we must pay to become adepts.

With the greatest humility, let us affirm that God is the doer, recognizing that it is not even our hands or our voice doing the work; they are but instruments of God. God is the doer. It is God! God! God! Therefore, let us garner enough sacred fire in our beings to let go of the human and put on the Christ. Let our love for God be greater than the need to "be right" or to be anything that is not God's will for us. Let us strive to imitate Christ in everything we do. Let us not make excuses for our human actions that are not Christlike, but simply own them, ask for forgiveness, put them into the violet flame, and move on. This is our daily attentiveness to the Path and the work of our soul in putting on the garments of our Christ Self and becoming an adept.

In her dictation, Mother Mary gives us a precious gift.

> *I therefore now place upon you the full Electronic Presence of my Son at the age of thirty-three. Beloved ones, know that masterful Presence. Desire to become it. Fear not the initiations but know that through your heart of Christ and through your life and mission many shall be saved, should you decide to become that masterful Presence.*
>
> *Precious hearts, I recommend that you do. For you labor in love, in such worthiness, in such sacrifice, in such long-suffering. You labor in all these things. Your labor has its*

reward, but you must claim that reward. And that reward is adeptship.[225]

Let us *claim* our reward of adeptship! It is who we are in our Christ Self. And if we pursue the Path and gain our adeptship, the future of the Church, the nations and this planet will be very, very different. We know there is pain on this planet almost beyond comprehension, but this does not have to be if we choose to pass our initiations and thereby make a difference.

We claim our adeptship in the absolute knowledge that our human self or human mind can never, ever be the true adept. Christ in us is the adept. God in us is the adept. And as we walk forward, we can be in the masterful Presence of Jesus when he was thirty-three—his attainment, love and mastery. This is the path we are to walk.

We can take the hand of our Father-Mother God and trust as a little child that they will lead us on that path. We can begin today by becoming the newborn child in the arms of Mother Mary, nestled to her heart as she bids us to *"enter in to the ineffable love of our oneness."*[226] It's entering in to unconditional love.

If we want to finally experience soul freedom and the indescribable love of oneness, then let us earnestly pursue the path before us and claim our adeptship.

As we honor the Christ Child in our beloved Jesus this season, let us also honor the Christ Child in ourselves and in others. And as Jesus was about his "Father's business,"[227] let us be also.

For we have other worlds to conquer....

KARMA, HONOR, AND VICTORY

Precious ones, never, never, never compromise your honor. For your honor is your sacred name and your sacred identity. If you allow that honor to be trampled upon, you have no identity; you are counted among the herds of the cattle upon the hillsides. Honor is the flame that differentiates man and beast.

—GODFRE

FIFTEEN

Karma, Honor, and Victory

Diogenes was a man with a mission! Although the ancient Greek philosopher lived in an old wine casket and gave away his only possession—a drinking cup—when he saw a child drink with the cup of his hand, he is perhaps best known for roaming the streets of ancient Athens with a lantern searching for an honest man![228] We don't know if he ever found one, since it seems that in ancient Greece honest men were in short supply.

We all value honesty, and it is a required virtue on the spiritual path. At the same time, it is possible to be honest but not have integrity. For example, a person can be honest about their misdeeds yet show no remorse.

Having integrity adds another dimension to honesty. The Cambridge dictionary defines "integrity" as "the quality of being honest and having strong moral principles."[229] It is wonderful to have strong moral principles, but do we always live by them? Not just when it's convenient, but when it becomes costly to us? Sophocles, the ancient Greek playwright, wrote, *"I would prefer even to fail with honor than win by cheating."*[230]

Elohim Heros and Amora help us understand honesty as being vital to the honor of Christ:

> *Remember the honor of Christ and you will have right thought, right action, right desire, right motive and purpose. The honor of Christ is always loving, kind, wise and tethered to the Law without compromise. The honor of Christ is the shaft of white fire. The first virtue of that honor is self-honesty and honesty toward all.*[231]

A *"shaft of white fire"*—can't you just feel the power and the intensity of such honor?

Honesty before God

Heros and Amora tell us that the *"first virtue of that honor is self-honesty and honesty towards all."*[232] Self-honesty takes courage and a willingness to see ourselves as we really are—without self-condemnation or the flattery of the ego or the self-justification of the dweller-on-the-threshold. Self-honesty implies honesty before God. It's a form of self-delusion to think we can fool him, for how can we be dishonest with God when he knows everything anyway!

Sometimes we may know we've got an issue or problem and we want to be honest with God, but we're embarrassed to acknowledge it before him. We're embarrassed to bring it up because we don't like it and may not be sure what to do about it. In addition, projections of condemnation or shame amplify our embarrassment. Yet when it comes down to it, what good does it do to pretend to ourselves or God that we don't have a problem?

How many times did the messenger implore us to talk to God? Every day of our lives we need to set aside a space and time when we can talk to God. Maybe it will be praising him or simply sending him our love and gratitude or maybe it's bringing an issue before him. Whatever it is, we need to talk to God. We might say, "God, I know I have a problem with anger (or any other issue). I want to be free of it, and I am making calls to be delivered of it. I ask your help in clearing the cause and of core of it and overcoming it once and for all." As we say that prayer, we may still have vestiges of anger or another problem, but we are being honest with ourselves and God. And as long as we are striving to overcome the problem, we can face God and the world with honor.

Remember the story about the time El Morya came to Mark Prophet and asked him to become a messenger? Mark responded with something like, "I'm not perfect. How can I be a messenger?" Morya essentially said, "If we wait until you're perfect, all will be lost."

The same is true of us. We don't have to wait to be perfect to come before God in honor. We are still on earth so that we can deal with our mis-creations, our psychology, mistaken thought patterns, or any number of things that have been our stumbling blocks. If we're honorable in recognizing them and working on them, then we can trust that we can come before the throne of God in honor. Let us not allow our shortcomings to keep us away from God or our precious inner communion with him.

Honesty Before Others

The need to be honest toward others should be self-evident. However, it's good to remember that dishonesty can manifest in many ways, such as telling lies, slanting the facts in one way or another, or withholding information. I've witnessed situations where everything individuals have said is the absolute truth, but they've left out a few details that would have clearly changed the picture of what was being presented. So it's not enough just to tell the truth; we have to give the *whole* truth, not a selective truth.

Another more subtle form of dishonesty is exaggerating. Many of us love to make a good story better or emphasize our position in an argument by exaggerating. If you are sharing a funny story, you might wonder, "How bad is it to exaggerate a few details to make this even funnier? Who could possibly be hurt?" Simple—the truth is hurt. When we exaggerate, we are establishing a pattern in thought and speech that allows us to tell "little lies." It's simply not honorable. That doesn't mean we cannot enjoy a good story or laugh at ourselves, but we must recognize when we are about to cross the line between truth and exaggeration. Failure in these subtle, seemingly small types of tests can lead to more serious negative patterns in our psychology.

The Cosmic Honor Flame

When I was preparing this sermon, I learned something new about the cosmic honor flame that is so profound and all-encompassing that it causes one to pause and deeply reflect. Archangel Chamuel with Covering Cherubim said, "*Yes, beloved, do not fear the piercing of the heart. Mary the Mother knew the piercing of the heart, as have so many saints who chose to suffer for a time that burden of world condemnation that they might enter in to the cosmic honor flame, which you know as the ascension flame.*"[233]

The cosmic honor flame is the ascension flame! Think about that—they are one and the same! When we have the cosmic honor flame in our auras, we have the ascension flame as well! We have been taught that we ascend daily and doesn't that imply the presence of the ascension flame? This is an exciting teaching that gives us another powerful incentive to strive to wear the mantle of the cosmic honor flame.

The Ascended Master Godfre told us the following about the cosmic honor flame:

> *Precious ones, never, never, never compromise your honor. For your honor is your sacred name and your sacred identity. If you allow that honor to be trampled upon, you have no identity; you are counted among the herds of the cattle upon the hillsides. Honor is the flame that differentiates man and beast.*
>
> *Therefore keep the cosmic honor flame. Keep it as burnished steel, as white-fire light.*[234]

That's quite an explanation: honor is our sacred name, our sacred identity, and it's the difference between man and beast. Honor is an unusual way to differentiate that, isn't it? I was in Dallas recently and visited a science exhibit that was very well done. It had a lot about ancient man, including a display which showed various models of the supposed evolution of modern man from an animal. The depiction was very neat and tidy, showing what started out as a monkey gradually developing into a man. As it was presented, it left no question that it was true that we've just evolved from the primordial soup, so to speak. Now we know that is *not* true. But imagine all the children and people who see this display and think, "Well, this is their explanation from a scientific point of view and it seems to make sense, so it must be true." And save for a few Christians, how many people really believe that we are descendants of God and did not evolve from animals? And who would say honor is what makes us different?

Godfre also tells us that we must "*never, never, never*" compromise our honor. Yet sometimes it's easy to think, "This is such a little thing. Maybe it's not the highest action, but it's what I need to do right now," and so we do it and compromise our honor. Then we rationalize it as being okay because we think it's either too small or not important, "Well, if it really matters I can always ask for forgiveness later, but I think it will do a lot of good." Or maybe we do it and don't ask forgiveness at all. Either way, the ends don't justify the means and we have compromised our honor.

Resolving Karma by the Cosmic Honor Flame

In the dictation we will hear today, Sanat Kumara admonishes, "*You must resolve the issues of your karma by the cosmic honor flame.*"[235]

By now it's clear that honor is key to our Christhood and our ascension. Honor is a flame, our sacred name, our sacred identity, *and* it is the way that we must resolve our karma. We can't just go slugging through our karma day after day, hoping we do the right thing to balance it. We need to approach it with the concept of integrity—God-integrity, God-honor. Honor is not only worthy of our attention; it is essential for us to be victorious on our path of karma yoga.

Ah, yes, our karma—that looming substance that never seems to go away. It might feel like there is no end to it. If we wonder why we are not ascended masters at this moment instead of still living on this dark star, with few exceptions the answer is our karma. At the same time, let us be balanced in our perspective and not consider our karma so great that we cannot overcome it or so little that we can while away the hours in human pursuits.

Recently, I decided to reread the first two books from the I AM Movement, *Unveiled Mysteries* and *The Magic Presence*. If you haven't read them or reread them for a while, I strongly recommend it. It has been close to fifty years since I first read them, and I remember so well the profound effect they had on me. I recall waiting patiently for a bird with an engraved invitation from Saint Germain to appear at my windowsill! But, alas, it never came. As I read them this time, it was with a very different perspective. I wasn't expecting the invitation from the bird this time, but I was struck anew at how different our lives seem to be on this planet today compared to the lives of those portrayed in the books: Guy Ballard, Rex and Nada, Bob and Pearl, Alexander Gaylord, and so on. A difference in attainment perhaps, probably even in dispensation, but more importantly, I believe the difference is in the amount of karma they had balanced. And though we don't know what attainment they had up to that point, clearly it was great.

Sanat Kumara reminds us of the complexity of our karma that can go back to Lemuria, Atlantis, and even to other times and planets before we came to Earth. That's a sobering thought, isn't it? It's not just karma we made on Earth, but for some of us it's from other planets as well! Karma is complex beyond the ability of anyone to ever hope to resolve it without God's help. There are intricacies of time and space and cycles, there are ongoing free-will choices, and not everything that we are dealing with is black and white. It definitely takes the mind of God to sort it all out.

Haven't we all felt at one time or another, "I must have been a really bad person to have this karma. I'm not sure I ever want to know what I did to cause it." Well, when you know karma is not your reality and you are willing to do whatever it takes to balance it, there is no reason for you to be afraid of it. It's good to remember that God is not punishing us with returning karma but is giving us precious opportunity to resolve it.

If we condemn ourselves for our mistakes and karma, that will only separate us from God. Self-condemnation can also be a tool to escape responsibility. Thinking, "Oh, I'm such a bad person. I can't be a chela of the ascended masters, so I won't even try," is a sneaky way to let yourself off the hook. Thinking, "I'm not worthy. My sins are so great that I just shouldn't be here," is a cop-out. *Whatever* our sins, there is a way to balance them and move on.

Karma may define who we are or what we are experiencing in a temporal sense, but never ultimately. Karma is finite, so as we balance our karma it will be no more. It will be gone just as a terrible head cold that dominated our lives for a time is quickly forgotten when it has passed. The book of Hebrews outlines God's promise to us: *"For I will be merciful to their unrighteousness, and their sins and their iniquities will I remember no more."*[236] God will forget them! It will be as if they never existed. So if God will not remember our sins any more, then surely once we balance our karma we don't want to revolve it or recreate it.

We need to have the cosmic honor flame to resolve and balance our karma. It is the white fire light that shines into the dark complexity of our karma. If we embody that honor flame, then as we balance our karma, we will surely arrive at the Promised Land.

Honor is the Majesty of God

If you are wondering what the honor flame looks like in practice, look no further than Thomas Becket and Thomas More—embodiments of our own beloved El Morya. If anyone can teach us about the cosmic honor flame, he can.

In the movie *Beckett*, King Henry II asks Thomas Beckett if he loved him.

> King: *You never loved me, did you, Thomas?*
> Thomas: *Insofar as I was capable of love, yes, I did.*
> King: *Did you start to love God? You mule! Answer a simple question!*
> Thomas: *Yes. I started to love...the honor of God.*[237]

What power and beauty in that concept—the honor of God! I get chills thinking about it. It's so strong, so pure, so powerful!

Thomas More was an ultimate threat to King Henry VIII not simply because of what he did or didn't do, but because of who he was. Diogenes' search would have been over very quickly if he had met Thomas; he would have found his honest man! More's embodiment of honor—which all could feel—was a challenge to the king's actions and therefore the king felt it had to be stopped.

If Beckett and More had not chosen the honor of God first, even over their lives, would they be remembered today at all? Yet they are continually recognized as pillars of virtue in history.

As we aspire to manifest the cosmic honor flame in our day-to-day lives, let us take a closer look at what the masters have to say about it.

Jesus admonishes us to call for the protection of our soul's spiritual garment,

> ... as both the undergarment of humility and the outer garment of honor. For is not honor born of humility?
> For when one comes to comprehend the honor of God, is one not humbled before the great light, the dazzling white light of the presence of the cosmic honor flame?
> Honor, then, is an homage that you pay unto the living Christ that I AM and unto your God. It is the honoring of the Light that is unsullied and untainted, the Light that is the strength that holds together the Matter cosmos.
> Honor is a strength beyond other strengths. Honor is purity. Honor is the majesty of God. It is the single-eyed vision and the adoration of the one true God. Honor is oneness. It is wholeness.[238]

What a powerful image—to see ourselves going forth each day with the "undergarment of humility and the outer garment of honor!"

The Maha Chohan tells us that his sternness *"is the sternness of the white flame of honor.*[239] The white flame of honor is uncompromising. That is why it is intense and why it is so pure. It does not compromise.

So now we know what honor looks like on a spiritual level, and when souls have honor, hopefully we will perceive it in their auras. And when we embody honor, we will be able to shed that light to others.

Our Word Is Our Bond

I recently read an obituary of a former coal company executive. It said that he was tough on the unions, but both the current and former union heads said that when he said he was going to do something, he did it. Even his adversaries recognized that he was a man who honored his word. Isn't that our goal as well?

The Roman writer Publilius Syrus wrote two thousand years ago, "*What is left when honor is lost?*"[240] Indeed, what is left? I remember my father saying on numerous occasions, "My word is my bond." And so it should be.

We must also keep our word to God and the ascended masters. Kuan Yin addressed this in a 1996 dictation.

> *If you could see, beloved, how some of you have not kept your promises to God over the ages or even to the messengers in this life—you must stop this. When you make a promise, even if all hell breaks loose, you keep that promise. Therefore you do not make a promise that you are not determined to keep. Espouse the cosmic honor flame and know your victory.*[241]

Perhaps many of us have been swept up in great enthusiasm and have over-promised and under-delivered to the masters. When we are at a conference or some event where the light is great and the call goes forth to do a certain thing, we may become overly optimistic about our ability to fulfill the promises that we make to God. But when we don't fulfill the promises, how likely is it that God will grant us dispensations for our requests in the future?

Keeping our word to God and man is part of the cosmic honor flame. If we know of promises we have broken to God and the masters, then we should confess the sin and do everything possible to make it right. It if is not possible to specifically do that, assign yourself a penance and ask God to show you how to balance the karma. Then in the future be *fastidious* in keeping your word to God and others!

This is an important point. While I believe every one of us has good intentions, where we often fall short is in following through with the details. The details are an important part of keeping our word. Perhaps we think, "Well, I meant to do this for God, and I did about half of it. That's probably good enough." What is missing in that attitude (besides the other half that we promised to do for God) is an awareness that we have compromised the cosmic honor flame. The danger is that we will continue to compromise our word in other areas as we rationalize this type of behavior.

As Morya says, he overlooks a lot of things that we do (thank goodness!), but there comes a time when he doesn't overlook them anymore. The line is drawn; it's "thus far and no farther," and he withdraws. If we indulge ourselves in little compromises, we may cause that hammer to fall when we least expect it. That's why we must pay attention to the details, not because we're fanatical but because we keep our word.

Our Office in Hierarchy

When we think of an office in hierarchy, we may think of the office of the messenger or the chohan of the first ray or any of the positions that the masters hold. However, we tend to forget the offices that *we* might hold. For example, being a Keeper of the Flame is an office, providing we keep the disciplines of the fraternity. Being a Communicant represents an office in hierarchy that comes with various benefits if we uphold the attendant standards. Even more important is the office of Chela with a capital "C"; there is no greater honor on this planet than to be accepted as a Chela by an ascended master. We can continue to hold these offices in honor as long as we do not compromise the mantle we have been given.

Whatever office we hold or aspire to in the Great White Brotherhood, there are some things we simply do not do and there are places we would not go. For instance, I think we can all agree that a casino in Las Vegas is not our place, nor are any number of other places with astral vibrations.

We know that as we walk the earth with the office that is upon us—such as Keeper of the Flame or Chela of an ascended master—we have the presence of the sponsoring master with us, and what we do matters. That doesn't mean we never make a mistake. But it does means that we live differently and are continually striving to uphold the office. And the key to living differently and upholding the mantle of our office is the cosmic honor flame.

Compromising Honor Brings Failure

Ah, but what if we compromise a point of the law because of all the good we think it might bring? It's an interesting question, isn't it? "God, I see a way to do a really wonderful thing for this church or for the Brotherhood on the planet. But to do this, I need to do a certain thing, and I know it isn't the best, but I think it's expedient." And so we rationalize and do it because we think *we* have to fix something, not remembering that *God in us* is the real doer. Beware of that word "expedient" and what it means.

The Goddess of Freedom gave us some perspective on this:

> Let every Keeper of the Flame be staunch in the cosmic honor flame, in the understanding that where there is compromise, the least compromise, in the individual life of the Keeper of the Flame, there will be failure. There, whatever project, whatever plan you are engaged in is doomed to fail.
>
> You know that many of the great churches and movements of the world have pursued that Machiavellian concept of the end justifying the means. Keepers of the Flame dare not! ... for that which compromises truth and cosmic law is the inception of a degeneration spiral and a disintegration spiral, and it is doomed to failure from the start.[242]

Pretty strong words, aren't they? When I read them it felt like an alignment of my consciousness. I realized the masters are not kidding about this. It is quite serious. If we're going to be students on this path, if we're going to have the sponsorship of the ascended masters, if we're going to make our ascension, then we must beware of compromising honor.

Look what happened to More and Becket; they kept the honor flame and paid the price with their very life. They could have lived if they had compromised and bent a little bit. Imagine if Thomas More had thought, "Well, I don't really agree with the king divorcing his wife and marrying Anne just to have an heir. But if I compromise on that one point, I can continue my work, and think of how much more good I can do." Many people would have rationalized that way, but he upheld God's honor.

When we are faced with a difficult situation, it's good to ask ourselves, "Is there a compromise here?" I'm not talking about mistakes people make. We all make mistakes. But there's a difference between an honest mistake and a compromise of vibration or honor. The masters don't expect us to be perfect, but they expect us to do our very best to stay in alignment with the integrity and honor of God.

We dare not take honor casually, as if it's not important or as if it's something we may live by today but perhaps not always! *If we're going to put on our Christhood, we cannot compromise the honor flame.* Some small things in life don't affect our spiritual path, but there are also *seemingly* small things that *do* matter spiritually, and we must develop the attunement to recognize them.

Never Shirk or Shun the Difficult

Several years ago I did a sermon‡‡‡ on a 19th century engraving that depicted the following teaching from Jesus: *Enter ye in at the strait gate: for wide is the gate, and broad is the way, that leadeth to destruction, and many there be which go in thereat: Because strait is the gate, and narrow is the way, which leadeth unto life, and few there be that find it.* [243]

Sanat Kumara admonishes us to be aware of the choices we make and *"the road not taken."* [244] If we are going to balance our karma, we must be willing to take the hard road and not the easy one followed by the masses. It's the name of the game for us. We aren't like other people who have chosen a different path than the one we have chosen, and we need not compare our life with the easy life they have.

Sanat Kumara also tells us to *"never shirk or shun the difficult."* [245] Some people do shun it, and one example stands out in my memory. When I moved to Los Angeles in the 1970s, I had a friend who was a nurse at the Children's Hospital there. She saw the most heart-rending cases of children with extremely

---
‡‡‡ The 49 Percent Challenge, page 205.

serious and even fatal health issues. I was so surprised when she told me how often, in some of the most tragic cases, a father could not handle the difficulty and the pain of dealing with the child's illness, and he would simply leave the child and the mother. It was a terrible avoidance of the difficult and was a tragedy for all concerned.

That's an attempt to evade karma. The fallen angels are karma dodgers, which works for a while, but there comes a time when karma cannot be dodged. Chelas of the ascended masters do not want to be karma dodgers; we *want* our karma to return so we can balance it. That is why we're here on this path—it is opportunity! Let's not slumber while we have this opportunity. Let us prepare ourselves for our returning karma, for we never know when we will have to face a large bundle, so to speak.

Joe Louis, the famous boxer, when commenting on how he would deal with an opponent in an upcoming fight, said, *"He can run, but he cannot hide."*[246] The same might be said of facing our returning karma; we might try to temporarily evade it, but we cannot continually hide from it.

In 1 Thessalonians we read, *"But of the times and the seasons, brethren, ye have no need that I write unto you. For yourselves know perfectly that the day of the Lord so cometh as a thief in the night."*[247] The phrase "cometh as a thief in the night" could be applied to our returning karma since we never know what to expect or when it will come. The verse continues: *"For when they shall say, Peace and safety; then sudden destruction cometh upon them..."*[248] The Masters have taught us to be prepared for our returning karma. We don't know when it's coming, but as we're reminded in the dictation we're hearing today, it comes! It's not going away, but we can greet it with honor and work to mitigate it by using the violet flame.

The equation of our path Home includes finally balancing complex and intricate karma. Because of this complexity, just imagine the challenge that the angels and masters have to bring everyone and everything into place at exactly the right time to afford us the opportunity to balance a certain karma. It's mind boggling to just think about all that's involved! Only God can do that, and he does it out of love for us and his desire for us to be victorious.

If we miss a cycle, it may not reappear for lifetimes. *This* is the hour when we have the tools to face the most difficult situations and dynamics. *Now* is our opportunity and the gift that God has given to us.

Even with daily diligence using all the spiritual tools at our disposal, it is not an easy path. But God has given us extraordinary graces. And if we keep striving and keep working and getting up when we fall down, Saint Germain has promised to help us. For example, in re-reading *The Magic Presence* I was reminded of the atomic accelerator. Saint Germain has said that he will give us the opportunity to sit in the atomic accelerator. If we strive to the very best of our ability and yet we still have not balanced 51 percent of our karma, the atomic accelerator could make up the difference. Such graces give us renewed hope and inspiration to carry on!

Communing with Our Divine Mother and Father

As I was preparing today's service, a friend sent me a dictation they thought I should read. It was from beloved Omega and offers profound comfort in this hour of descending personal and planetary karma.

In her dictation given in 1992, beloved Omega said,

> *I would remind you that the divine spark within... truly does have a name and that name is Alpha-Omega. We are the Divine Presence in your heart...*
>
> *Therefore, as we can understand even the dilemma of living in this octave, so will you not understand that there is also the very present possibility for you to live in that holy aura, truly the universe of Light that is in the secret chamber of your heart?*[249]

Let's ponder this for a minute. We've been taught over and over that the presence of God is within us. But I tended to only think of that in generic and not personal terms. In other words, I believed that God was in me as light, but if I really wanted to talk to Alpha and Omega, I had to reach them from afar with my prayers because they were in the Great Central Sun. Omega telling us that the presence of God within us *is* Alpha and Omega can be life-changing. When we meditate and enter into the secret chamber of our heart and bow before the Christ flame within us, we are in the very presence of the Father-Mother God. Isn't it comforting to know that we may enter into that secret chamber and find them there—so very close and personal?

Omega continues to explain how to safely establish our communion with them:

> *There are boulders and mountains of karma that stand between you, as the soul seated in the seat-of-the-soul chakra, and that secret chamber that is the replica of our Home...*
>
> *Therefore, under the old dispensation, you could not have lawfully risen to such a holy place without having balanced that karma, but in this day and hour the Archangel*

> *Michael does place his Presence over you. And therefore, in the presence of that God-free, wondrous manifestation of I AM THAT I AM, your soul may rise to that level (as she has not done in many centuries) and be tutored, beloved ones.*
>
> *Is this not the mighty grace of the Lord, who weeps for you, who loves you, who desires you not to be absent but with him, with him in the very heart of Brahman?*[250]

We are so loved by God, and he wants us to be with him! While we still have to clean up our karma, we don't have to wait until every jot and tittle is balanced to be with our Divine Mother and our Divine Father. We have a dispensation to enter the secret chamber of our heart if we will take the time and the effort, and it doesn't have to take hours. We can kneel by our bed at night and ask Archangel Michael to take us to the secret chamber of our heart, to be in the presence of Alpha and Omega, to feel their comfort and love, to honor the light and to surrender ourselves to that light. We can directly experience the blessing and the bliss of being in the presence of God, of being in the presence of honor and the honor flame.

Let us not think of ourselves as unworthy. Remember the fiat, "*Lord, I am worthy; make me worthier still.*" Omega tells us that if we will make the effort, we can go into the secret chamber of our heart, and then lay our bodies to rest and go wherever our business is in cosmos that night. Then when we awaken in the morning, we take up our karma again and go out to fulfill our responsibilities. But that night when we are ready to sleep once more, *if we choose*, we may again enter into that holy Presence.

What will come of this? That is for each one of us to find out for our self. But Omega offers encouragement that once we do this, we will experience "*a new tenderness, a kind of tenderness so rare whereby you can hardly find a harsh feeling or a harsh word thereafter—so wondrous, so loving [is the Presence and] so much love do you find in that [secret place] where the threefold flame does burn."*[251]

The challenges of the day are real and can be significant. But we are not going into this spiritual battle without armor. We have the armor of the cosmic honor flame, we have sponsorship and the support of the sacred light within us. If we will make the effort, if we will confess, if we will embrace the will of God, if we will surrender and let go of those things that we thought we had to have (our human personality, our dweller, this or that thing or relationship), we can be sure that our Father-Mother God will love and care for us.

There is a *freedom* in that! I don't think there's any way you can have a greater freedom on this planet than to rest in the bosom of our Father-Mother God, knowing you are doing what you need to do in this time and place to maintain the cosmic honor flame and balance your karma. It's a glorious freedom.

The Rewards Promised to Him That Overcometh

The masters define courage as the coming of age of the heart. It takes courage to walk this path—courage to face our karma, courage to recognize and challenge the darkness within ourselves, courage to let go of the familiar, courage to move forward while knowing we are still less than perfect. It takes courage to wear the mantle of the cosmic honor flame, to be as Thomas Beckett or Thomas More. It takes courage to stand and face the opposition to all that we hold dear. It takes courage to surrender our human will and replace it with the divine will.

The masters have taught us that the Path is often an endurance test. They have told us to keep on keeping on when the clouds cover our I AM Presence and all seems lost. As we pray and summon the fire and the will to complete all that God has given us to do, they are with us, and our Father-Mother God is as close as the secret chamber of our heart.

Let us take courage, take heart. Let us remember and look forward to receiving the reward for those who diligently seek God.

The Book of Revelation has eight verses that refer to the rewards given to "him that overcometh." Our path is surely a path of overcoming—overcoming our karma, our psychology, our dweller, the forces of death and hell—*everything* within and without that would hinder our victory.

Let us ponder three of these precious promises given to those who persevere, for these words make plain that there are incomparable rewards waiting for us if we continue on the path of overcoming.

Revelation 3:12

Him that overcometh will I make a pillar in the temple of my God, and he shall go no more out: and I will write upon him the name of my God, and the name of the city of my God, which is new Jerusalem, which cometh down out of heaven from my God: and I will write upon him my new name.

Revelation 3:21

To him that overcometh will I grant to sit with me in my throne, even as I also overcame, and am set down with my Father in his throne.

Revelation 21:7

He that overcometh shall inherit all things; and I will be his God, and he shall be my son.

We have a glorious future, for the Lord has told us so. He said: "*In my Father's house are many mansions: if it were not so, I would have told you. I go to prepare a place for you.*"[252]

Let us embrace the honor of God as the beacon that will lead us to our Father's mansions.

Our Lord awaits us.

Dictations Played After the Sermons

1. Practicing Sainthood

Beloved Gautama Buddha, "Master One Petal *Keep On Climbing* Wesak Address 1994," *Pearls of Wisdom*, vol. 37, no. 22, May 29, 1994.

2. Love As a Choice

Beloved Paul the Venetian, "Love Is the Great Challenge, '*Comfort Ye, Comfort Ye My People,*' Saith Your God," *Pearls of Wisdom*, vol. 38, no. 3, January 15, 1995.

3. Pleasing God

Beloved Saint Germain, "Pleasing Your Own Mighty I AM Presence Is the Greatest Honor You Can Ever Achieve," *Pearls of Wisdom*, vol. 60, no. 7, February 15, 2017.

4. Next Year in Jerusalem

   Beloved Akshobhya, "Becoming Real! In the Heart of Mirrorlike Wisdom," *Pearls of Wisdom*, vol. 37, no. 4, January 23, 1994.

5. Nine Mindsets for Your Soul's Victory, Part I

   Beloved Hercules and Amazonia, "Know the Law and You Shall Conquer *In Defense of the Messengers of God* May You Pass Every Test of the Will of God! *Beware the Dweller-on-the-Threshold,*" *Pearls of Wisdom*, vol. 36, no. 28, July 11, 1993.

6. Nine Mindsets for Your Soul's Victory, Part 2

   Beloved Victory, "Indomitable Greetings of Cosmic Victory," *Pearls of Wisdom*, vol. 19, nos. 45 & 46, November 7 & 14, 1976.

7. The Poison of Pride

   Beloved Sanat Kumara with the Seven Holy Kumaras, "*The Convening of the Stars* Purge the Earth of Pride," *Pearls of Wisdom*, vol. 42, no. 11, March 14, 1999.

8. A Buddha's Christmas Vow

   Beloved Godfre, "Godfre's Birthday Address!" *Pearls of Wisdom*, vol. 19, nos. 16 & 17, April 18, 1976.

9. Who Am I in God?

Beloved Mighty Victory, "Victory Way of Life," *Pearls of Wisdom*, vol. 43, no. 2, January 9, 2000.

10. The 49 Percent Challenge

Beloved Mother Mary, "Guard the Great Light That You Have! Stray Not from the Almighty One!" *Pearls of Wisdom*, vol. 37, no. 46, November 13, 1994.

11. Seven Ways to Bring Light to the Dark Night

Beloved Mighty Victory, "Victory over the Dark Night of the Soul," *Pearls of Wisdom*, vol. 43, no. 16, April 16, 2000.

12. Sweet Surrender

Beloved El Morya, "The Light of the Guru and the Chela: Surrender for a More Perfect Love," *Pearls of Wisdom*, vol. 23, no. 45, November 9, 1980.

13. A Walk with the Buddha

Beloved Gautama Buddha, "A Rescue Mission *"I Will Fulfill My Mission Come What May!"* Cherish the Flame Wesak Address 1995," *Pearls of Wisdom*, vol. 38, no. 21, May 14, 1995.

14. Claim Your Adeptship!

> Beloved Mother Mary, "The Ineffable Love of Our Oneness *The Challenge of Every Day Is to Separate the Unreal from the Real* The Reward of Your Labor Is Adeptship Christmas Eve Address 1993," *Pearls of Wisdom,* vol. 36, no. 70, December 29, 1993.

15. Karma, Honor, and Victory

> Beloved Sanat Kumara, "*The Fulfillment of the Twentieth Century Portents for Maitreya's Mystery School* You Must Resolve the Issues of Your Karma by the Cosmic Honor Flame," *Pearls of Wisdom,* vol. 37, no. 10, March 6, 1994.

Notes

1. *My Soul Doth Magnify the Lord!* (Colorado Springs, CO: The Summit Lighthouse, 1974), pp. 249-50.
2. Beloved Gautama Buddha, "Practice Sainthood Daily *Walk in the Footsteps of the Great Saints of East and West*," *Pearls of Wisdom*, vol. 46, no. 40, October 5, 2003.

Practicing Sainthood

3. Thomas à Kempis, *The Imitation of Christ* (Boston, MA: Saint Paul Editions, 1962, 1978), p. 141.
4. Beloved Gautama Buddha, "Master One Petal *Keep on Climbing*," *Pearls of Wisdom*, vol. 37, no. 22, May 29, 1994.
5. Beloved Gautama Buddha, "Practice Sainthood Daily *Walk in the Footsteps of the Great Saints of East and West*," *Pearls of Wisdom*, vol. 46, no. 40, October 5, 2003.
6. Beloved Jesus Christ, "I Love You! My Heart/Thy Heart *'Jesus, I Bid You Enter My Whole Temple Now!'*," *Pearls of Wisdom*, vol. 34, no. 41, August 25, 1991.
7. Mother Teresa, *Come Be My Light: The Private Writings of the Saint of Calcutta* (New York: Doubleday, 2007), p. 194.
8. Ibid, p. 164.

9. Ibid, p. 33.
10. Ibid, p. 235.
11. C.B. Ruffin, *Padre Pio: The True Story* (Huntington, Indiana: Our Sunday Visitor Publishing Division, 1991), p. 119.
12. This line was spoken by Linus Van Pelt in the November 12, 1959 comic strip of *Peanuts*, written and drawn by Charles Schulz (1950-2000).
13. Sister Faustina Kowalska, *Diary, Divine Mercy in My Soul* (Stockbridge, MA: Marians of the Immaculate Conception, 1996), p. 34.
14. Mother Teresa, *Where There Is Love, There Is God: Her Path to Closer Union with God and Greater Love for Others* (New York: Random House, 2010), p. 298.
15. Ibid, pp. 20, 174.
16. Caccioppoli, "Padre Pio in His Own Words," http://caccioppoli.com/, accessed November, 2014.
17. C.B. Ruffin, *Padre Pio: The True Story* (Huntington, Indiana: Our Sunday Visitor Publishing Division, 1991), p. 76.
18. Sister Faustina Kowalska, *Diary, Divine Mercy in My Soul* (Stockbridge, MA: Marians of the Immaculate Conception, 1996), p. 29.
19. Beloved Gautama Buddha, "Master One Petal *Keep on Climbing*," *Pearls of Wisdom*, vol. 37, no. 22, May 29, 1994.
20. Ibid.
21. C.B. Ruffin, *Padre Pio: The True Story* (Huntington, Indiana: Our Sunday Visitor Publishing Division, 1991), p. 142.

Love As a Choice

22. The Four Chaplains Memorial Foundation, "The Story," www.fourchaplains.org, accessed December, 2014.
23. John 15:13.

24. Beloved Paul the Venetian, "Love Is the Great Challenge 'Comfort Ye, Comfort Ye My People,' Saith Your God," *Pearls of Wisdom*, vol. 38, no. 3, January 15, 1995.
25. Ibid.
26. *100 Letters for You*, ed. Fr. Francesco D. Colacelli (Italy: Edizioni Padre Pio Da Pietrelcina, 2010), p. 179.
27. Beloved Paul the Venetian, "Love Is the Great Challenge 'Comfort Ye, Comfort Ye My People,' Saith Your God," *Pearls of Wisdom*, vol. 38, no. 3, January 15, 1995.
28. Matt. 22:39.
29. Beloved Paul the Venetian, "Love Is the Great Challenge 'Comfort Ye, Comfort Ye My People,' Saith Your God," *Pearls of Wisdom*, vol. 38, no. 3, January 15, 1995.
30. Isa. 40:1.
31. Beloved Kuthumi, "The Vessel of Kindness," *Pearls of Wisdom*, vol. 34, no. 33, July 1, 1991.
32. Memo from Mother to staff dated June 3, 1994.
33. Great-Quotes.com, Mother Teresa, http://www.Great-Quotes.com/quote/25214, accessed December, 2014.
34. Beloved Lanello, "The Covenant of Compassion Ascension Day Address," *Pearls of Wisdom*, vol. 27, no. 35, July 1, 1984.
35. Beloved Paul the Venetian, "Love Is the Great Challenge 'Comfort Ye, Comfort Ye My People,' Saith Your God," *Pearls of Wisdom*, vol. 38, no. 3, January 15, 1995.
36. 1 Cor. 13:1.
37. Beloved Paul the Venetian, "Love Is the Great Challenge 'Comfort Ye, Comfort Ye My People,' Saith Your God," *Pearls of Wisdom*, vol. 38, no. 3, January 15, 1995.
38. Catholic Online, Mother Teresa quotes, www.catholic.org/clife/teresa/quotes.php, accessed December, 2014.

Pleasing God

39. Wommack, Andrew, Andrew Wommack Ministries, "What Pleases God," https://www.awmi.net/reading/teaching-articles/pleases_god/, accessed July, 2017.
40. *Common English Bible.*
41. Ibid.
42. Beloved Lanello, "Points of Darkness *Oh, the Heart of Kindness!* Call to Lanello to Descend the Spiral Staircase 33 Days *I Have Broken the Chain of Mortality! Call to Me: I Will Show You How to Do It!*" *Pearls of Wisdom,* vol. 36, no. 2, January 10, 1993.
43. Ibid.
44. Luke 10:42.
45. *Beloved Jesus the Christ,* "DISCIPLESHIP Corona Class Lesson 25 Requirement 'Here I am, Send Me!'," *Pearls of Wisdom,* vol. 5, no. 12, March 23, 1962.
46. Beloved Kuthumi, "Understanding Yourself *12* Action and Reaction," *Pearls of Wisdom,* vol. 12, no. 36, September 7, 1969.
47. Sister Maria Antonia, *Under Angel Wings: The True Story of a Young Girl and Her Guardian Angel* (Rockford, Illinois: Tan Books and Publishers, Inc., 2000), p. 20.
48. *Beloved Jesus the Christ,* "DISCIPLESHIP Corona Class Lesson 25 Requirement 'Here I am, Send Me!'," *Pearls of Wisdom,* vol. 5, no. 12, March 23, 1962.
49. Elizabeth Clare Prophet, Tenth Anniversary of Lanello's Ascension, Event #5 B. Mother's Teaching from Corona Class Lesson Number 25, February 27, 1983.

Next Year in Jerusalem

50. Beloved Lord Maitreya, "To Restore the Christhood of America! Return to the One God The Question Is Not Can You but Will You Turn the World Around?" *Pearls of Wisdom*, vol. 35, no. 42, October 11, 1992.
51. Aron Moss, "Next Year in Jerusalem...Really!", https://www.chabad.org/library/article_ cdo/aid/274826/jewish/next-year-jerusalem.htm, accessed March, 2018.
52. Rev. 10:9.
53. Beloved Jesus Christ, "The Descent of the Crystal Fire Mist *From My Sacred Heart I Pour Out the Vial* Do Not Postpone the Day of Your Initiation," *Pearls of Wisdom*, vol. 35, no. 18, May 3, 1992.
54. Goddess of Purity, "The New Order of the Ascension Flame *Part 2*," *Pearls of Wisdom*, vol. 54, no.14, July 15, 2011.
55. Beloved El Morya, "*Give Me Your God-Controlled Attention!* You Are Worthy to Be Infired with God The Gift of the Thread of Contact," *Pearls of Wisdom*, vol. 35, no. 19, May 10, 1992.
56. Beloved Gautama Buddha, "Enter into the Heart of the Oneness with God *Wesak Address*," *Pearls of Wisdom*, vol. 55, no. 9, May 1, 2012.
57. 1 Peter 1:7.
58. Beloved Jesus Christ, "The Descent of the Crystal Fire Mist *From My Sacred Heart I Pour Out the Vial* Do Not Postpone the Day of Your Initiation," *Pearls of Wisdom*, vol. 35, no. 18, May 3, 1992.
59. Ibid.
60. John 10:9.

61. Beloved Jesus Christ, "The Descent of the Crystal Fire Mist *From My Sacred Heart I Pour Out the Vial* Do Not Postpone the Day of Your Initiation," *Pearls of Wisdom*, vol. 35, no. 18, May 3, 1992.
62. 1 Cor. 13:12.
63. Elizabeth Clare Prophet, "*Darshan with the Messenger* The Guru-Chela Relationship 'Nothing Will Ever Allow Me to Stop Loving You' Part 4," *Pearls of Wisdom*, vol. 51, no. 23, October 15, 2008.
64. Beloved Akshobhya, "Becoming Real! In the Heart of Mirrorlike Wisdom," *Pearls of Wisdom*, vol. 37, no. 4, January 23, 1994.
65. Elizabeth Clare Prophet, "*Darshan with the Messenger* The Guru-Chela Relationship 'Nothing Will Ever Allow Me to Stop Loving You' Part 4," *Pearls of Wisdom*, vol. 51, no. 23, October 15, 2008.
66. Elizabeth Clare Prophet, "*Darshan with the Messenger* The Guru-Chela Relationship 'Nothing Will Ever Allow Me to Stop Loving You' Part 3," *Pearls of Wisdom*, vol. 51, no. 22, October 1, 2008.
67. Beloved Jesus Christ, "The Descent of the Crystal Fire Mist *From My Sacred Heart I Pour Out the Vial* Do Not Postpone the Day of Your Initiation," *Pearls of Wisdom*, vol. 35, no. 18, May 3, 1992.
68. Mark L. Prophet and Elizabeth Clare Prophet, *Morya I* Teachings of the Ascended Masters (Corwin Springs, MT: Summit Lighthouse Library, 1982, 1983, 2001), p. xiii.
69. Ibid, p. 281.
70. Beloved El Morya, "*Give Me Your God-Controlled Attention!* You Are Worthy to Be Infired with God *The Gift of the Thread of Contact*," *Pearls of Wisdom*, vol. 35, no 19, May 10, 1992.

71. Ibid.
72. Ibid.
73. Ibid.
74. Beloved Akshobhya, "Becoming Real! In the Heart of Mirrorlike Wisdom," *Pearls of Wisdom*, vol. 37, no. 4, January 23, 1994.
75. Elizabeth Clare Prophet, "*Darshan with the Messenger* The Guru-Chela Relationship 'Nothing Will Ever Allow Me to Stop Loving You' Part 4," *Pearls of Wisdom*, vol. 51, no. 23, October 15, 2008.
76. Mark L. Prophet and Elizabeth Clare Prophet, *Morya I* Teachings of the Ascended Masters (Corwin Springs, MT: Summit Lighthouse Library, 1982, 1983, 2001), pp. 84-85.

Nine Mindsets for Your Soul's Victory Part 1

77. Naval History and Heritage Command, "John Paul Jones," www.history.navy.mil, accessed November, 2013.
78. Ibid.
79. Ibid.
80. James Reed and Paul G. Stoltz, *Put Your Mindset to Work: The One Asset You Really Need to Win and Keep the Job You Love* (New York: Penguin Books, 2011), p. 6.
81. Ibid, p. 7.
82. Douay-Rheims Bible, 1899 American Edition (DRA), public domain.

83. "A Back-up Burglar Alarm With A Digestive Problem," column by Dave Barry, Miami Herald, November 29, 1992.
84. 1 John 4:18.
85. Elizabeth Clare Prophet, "On Healing and the Four Types of Fear, Teachings of the Divine Mother," April 3, 1991.
86. Ibid.
87. Beloved Hercules & Amazonia, "Know the Law and You Shall Conquer In Defense of the Messengers of God May You Pass Every Test of the Will of God! *Beware the Dweller-on-the-Threshold*," *Pearls of Wisdom*, vol. 36, no. 28, July 11, 1993.
88. Ibid.

Nine Mindsets for Your Soul's Victory Part 2

89. C.B. Ruffin, *Padre Pio: The True Story* (Huntington, Indiana: Our Sunday Visitor Publishing Division, 1991), p. 65.
90. Beloved Victory, "Indomitable Greetings of Cosmic Victory," *Pearls of Wisdom*, vol. 19, nos. 45 & 46, November 7 & 14, 1976.
91. Djwal Kul, *Only Mark*, album 6, track 25, dictation given March 27, 1970.
92. Douay-Rheims Bible, 1899 American Edition (DRA), public domain.
93. Patricia Kirmond, *Messages from Heaven* (Corwin Springs, MT: Summit University Press, 1999), p. 32.
94. Elizabeth Clare Prophet, *Inner Perspectives* (Corwin Springs, MT: Summit University Press, 2003), p. 315.
95. Ibid.
96. Ibid.
97. Ibid, pp. 313-14.

98. Llanya Vanzant, *Forgiveness: 21 Days to Forgive Everyone for Everything* (Carlsbad, CA: Smiley Books, 2013).
99. Matt. 18:21-22.
100. Elizabeth Clare Prophet, "The Torch Is Passed! Event 3" October 5, 1979, Audio and video.
101. Luke 22:53.

The Poison of Pride

102. Beloved Sanat Kumara with the Seven Holy Kumaras, "Purge the Earth of Pride," *Pearls of Wisdom*, vol. 42, no. 11, March 14, 1999.
103. The Beloved God and Goddess Meru, "Run to the Heart of the Little Child *The Empowerment of Those Who Would Teach the Little Children*," *Pearls of Wisdom*, vol. 34, no. 34, July 7, 1991.
104. Ibid.
105. Marilyn Barrick, *Everything is Energy* (Gardiner, MT: Summit University Press, 2005), pp. 9-10.
106. Prov. 16:18; James 4:6.
107. Djwal Kul, *Only Mark*, album 6, track 25, dictation given March 27, 1970.
108. Maha Chohan, "Conquer Pride and Receive the Gifts of the Holy Spirit Part 2," *Pearls of Wisdom*, vol. 48, no. 2, January 9, 2005, endnote 4.
109. Decree insert 6.04D, "Bind the Pride of the Fallen Ones."
110. See Igino Giordani, *Saint Catherine of Siena—Doctor of the Church*, trans. Thomas J. Tobin (Boston: Daughters of St. Paul, St. Paul Editions, 1975), pp. 35, 36. (Referenced in Sanat Kumara with the Seven Holy Kumaras, "Purge the Earth of Pride," *Pearls of Wisdom*, vol. 42, no. 11, March 14, 1999, endnote 2.)

111. C.B. Ruffin, *Padre Pio: The True Story* (Huntington, Indiana: Our Sunday Visitor Publishing Division, 1991), p. 111.

A Buddha's Christmas Vow

112. Carbone, Gerald M., "December 1776: Victory or Death," https://www.thehistoryreader.com/modern-history/december-1776-victory-death/, accessed February, 2020.
113. Gerald M. Carbone, *Nathanael Greene: A Biography of the American Revolution* (New York: Palgrave Macmillan, 2008), p. 53.
114. Beloved Jesus Christ, "The Day of Thy Christhood *Keep the Flame of Eternal Life,*" *Pearls of Wisdom,* vol. 30, no. 74, December 13, 1987.
115. Prov. 16:25.
116. Beloved Godfre, "Godfre's Birthday Address Part 1," *Pearls of Wisdom,* vol. 19, no. 16, April 18, 1976.
117. Rev. 10:9.
118. In the novel *The Strange Case of Dr. Jekyll and Mr. Hyde* by Robert Louis Stevenson, Dr. Jekyll is a respectable and virtuous citizen who is fascinated by the idea of isolating the good and evil in human nature. He develops a drug to periodically transform himself into Mr. Hyde, a separate personality through whom he gives vent to evil impulses. When he commits murder, Dr. Jekyll realizes his creation has overpowered his own instincts for good. No longer able to restore his original personality at will, Dr. Jekyll takes his own life just before he is to be arrested. On November 26, 1987, the messenger gave teaching on the confrontation with the dweller-on-the-threshold in which she commented on the story of Dr. Jekyll and Mr. Hyde, describing Mr. Hyde as the embodiment of

Dr. Jekyll's dweller-on-the-threshold. See endnote 39, Beloved Jesus Christ, "The Second Coming of Christ Receive Me and Become Who You Are," *Pearls of Wisdom*, vol. 32, no. 60, December 10, 1989.

119. Beloved Jesus Christ, "The Second Coming of Christ Receive Me and Become Who You Are," *Pearls of Wisdom*, vol. 32, no. 60, December 10, 1989.
120. Beloved Godfre, "Godfre's Birthday Address Part 1," *Pearls of Wisdom*, vol. 19, no. 16, April 18, 1976.
121. Catholic Online, Mother Teresa quotes, www.catholic.org/clife/teresa/quotes.php, accessed December, 2014.

Who Am I in God?

122. Wurmbrand, Richard and Sabina, "The Voice of the Martyrs," www.persecution.org, accessed October, 2016.
123. Ibid.
124. *With God In Solitary Confinement*, eBook, by Richard Wurmbrand, (Bartlesville, OK: Livingston Sacrifice Book Company, 1969, 2001).
125. El Morya, "The Chela and the Path Letter 4," *Pearls of Wisdom*, vol.18, no. 4, January 26,1975.
126. Elizabeth Clare Prophet, "Mighty Victory on the Four Lower Bodies and the Threefold Flame Part 1," *Pearls of Wisdom*, vol. 43, no. 3, January 16, 2000.
127. Ibid.
128. Ibid.
129. Luke 12:32.
130. Elizabeth Clare Prophet, "Mighty Victory on the Four Lower Bodies and the Threefold Flame Part 3," *Pearls of Wisdom*, vol. 43, no. 5, January 30, 2000.

131. Mark L. Prophet, "Meeting Your Inner Master Part 2," *Pearls of Wisdom*, vol. 43, no. 28, July 9, 2000.
132. Beloved Jesus Christ, "It Is a Matter of Heart! *I Summon My true Chelas* I Can Save You Only If You and I Are One," *Pearls of Wisdom*, vol. 36, no. 26, June 27, 1993.
133. Richard Wurmbrand, *With God in Solitary Confinement* (Bartlesville, OK: Living Sacrifice Book Company, 1969), p. 5.
134. Richard Wurmbrand, *If Prison Walls Could Speak* (Plainfield, NJ: Logos International, 1972), pp. 13-14.
135. Beloved Mighty Victory, "Victory's Way of Life," *Pearls of Wisdom*, vol. 43, no. 2, January 9, 2000.
136. Ibid.

The 49 Percent Challenge

137. Beloved Archangel Michael and Kuthumi, "Pierce the Veil, O My Soul!," *Pearls of Wisdom*, vol. 29, no. 46, October 5, 1986.
138. The Summit Lighthouse, *The Open Door* internet radio program, episode number 238, www.tsl.org, aired July 11, 2017.
139. Elizabeth Clare Prophet, lecture on Discipleship delivered to Summit University, March 17, 1983.
140. Lanello, dictation given April 8, 1979, available on the Ascended Master Library, www.tsl.org.
141. Beloved Archangel Zadkiel, December 15, 1978, referenced by Beloved Archangel Zadkiel in *Pearls of Wisdom*, vol. 24, no. 6, February 8, 1981, endnote 1.
142. Phil. 2:5.
143. Beloved Purity and Astrea, "*The Sweetness of the Light* The Way of Self-Indulgence Take on the Challenge of the

Selfish Self *'Take It or Leave It!'*," *Pearls of Wisdom*, vol. 36, no. 23, June 6, 1993.
144. Elizabeth Clare Prophet, "Now Is the Time for Us to Make Our Ascension," *Pearls of Wisdom*, vol. 45, no. 38, September 22, 2002.
145. Luke 22:31.
146. Luke 4:8; Matt. 16:23.
147. Kuthumi and the Brothers of the Golden Robe, "An Exposé of False Teachings," *Pearls of Wisdom*, vol. 19, no. 13, March 28, 1976.
148. Ibid.
149. Ibid.
150. Ibid.
151. Ibid.
152. Beloved Mother Mary, "Guard the Great Light That You Have! *Stray Not from the Almighty One!* Christmas Eve Address 1994," *Pearls of Wisdom*, vol. 37, no. 46, November 13, 1994.
153. Beloved Maha Chohan, "Chelaship under the Tutelage of the Holy Spirit *First Earn Your Stripes under the Seven Chohans*," *Pearls of Wisdom*, vol. 46, no. 15, April 13, 2003.
154. Elizabeth Clare Prophet, "The Thirty-Sixth Anniversary of the Founding of the Summit Lighthouse *Bond Your Heart to the Heart of a Master*," *Pearls of Wisdom*, vol. 51, no. 17, July 15, 2008.

Seven Ways to Bring Light to the Dark Night

155. Matt. 27:46
156. John Ferling, *The Ascent of George Washington: The Hidden Political Genius of an American Icon* (New York, NY: Bloomsbury Press, 2009), p. 115.

157. John 15:20.
158. Beloved Listening Angel, "Strength in the Union of the I AM THAT I AM *You Can Place the Capstone on the Pyramid*," *Pearls of Wisdom*, vol. 30, no. 62, December 1, 1987, endnote 1.
159. Elizabeth Clare Prophet, Summit University, Levels I and II, Questions and Answers, Audio and video, April 16, 1986.
160. Saint John of the Cross, "Dark Night," II.5.1, in *Collected Works*, p. 335, and Saint John of the Cross, "Dark Night," II.6, in *Mystical Evolution*, p. 197. Referenced in Mark L. Prophet and Elizabeth Clare Prophet, *Climb the Highest Mountain Series: The Path to Attainment* (Gardiner, MT: Summit Publications, Inc., 2008), p. 244, endnotes 33, 34, p. 395:
161. Beloved Jesus Christ, "The Descent of the Crystal Fire Mist *From My Sacred Heart I Pour Out the Vial* Do Not Postpone the Day of Your Initiation," *Pearls of Wisdom*, vol. 35, no. 18, May 3, 1992.
162. Ibid.
163. Beloved El Morya, "*Give Me Your God-Controlled Attention! You Are Worthy to Be Infired with God The Gift of the Thread of Contact*," *Pearls of Wisdom*, vol. 35, no. 19, May 10, 1992.
164. Beloved Archangel Raphael and Mother Mary, "Healing, Karma and the Violet Flame *The Law and the Fiery Trial*," *Pearls of Wisdom*, vol. 30, no. 7, February 15, 1987.
165. Beloved Mother Mary, "You Have Won the Prize! Now Pass Your Tests!," *Pearls of Wisdom*, vol. 33, no. 23, June 17, 1990.
166. 2 Cor. 12:9.

167. Saint Teresa of Avila, "Brides of Christ *Your Bridegroom Is Waiting* A Secret Pact *In the Ecstasy of the Lord* Rejoice In Opportunity!," *Pearls of Wisdom*, vol. 35, no. 61, December 6, 1992.
168. Isa. 6:3.
169. The Beloved Maha Chohan, "The Journey of a Lifetime *A New Life in the Holy Spirit*," *Pearls of Wisdom*, vol. 37, no. 28, July 10, 1994.
170. Beloved Archangel Michael, "Planetary Cataclysm or World Transmutation: You Decide *The Earth Is the Lord's and the Fullness Thereof, the World and All They That Dwell Therein*," *Pearls of Wisdom*, vol. 36, no. 35, August 29, 1993.
171. Luke 22:42.
172. Luke 23:46.
173. Elizabeth Clare Prophet, *The Fourteenth Rosary: The Mystery of Surrender* (Gardiner, MT: Summit University Press, 2010).
174. Ibid.
175. Beloved Mighty Victory, "Victory Over the Dark Night of the Soul," *Pearls of Wisdom*, vol. 43, no. 16, April 16, 2000.
176. Fischer, David H., *Washington's Crossing*, ed. James M. McPherson, (New York, Oxford Press, 2004), p. ix.
177. Beloved Mighty Victory, "Victory Over the Dark Night of the Soul," *Pearls of Wisdom*, vol. 43, no. 16, April 16, 2000.

Sweet Surrender

178. Beloved El Morya, "The Light of the Guru and the Chela: Surrender for a More Perfect Love," *Pearls of Wisdom*, vol. 23, no. 45, November 9, 1980.
179. Ibid.

180. Ibid.
181. Ibid.
182. Ibid.
183. Elizabeth Clare Prophet, "Discipleship: Five Steps of Initiation under the Living Word Part 5 Christ II," *Pearls of Wisdom,* vol. 52, no. 6, March 15, 2009.
184. Beloved El Morya, "The Light of the Guru and the Chela: Surrender for a More Perfect Love," *Pearls of Wisdom,* vol. 23, no. 45, November 9, 1980.
185. Rom. 8:28.
186. Beloved El Morya, "The Light of the Guru and the Chela: Surrender for a More Perfect Love," *Pearls of Wisdom,* vol. 23, no. 45, November 9, 1980.

A Walk with the Buddha

187. Luke 24:13-16, 28-32.
188. Beloved Saint Germain, "Spirals of Selflessness for the Madonna and Child Part 2," *Pearls of Wisdom,* vol. 20, no. 27, July 3, 1977.
189. Beloved Gautama Buddha, "A Rescue Mission 'I Will Fulfill My Mission Come What May!' Cherish the Flame Wesak Address 1995," *Pearls of Wisdom,* vol. 38, no. 21, May 14, 1995.
190. Ibid.
191. Ibid.
192. Ibid.
193. I Cor. 13:11.
194. Beloved Gautama Buddha, "A Rescue Mission 'I Will Fulfill My Mission Come What May!' Cherish the Flame Wesak Address 1995," *Pearls of Wisdom,* vol. 38, no. 21, May 14, 1995.

195. Beloved Godfre, ""Do Not Give Up the Ship!" Let Liberty's Voice Be Heard," *Pearls of Wisdom*, vol. 30, no. 45, November 8, 1987.
196. The Beloved Maha Chohan, "Initiations of the Holy Spirit from the Mount of Salvation *The Ladder of Chelaship* Pentecost address 1993," *Pearls of Wisdom*, vol. 36, no. 31, August 1, 1993.
197. Ibid.
198. Ibid.
199. Ibid.
200. Beloved Gautama Buddha, "A Rescue Mission *'I Will Fulfill My Mission Come What May!'* Cherish the Flame Wesak Address 1995," *Pearls of Wisdom*, vol. 38, no. 21, May 14, 1995.
201. Ibid.
202. Beloved Godfre, ""Do Not Give Up the Ship!" *Let Liberty's Voice Be Heard*," *Pearls of Wisdom*, vol. 30, no. 45, November 8, 1987.
203. Beloved Gautama Buddha, "A Rescue Mission *'I Will Fulfill My Mission Come What May!'* Cherish the Flame Wesak Address 1995," *Pearls of Wisdom*, vol. 38, no. 21, May 14, 1995.
204. The Beloved Maha Chohan, "Initiations of the Holy Spirit from the Mount of Salvation *The Ladder of Chelaship* Pentecost address 1993," *Pearls of Wisdom*, vol. 36, no. 31, August 1, 1993.
205. Ibid.
206. Ibid.

Claim Your Adeptship!

207. Thomas à Kempis, *The Imitation of Mary* (New Jersey: Catholic Book Publishing Corp., 2005), pp. 73-74.
208. Beloved Mother Mary, "The Ineffable Love of Our Oneness *The Challenge of Every Day Is to Separate the Unreal from the Real* The Reward of Your Labor Is Adeptship," *Pearls of Wisdom*, vol. 36, no. 70, December 29, 1993.
209. Ibid.
210. Ibid.
211. Robert J. Edmonson, *The Practice of the Presence of God: A New Translation*, (Orleans, MA: Paraclete Press, 1985), pp. 61-63.
212. Beloved Mother Mary, "The Ineffable Love of Our Oneness *The Challenge of Every Day Is to Separate the Unreal from the Real* The Reward of Your Labor Is Adeptship," *Pearls of Wisdom*, vol. 36, no. 70, December 29, 1993.
213. John 14:10.
214. Beloved Mother Mary, "The Ineffable Love of Our Oneness *The Challenge of Every Day Is to Separate the Unreal from the Real* The Reward of Your Labor Is Adeptship," *Pearls of Wisdom*, vol. 36, no. 70, December 29, 1993.
215. Beloved Archangel Gabriel, "Called to an Unusual Sacrifice *Violet Flame for an Extraordinary Transmutation*," *Pearls of Wisdom*, vol. 30, no. 53, November 22, 1987.
216. Archangel Jophiel and Archeia Hope, "Is Anything Too Hard for the Lord? "I Say No!" *Bypass the Carnal Mind and Pursue the Imitation of Christ Pierce the Veil of Ignorance by*

the Circle of Illumination's Fire!," Pearls of Wisdom, vol. 32, no. 36, September 3, 1989.
217. Ibid.
218. Ibid.
219. Ibid.
220. Ibid.
221. Elizabeth Clare Prophet, "Teachings of Jesus Christ on Your Path of Personal Christhood," June 27, 1993. Available on DVD "The Path of Personal Christhood" from www.SummitLighthouse.org
222. Ibid.
223. Beloved Mother Mary, "The Ineffable Love of Our Oneness *The Challenge of Every Day Is to Separate the Unreal from the Real* The Reward of Your Labor Is Adeptship," *Pearls of Wisdom*, vol. 36, no. 70, December 29, 1993.
224. Ibid.
225. Ibid.
226. Ibid.
227. Luke 2:49.

Karma, Honor, and Victory

228. Wikipedia, "Diogenes," https://en.wikipedia.org/wiki/Diogenes, accessed November, 2019.
229. Cambridge Dictionary, "Integrity," https://dictionary.cambridge.org/us/dictionary/english/integrity, accessed November, 2019.
230. Brainy Quote, "Sophocles," https://www.brainyquote.com/quotes/sophocles_155151, accessed November 12, 2019.

231. Beloved Heros and Amora, "Our God Is Love The Power of the Three-Times-Three of Elohim A Child's Rosary and the Ruby Ray Judgment Call," *Pearls of Wisdom*, vol. 31, no. 81, November 27, 1988.
232. Ibid.
233. Archangel Chamuel with Covering Cherubim, "Open Your Heart to God The Initiation of the Piercing of the Heart," *Pearls of Wisdom*, vol. 36, no. 9, February 28, 1993.
234. Beloved Godfre, "*I Come to Originate a Plan for the Expansion of the Light of America to Ignite Hearts the World Around,*" *Pearls of Wisdom*, vol. 55, no. 15, August 1, 2012.
235. Beloved Sanat Kumara, "*The Fulfillment of the Twentieth Century Portents for Maitreya's Mystery School* You Must Resolve the Issues of Your Karma by the Cosmic Honor Flame," *Pearls of Wisdom*, vol. 37, no. 10, March 6, 1994.
236. Heb. 8:12.
237. Scripts.com, Stands4 LLC, 2019. "Beckett," https://www.scripts.com/script/becket_3783, accessed November 30, 2019.
238. Beloved Jesus Christ, "The Call of Love In Preparation for the Wedding Day Your Marriage to Jesus Christ," *Pearls of Wisdom*, vol. 34, no. 66, December 22, 1991.
239. The Beloved Maha Chohan, "The Sacred Science of the Mother *Unto God Is Reserved the Worship of Your Soul,*" *Pearls of Wisdom*, vol. 57, no. 8, April 15, 2014.
240. https://quotefancy.com/quote/490536/Publilius-Syrus-What-is-left-when-honor-is-lost, accessed November 30, 2019.
241. Beloved Kuan Yin, "Do You Have the Will to Save This Planet? Go Forth and Fulfill What You Have Promised God Espouse the Cosmic Honor Flame and Know Your Victory," *Pearls of Wisdom*, vol. 46, no. 14, April 6, 2003.

242. The Beloved Goddess of Freedom, "Releasing the Flame of Freedom Enshrined in the Capitals of the Nations Part 2," *Pearls of Wisdom*, vol. 44, no. 21, May 27, 2001.
243. Matt.7:13-14.
244. Beloved Sanat Kumara, "*The Fulfillment of the Twentieth Century Portents for Maitreya's Mystery School* You Must Resolve the Issues of Your Karma by the Cosmic Honor Flame," *Pearls of Wisdom*, vol. 37, no. 10, March 6, 1994.
245. Ibid.
246. Book Browse, "You Can Run but You Can't Hide, https://www.bookbrowse.com/expressions/detail/index.cfm/expression_number/238/you-can-run-but-you-cant-hide, accessed November, 2019.
247. 1 Thess. 5:1-2.
248. 1 Thess. 5:3.
249. Beloved Omega, "Do Not Doubt God! Love God and Love One Another *Go Daily to the Secret Chamber of the Heart Become a Chela of the Messenger*," *Pearls of Wisdom*, vol. 35, no. 32, August 9, 1992.
250. Ibid.
251. Ibid.
252. John 14:2.

www.ingramcontent.com/pod-product-compliance
Lightning Source LLC
LaVergne TN
LVHW021650060526
838200LV00050B/2294